£6.50

D0178448

Butterflies and Moths
in
Britain and Europe

for James, Edward, William and Catherine

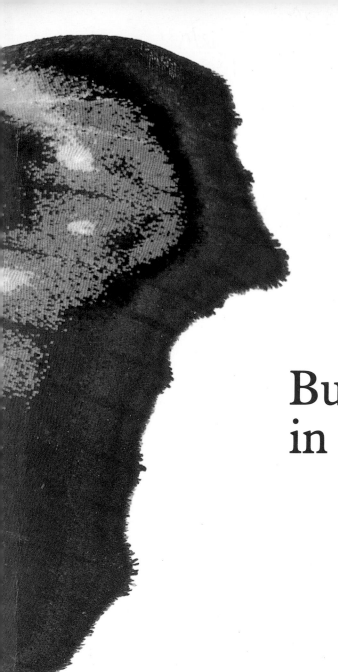

Butterflies and Moths
in Britain and Europe

by

David Carter
British Museum (Natural History)

Designed by Roger Phillips

Pan Books
in association with William Heinemann
and the British Museum (Natural History), London

#Ref82 22067 9.82
y/ F Ref82/Addition
595.789 CAR

Acknowledgements

My special thanks are due to my wife Brenda for typing and checking the main text, to Kate Penoyre for her painstaking work on the page layouts, to Kyle Cathie, Ros Edwards and Chris Owen for editorial advice, to Sheila Halsey for preparing the indexes and above all to the photographers listed below, without whose excellent work this book would not have been possible. I am also grateful to the Royal Horticultural Society for permission to photograph butterflies in its gardens at Wisley.

Photographic acknowledgements
The plates of set specimens are all by **Colin Keates** of the British Museum (Natural History) Photo Unit.

Photographs of living specimens were mainly provided by **Natural Science Photos:** P. A. Bowman 111c1 123belowcr 135cr, J. D. Bradley 117tl+r 123abovecr,br 125br 127b 155br 157br 161bl 180b 181tl 183cl, M. Chinery 17tr 72br 111tr,b 112tr 113bl&r 117cr 121tr 122tr 123cl 124tr,cr 125belowcr 127tr 133cr 135tl 137tr,br 139t,br 141t,c,br 142br 143cr 144br 145t 147t,br 151br 155cr 163tr,b 165br 170cr 177bl 187tl, J. A. Grant 131tl 169bl, R. C. Revels 10cl 17bl 18tr 23t 26 27t 33t,bl 34t 35tr,b 41bl 43cl 44tc,br 50tr 51tr,bl 52tr,cr 53bl&r 55bl&r 56c 57tl,b 59cl 61 63c,tr 65bl 70br 73tr,bl 74br 75cr 77br 79bl 83b 85tl 86r 87t 88tr 89t 90b 91t,bl&r 92r 93b 94tr 95 96cr 97t 98tr 103br 105bl 107 109tr 113t 117tl 121b 123tr 126tr 131bl 137bc 139belowcl 141bl 149tr 151tr,cr 153t 155tr 158tr 159tl,r,c 161tl 165tr 166rb 171tr,cl 172tr 173tr 185bl 187cr, T. Ruckstuhl 31t,c,b 34b 36tr 37bl&r 39t,b 41t,c 43t,b 45t,b 47bl 49br 51br 54tr 55t 56t 58tr 59tl,b 60tr 63tl,bl 64br 65br 67t 68tr 69b 71tr,b 73tl 75tl,r,b 77bl 81t,b 84r 85tr,cr 87b 88b 89b 91cl 93t 95tr 97b 99 101 103tl 104tr 105t 109br 121cr 123tl 131tr 137bl 147cr 151tl 153bl 182tr 183tr,cr 185t 187tr, K. Rumbucher 73br, A. Shears 18cl, I. Sivec 137ct, 152tr, P. H. Ward 15bl 16 19 20bl&r 22 27b 33br 35tl,cl 37t 41br 42cr,br 46tr 48tr,cr 59tr 77c,bc 79cr,br 83tr 85b 95tl 102tr 103cl,bl 105br 106c,b 109bl 111tl 117cl 119tr,c,b 121tl,cl 125tl,cl,tr,abovecr 128tr 129bl 131br 133tl,cl,b 135bl,tr,br 137tl 139abovecl,bl,cr 143t,cl 145bl 148tr 149tl 150tr 151bl 153br 155bl 159c,cr 161cl,cr,br 163cr 165tl 167tl,cl&r 169rt,c&b 170tr 171tl 172cr 173tl 175tl,tr,br 177cl,br 179tl 181tr 183tl 184tr 185cl 187cl, S. L. Ward 24bl, D. Yendall 109cl 129br 133br 143br.

Other photographs by D. J. Carter 23b 47t 109tl 115tl,c,bl 116bl&r 142tr 147bl 155cl 165cl 167tr 172rb 175cl 183br, R. C. Goodden 68br 69t, F. Greenaway [BM (NH) Photo Unit] 8 9t,bl 10tr 13t 15br 21 24tr 29 47br 49t,bl 53t 57tr 63br 65t 77t 79t 127tl 129t 149b, J. D. Holloway 67bl 70bl 71tl 83tl, M. R. Honey 66cr 67br 118tr 130tr 144tr 147cl 164tr 165lb 166tr 167br 169tl, P. Lund 6 7 96tr, M. W. F. Tweedie 145br 157t,c 163tl 177t 179tr,b 181b 185br.

First published 1982 by Pan Books Ltd,
Cavaye Place, London SW10 9PG
in association with William Heinemann Ltd
and the British Museum (Natural History), London

© David Carter 1982

ISBN 0 330 26642 X

Photosetting by Crawley Composition Ltd

Printed by Toppan Printing Company (HK) Ltd,
Hong Kong

This book is sold subject to the condition that it shall not, by way of trade or otherwise, be lent, re-sold, hired out or otherwise circulated without the publisher's prior consent in any form of binding or cover other than that in which it is published and without a similar condition including this condition being imposed on the subsequent purchaser

Contents

Introduction

Butterflies are universally loved as symbols of life and beauty and are frequently associated with sunshine, flowers and the countryside. Moths on the other hand are seldom popular and are often regarded as dull-coloured pests which eat holes in clothes or damage vegetables in the garden. Both of these concepts are in part true although butterflies are not really so distinct from moths and share with them many aspects of appearance and behaviour. Butterflies may be regarded as specialised day-flying moths, generally recognised by their bright colours and clubbed antennae. Although a great number of moths are dull in colour and nocturnal in habit, there are many that are day-flying and brightly coloured. Although some butterflies and moths are pests, the vast majority of Lepidoptera are harmless and may play an important part in maintaining the delicate balance of our natural environment.

STRUCTURE OF THE ADULT

Eyes

The most obvious feature of the head is the pair of large compound eyes, so called because each comprises a large number of individual facets or lenses (up to about 6000) which build up a compound image in the insect's brain. In moths, pigment cells within the eye can be arranged in different ways to regulate the amount of light received. This is important to insects that are largely nocturnal and sometimes have to cope with a wide range of light intensity. Butterflies which are mostly active in sunlight do not have or require this ability. The structure of the insect eye has certain disadvantages in that it cannot alter its focus and only a few lenses will keep an object in focus at any one time. The point of focus is fairly close so that Lepidoptera may be regarded as short-sighted although this type of eye is very effective in sensing range and movement. These facilities are very important to an insect which has to detect the approach of its enemies and manoeuvre rapidly when in flight.

The eyes of Lepidoptera are sensitive to a different colour range from that of the human eye. While butterflies and moths are relatively insensitive to red light, they can perceive ultra-violet light. Butterflies can recognise colour patterns on flowers and on the wings of other butterflies which are undetectable to the human eye, while nocturnal moths are attracted to the 'black light' of an ultra-violet lamp. Some moths have an additional pair of ocelli, or simple eyes, on the head, not capable of registering a complete image but sensitive to relative light intensity and probably able to regulate the light sensitivity of the compound eyes.

Antennae

The antennae are the main organs of smell and are richly supplied with nerve receptors which can respond to minute dilutions of particular scents undetectable to the human nose. They are probably also sensitive to touch and are often used to tap an object that is being examined. The antennae of some moths are strongly modified with side branches or tufts of hair which give a feathery appearance. These modifications increase the surface area for scent reception and probably enable the insect to get a more positive 'fix' on the source of a smell. Feathery antennae are particularly noticeable in some male moths that locate their mates at long distances by their sense of smell. Female Lepidoptera almost certainly use the sensitive powers of their antennae in selecting the correct plants on which to lay their eggs. Antennae are also capable to some degree of perceiving taste and temperature change.

Mouthparts

In all but the most primitive Lepidoptera which feed on pollen and still retain functional biting mouthparts, butterflies and moths feed through a specialised sucking-tube called a proboscis. When not in use the proboscis is held coiled under the head like a watch spring, but when feeding takes place it can be uncoiled and extended to probe into flowers and other sources of liquid food. The proboscis is modified in different groups of Lepidoptera to cope with different feeding habits and in some cases where feeding does not take place in the adult stage may be absent or much reduced. In the case of hawk-moths which hover in front of flowers to feed, the proboscis is very long and in the Madagascan species *Xanthopan morgani* Walker which feeds from orchids with long slender nectaries, it extends up to 20cm. On the other hand, the proboscis of the Death's Head Hawk-moth is short and stout, enabling it to penetrate the waxen cells of a beehive in order to suck the honey.

On either side of the proboscis are two further sensory organs, the maxillary palpi and labial palpi. While the former are usually very small and inconspicuous, the labial palpi are sometimes very large and prominent, particularly in snout moths of the subfamily Hypeninae and butterflies of the family Libytheidae. The palpi are sensitive to touch and smell.

Legs

Behind the head is the thorax which is the powerhouse of the insect's body. It is divided into three parts called the prothorax, mesothorax and metathorax, each carrying a pair of jointed walking legs with claws at their ends which enable them to grip the surface to which they are clinging. In many species of Lepidoptera the feet (tarsi) possess sense organs which can taste certain food substances with a greater sensitivity than the human tongue. The legs of Lepidoptera are generally long and slender but in the Nymphalidae and some other butterflies the front pair of legs is very short and does not have a walking function. In other cases legs are furnished with large spines or tufts of hairs, as in the Fan-foot moth.

Wings

The mesothorax and metathorax each carry a pair of wings. Each wing consists of an upper and lower membrane separated by a system of supporting 'veins' which are strengthened tubes carrying air, nerve fibres and blood. Primitive moths have similar arrangement of the veins in both forewings and hindwings, whereas in more advanced groups they show striking differences and modifications.

Scales and coloration

Both upper and under surfaces of the wings are covered with overlapping scales, an important distinguishing feature of the Lepidoptera. These scales are specially modified, flattened hairs, each having a short stalk which fits into a socket. Scales vary in shape and size and some are adapted to act as scent distributors. These scales, called androconia, are connected to scent-producing glands and are generally long and slender with a tuft of fine hairs at the tip. Androconia are present on the wings of many male butterflies and moths and the scents produced, called pheromones, are used to attract females and to induce them to mate – a butterfly aphrodisiac. The wing scales are largely responsible for the bright colours of Lepidoptera and either contain colour pigments or are constructed in such a way that they produce colours by selective reflection and diffraction of light. In some species there are areas of deciduous scales which are shed during the first flight, leaving clear, window-like areas on the wings. Many Lepidoptera with deciduous scales are mimics of bees and wasps.

Flight

When Lepidoptera fly, the fore- and hindwings are linked together so that they beat in unison. Butterflies, and also a few moths, hold their wings together in flight by means of an expanded lobe on the

Head and thorax of **Privet Hawk-moth** *Sphinx ligustri*

Clouded Yellow *Colias croceus* feeding

hindwing which is overlapped by the base of the forewing. In most moths the wings are held together by a frenulum which in males consists of a single stout bristle projecting from the base of the hindwing and engaging with a catch-like flap, called the retinaculum, on the forewing. In females the frenulum consists of a group of bristles arising from the hindwing and engaging with a retinaculum made up of a group of stout hairs on the forewing.

Although the wings of butterflies and moths simply appear to flap up and down when in flight, the movement is more complex than this. The wings are twisted at the base as they move up and down so that the wing tips describe a figure of eight. This pushes a stream of air downwards and backwards, propelling the insect forwards. These wing movements are controlled by contractions of powerful muscles situated within the thorax.

Abdomen

The hindmost part of the body is called the abdomen and consists of ten segments that are very similar to each other and do not bear legs or wings. The abdomen is covered with scales and in some Lepidoptera it is brightly coloured or strongly patterned. The abdomen is very important as it contains the reproductive system and the major part of the digestive system. The external parts of the reproductive organs which are visible on the final segments of the abdomen are often useful in distinguishing closely similar species. The most prominent feature of the male is a pair of claspers which is used to hold the abdomen of the female during mating. The female is distinguished by the presence of an extendible egg-laying tube, or ovipositor, which in some species is long and flexible in order to insert eggs into crevices in bark or into flowers. Some female moths have a large tuft of hairs at the tip of the abdomen which they use to cover their eggs.

Hearing

Many Lepidoptera possess 'ears' but these are generally situated on the thorax or on the front part of the abdomen. These ears, called tympanal organs, consist of a thin membrane covering an air-filled depression in the body. The membrane acts as an ear-drum, vibrations sending messages to the brain via an auditory nerve. Moths are sensitive to high-pitched sounds such as those produced by bats.

Exoskeleton

One of the most significant features of insects is the fact that they do not have an internal supporting skeleton of bones as in birds and mammals, but have a tough outer coating, rather like a suit of armour, called an exoskeleton. The exoskeleton is composed of a substance called chitin which is combined with protein to produce a tough and flexible material. In places the exoskeleton is folded inwards to provide extra strength and attachment points for the muscles.

Respiratory system

Internally, the Lepidoptera have the typical insect form of blood circulatory, respiratory, digestive and reproductive systems. The blood is not contained in veins and arteries but bathes the organs within the body cavity. The blood is circulated by a long tubular heart which runs the length of the body and acts as a simple pump. Insect blood, unlike ours, does not distribute oxygen to the body or remove carbon dioxide. This is achieved by means of a system of minute air-carrying tubes, called tracheoles, which ramify throughout the insect's body and carry oxygen direct to the various organs. These fine tubes lead into larger tubes, called tracheae, which in turn connect with the outside atmosphere by means of breathing pores, called spiracles, along the sides of the body. Transmission of oxygen and carbon dioxide through this intricate network is by diffusion. Because this system of breathing is relatively slow and inefficient, it has a limiting effect on the potential size of insects and is one of the reasons why we do not have butterflies as big as eagles.

Nervous system

The nervous system consists of a solid double nerve-cord running the length of the body below the gut and connecting a series of nerve centres or 'brains' called ganglia. At the front of the body the nerve-cord loops around the gut to join the cerebral ganglia of the head. This central nerve-cord is connected to the various organs by a network of nerve fibres.

Digestive system

The digestive system consists of a muscular pharynx which pumps food from the mouth to the next section of the alimentary canal called the oesophagus. The oesophagus is a narrow tube which usually leads into a food reservoir, or crop, where food may be stored. The next section of the system, the mid-gut, is the region from which nutrients are absorbed into the blood, while the final section, the hind-gut, receives excretory products passed back from the blood and leads to the anus through which waste products are voided. Digested food that has been absorbed into the blood is stored in fat bodies which provide important energy reservoirs.

Reproductive system

The reproductive system of male Lepidoptera consists of a pair of testes which in some groups are fused together, connected by narrow tubes of the vas deferens to the ductus ejaculatorius through which sperms are passed into the body of the female during mating. Similarly in the female the ovaries are paired but lead into oviducts where the developing eggs are coated with a protective shell. The female also has a sac-like storage vessel called the bursa copulatrix where sperms received from the male during mating are stored until eggs are matured and ready for fertilisation.

The Life Cycle

Butterflies and moths undergo four stages of development: the egg, the larva, the pupa and the adult.

Life history

In the first stage the embryo develops to become a minute larva or caterpillar. When the larva has completed its initial development, it bites its way through the egg-shell and goes off in search of food. The caterpillar represents the main feeding and growth stage and is ideally constructed to perform these functions. The structure of the body is basically a cylindrical tube with a head at one end. The head is armed with powerful biting jaws with which it feeds and the body carries a series of legs to enable it to move about and cling to its foodplant.

Moulting

All caterpillars moult a number of times before completing their growth. This is because the cuticle (skin) of the exoskeleton, although tough and flexible, is not capable of much stretching and so must be replaced to allow for growth. At the onset of moulting the caterpillar swells up the front part of its body to split open the old skin and gradually sheds it by means of a series of muscular contractions. This sometimes takes a considerable time and during this period the insect is very vulnerable to its enemies. Caterpillars usually hide away before moulting and spin a silken pad to which they cling while freeing themselves of the old skin.

The phases between each moult are referred to as instars and the number of instars varies according to the species and sometimes also to environmental conditions. The typical number of instars is five or six.

Hairs and spines

Apart from an increase in size, various other changes may take place between instars, for example, a change in colour, an increase in the number of body hairs or the development of specialised outgrowths in the form of horns or tubercles. Changes in proportion may also be noticed, as in many hawk-moth caterpillars where the tail horn is relatively large in early instars, but becomes progressively smaller in proportion to the body as it grows. The Alder Moth is a fine example of a species with distinct caterpillar forms in early and late instars, each having a different protective function.

Pupation

When the caterpillar is full grown it undergoes its final moult to enter the chrysalis or pupa stage. This is the phase during which the ultimate transformation from caterpillar to butterfly or moth takes place and involves the complete breakdown and regrouping of the body cells which then develop into the adult organs. Before the final moult the caterpillar makes various provisions for the pupa stage such as choosing a suitable site, burrowing into the soil or spinning a silken cocoon. In many butterflies the pupa is suspended from a small pad of silk spun on a branch or twig and the pupa performs a remarkable series of manoeuvres to free itself from the old skin without losing its grip and falling to the ground.

Pupa

The pupa is enclosed in a strongly sclerotised outer shell with the wings, antennae and legs firmly fused to the body in most cases. The Latin name 'pupa' means a doll or puppet. The popular name 'chrysalis' is derived from a Greek word meaning gold and refers to the metallic golden spots to be seen on many butterfly pupae. Some pupae, particularly those suspended by their tails, will jerk violently if disturbed, while the pupae of the Small Copper butterfly and the Death's Head Hawk-moth are even capable of producing squeaking or scratching sounds.

Emergence of the adult

As the pupa stage nears its culmination it darkens and the wing pattern of the adult often becomes visible through the pupal shell. Suddenly the pupa splits open and the adult begins to emerge. It swallows air to expand its body and further split the pupal case, and with movements of its legs and abdomen struggles free. As the freshly emerged insect clings to a twig or other support it is a pathetic

sight with its damp wings hanging like shapeless bags on either side of its body. However, as soon as blood is pumped into the veins the wings begin to expand and are held open until they have dried and hardened. Before its first flight, the butterfly or moth has to void the excretory wastes that have built up during the pupa stage. These are expelled from the body in the form of a reddish liquid called meconium which is often mistaken for blood.

Finally the adult butterfly or moth flies away and brings the life cycle to its completion by mating and laying eggs.

A closer examination of the egg, larva and pupa will show some of the adaptations that enable them to fulfil their functions in the life cycle.

Peacock *Inachis io* emerging from pupa

Eggs

The eggs of Lepidoptera are extremely variable in shape, size and colour, ranging from the flattened, scale-like eggs of some Microlepidoptera to the ornately sculptured eggs of many butterflies of the family Lycaenidae. The egg contains an embryo with its nutrient yolk and is enclosed by a protective shell which is lined on the inside with a thin waterproofing layer of wax. In the eggs of Lepidoptera respiration takes place through a number of microscopic pores and also through a larger opening called the micropyle. The micropyle, a term literally meaning 'a little door', performs two important functions as it is also the pore through which the sperm enters during fertilisation. The area around the micropyle is frequently patterned, often in the form of an intricate rosette. The entire surface of the egg is sometimes heavily sculptured with ridges or network patterns, or may be entirely smooth and shining. While most eggs are dull in colour and blend into the background, a few are quite strikingly patterned or brilliantly coloured, usually as an indication that they are distasteful.

The way in which eggs are laid varies enormously and eggs are often specially modified. The eggs of some Microlepidoptera, such as the Carnation Tortrix, are laid in overlapping layers like tiles on a roof and are consequently flattened in shape. The round, smooth

Egg mass of the **Hebrew Character** *Orthosia gothica*

eggs of the Ghost Moth are laid by the female as she hovers over the foliage and they fall to the ground amongst the grass roots where the caterpillars will feed. The Lackey Moth lays her barrel-shaped eggs in neat rows around a twig so that they form a distinctive bracelet, while the European Map butterfly has the unusual habit of laying her eggs in strings, hanging one below the other from the underside of a leaf.

Caterpillar

Like the adult butterfly or moth the caterpillar is made up of a head, thorax and abdomen. The head which is enclosed in a horny head capsule is usually rounded but may be flattened or wedge-shaped as in the Leopard Moth. Although the head is usually smooth, in some moths it may be hairy and in some butterflies it may bear spines or even horns. One of the most important features of the head is the pair of robust biting jaws or mandibles. These are surrounded by two plate-like lips which help to direct food into the mouth. The lower lip carries a structure called the spinneret which is the outlet of the silk glands. Silk is extruded through the spinneret as a liquid but hardens on contact with the air to form a fine but tough thread. The small antennae situated on either side of the mandibles are important sensory organs.

Caterpillar of **Privet Hawk-moth**
Sphinx ligustri feeding

Prolegs of **Privet Hawk-moth**
Sphinx ligustri caterpillar

Eyes

The simple eyes or ocelli are arranged in semi-circles on either side of the head. There are usually six on each side but there are fewer in some species and caterpillars that spend most of their lives in darkness may have none at all. The ocelli are probably capable of little more than distinguishing between light and darkness and consequently the other sensory organs are highly developed to compensate for this.

Legs

The thorax has three pairs of jointed legs which vary in length and development but are more useful for holding food than for walking. The abdomen which consists of ten segments carries a number of sucker-like claspers or prolegs. These are the caterpillar's highly muscular walking legs and each has a ring or band of tiny hooks called crochets that enable the caterpillar to grip roughened surfaces.

On the side of many of the body segments is a round or oval spiracle which leads into the respiratory system. Many caterpillars are able to close their spiracles in an emergency and, in this way, some are able to withstand immersion in water for a considerable time, a useful ability for caterpillars feeding on foliage overhanging ponds and rivers. In the Brown China-mark moth which lays its eggs on aquatic plants, the young caterpillars do not have spiracles but breathe by diffusion of dissolved oxygen from the surrounding water. Later the spiracles develop and the caterpillar lives in a case of leaf fragments in which an air bubble is trapped. From time to time the caterpillar floats to the surface to replenish its oxygen supply.

Protective devices

The thorax and abdomen are covered with hairs which may be very small and few in number, as in the families Noctuidae and Geometridae, or long and dense as in the families Arctiidae, Lasio-campidae and Lymantriidae. Many butterfly caterpillars are strongly armed with stout spines, and similar structures may be found in some moth caterpillars of the family Saturniidae. Some caterpillars have horns and other protuberances which either serve to frighten predators or change the caterpillar's shape so that it becomes less conspicuous. Colour pattern may act as camouflage or in the case of brightly coloured, distasteful species as a warning to enemies.

Glands

The body may also carry various specialised glands. The caterpillar of the Swallowtail butterfly has a forked red gland, called an osmeterium, hidden immediately behind the head. This gland can be rapidly expanded if the caterpillar is threatened, emitting a pineapple-like scent that apparently acts as a deterrent to predators or parasites. Burnet moth caterpillars have poison glands that secrete cyanide compounds over the body, a very effective way of making themselves unpalatable. The caterpillar of the Puss Moth is even able to spray formic acid at its enemies from a gland at the base of the thorax. In contrast to this the caterpillars of many butterflies of the family Lycaenidae have glands on the upper surface of the body. These secrete a sweet honey-like liquid that is highly attractive to certain species of ants. In return for this liquid the ants afford protection to the caterpillars, sometimes to the extent of carrying them to their nests where they complete their development.

Structure of the pupa

The pupa also is divided into head, thorax and abdomen but the divisions are often more difficult to see. Many of the adult features may be distinguished on the surface of the pupa. The head can be seen to bear a pair of compound eyes although these are not functional, and a proboscis which is firmly fused to the body. The thoracic structures such as the wings and legs are similarly visible but fixed in position and non-functional. The abdomen has few distinctive features except at the tail where many species have a protuberance, called the cremaster, which bears a number of hooked spines and is used to anchor the pupa in position. Additionally a number of pupae have ridges or bands of spines that enable them to wriggle through the soil or out of a tunnel so that they are in a suitable position for the adult to emerge. Although the general form of pupae is smooth and rounded, some are strongly angular and resemble dead leaves or fragments of wood.

Classification
Linnean system

Many early naturalists attempted to describe and name butterflies and other insects but until the eighteenth century each worker adopted his own method of nomenclature. It was not until the Swedish naturalist Carl Linné, usually known by the latinised name Carolus Linnaeus, published the tenth edition of his *Systema Naturae* that we were provided with the basic system on which all modern animal nomenclature is based. The *Systema Naturae* was a descriptive catalogue of all animal life known to Linnaeus and employed the 'binomial' system of nomenclature. Under Linnaeus' binomial system each animal species was given two names: the first the generic name, and the second the specific name. Thus the Large White butterfly has the generic name *Pieris*, indicating the genus to which it belongs, followed by the specific name *brassicae* indicating its individual position within the genus (i.e. the *Pieris* butterfly which feeds on cabbage). When looking through this book it is interesting to notice how many of our common butterflies and moths Linnaeus named. This is all the more remarkable considering that he did the same for most other groups of animals and plants.

Species

The term 'species' is difficult to define and our concept changes as new evidence comes to light. A simple description of a species is a group of organisms which can freely interbreed and produce viable offspring. In recent times it has been shown that distinct species can sometimes be induced to interbreed and that viable offspring may be produced although this is extremely unlikely to happen in nature. Species are sometimes subdivided into races or subspecies. These terms usually apply to geographically isolated populations that show differences in patterning, structure or

Black-veined White *Aporia crataegi*

behaviour. Some species vary throughout a continuous range so that at the extremes they look very different but in between all forms of intermediates occur.

Varieties

Other terms that are frequently used with reference to butterflies and moths are varieties and aberrations. These usually apply to specimens in which the wing pattern deviates sufficiently from the normal to be readily recognisable and range from regularly recurring forms which are genetically controlled to rare mutants and developmental freaks which seldom, if ever, recur.

Characteristics and evolution

The characteristics most readily used in classifying Lepidoptera are those of the wing patterns but although very useful for initial identification they can be misleading. This is because many unrelated species adopt similar patterning, either for camouflage, as

Speckled Wood *Pararge aegeria*

warning coloration, to mimic other species, or for other reasons. In order to discover relationships between different groups of Lepidoptera it is necessary to make careful structural studies of the wing venation, mouthparts, eyes, legs and body. In addition a close study of biology and behaviour can be helpful. Some species may be grouped by the foodplants on which the caterpillars feed, an interesting case of coevolution, as many flowering plants and Lepidoptera are believed to have evolved together and may have reached their peaks of development at about the same geological time. The earliest known moths, over one hundred million years old, are Microlepidoptera preserved in Lebanese amber from the Lower Cretaceous period.

Family classifications

Drepanidae

Many moths of this family are known as Hook-tips because the tips of the forewings are characteristically hooked. They mostly resemble Geometridae but do not have looper caterpillars. The caterpillars of Drepanidae are tapered towards the tail and do not have a pair of anal claspers at the end of the body.

Thyatiridae

The moths of this small family closely resemble those of the family Noctuidae. They differ in fine structures – such as the arrangement of the wing veins – but European species can be recognised by their distinctive wing patterns.

Geometridae

Members of this very large family are often called Loopers or Geometers because of the looping progression of their caterpillars which is sometimes described as 'earth measuring'. This unusual method of walking results from the reduction in the number of functional clasper legs on the body. The moths are generally rather fragile, having large wings in relation to their slender bodies. A few of the more robust species may be confused with those of the Noctuidae but may easily be distinguished in the caterpillar stage. Some geometrid moths rest with their wings held together vertically over their bodies in the same way as butterflies.

Sphingidae

All the moths of this distinctive family are known as Hawk-moths. This is probably because of their large size and powerful flight. Many are capable of feeding from flowers while hovering in front of them like humming-birds. When at rest, they hold their streamlined wings sloping back from the body like the wings of a jet aircraft. Their large caterpillars are usually distinguished by the presence of a pointed horn at the tail end of the body.

Notodontidae

The Prominents, Puss Moths and the Lobster Moth belong to this large and varied family. They are medium to large-sized moths, many having a tuft of scales on the hind margin of the forewing which projects upwards when the wings are folded, thus giving rise to the term Prominent. The caterpillars of these moths are extremely varied in form, ranging from the hairy Buff-tip caterpillars to the grotesque caterpillars of the Lobster Moth.

Thaumetopoeidae
The members of this small but worldwide family are known as Processionary Moths. This name is derived from the processionary habit of the caterpillars which move about in companies and often live in communal nests. The moths are rather dull in colour, being either grey or brown marked with white. This group is considered by some to belong to the family Notodontidae.

Lymantriidae
Moths of this family are commonly known as Tussocks. This is because some of the caterpillars which are very hairy have distinctive tussocks of coloured hairs along their backs. The male moths usually have feathered antennae and often have very different wing patterns to those of the females. Unlike the closely related Noctuidae, these moths do not have developed mouthparts and so are unable to feed in the adult stage.

Arctiidae
The Tiger Moths, Ermines and Footmen are members of this large family that has a worldwide distribution. Many European species are large and brightly coloured although the Footmen which belong to a distinct subfamily, the Lithosiinae, are generally smaller and drabber in colour. The caterpillars are very hairy and those of the larger species are often known as 'Woolly Bears'.

Ctenuchidae
The one European species of this otherwise mainly tropical family (sometimes regarded as a subfamily of the Arctiidae) of narrow-winged, brightly coloured moths is the Yellow-belted Burnet. Many tropical moths of this family are superb wasp mimics while the European species is a mimic of distasteful moths of the family Zygaenidae.

Noctuidae
This is probably the largest family of moths with representatives throughout the world numbering in excess of 20000 species. They are generally small to medium-sized although the South American Giant Owl Moth, *Thysania agrippina* Cramer, has a wingspan of 30cm and is the largest moth in the world. Many moths of this family are dull brown and well camouflaged although some day-flying species are brightly coloured and others have brilliantly coloured hindwings that are displayed when the moths are disturbed. The caterpillars are generally smooth but certain groups are very hairy. Many are pests of agricultural crops and grassland and are known as cutworms or armyworms.

Hepialidae
This worldwide family of rather robust moths includes the Swift Moths, so called because they are powerful flyers. Unlike most moths the two pairs of wings are held together in flight by a lobe of the forewing which locks under the hindwing. The arrangement of the veins of the forewing is virtually the same as that of the hindwing, another unusual characteristic of these rather primitive moths. Their caterpillars either feed on roots or bore in wood.

Cossidae
The Goat Moth is a typical member of this worldwide family of generally large and robust moths. This is another group in which the adults have no proboscis and so are unable to feed. Their caterpillars characteristically tunnel in wood and are sometimes known as Carpenterworms. In Australia the caterpillars of some of these moths are eaten by the Aborigines and are known as 'Witchety Grubs'.

Zygaenidae
Many of the more brightly coloured members of this worldwide family of moths are distasteful and use their distinctive patterns to warn potential predators. They are mostly day-flying and the European species, which are known as Burnets and Foresters, are exclusively so. Their caterpillars are rather slug-like with the head retracted into the body. Like the adult moths many of the caterpillars are poisonous and distasteful. They pupate in papery cocoons on the ground or attached to the foodplant.

Hesperiidae
This large family of generally small, moth-like butterflies is worldwide in distribution. These butterflies are often referred to as Skippers because of their rapid darting flight. When at rest many fold their wings over their back in the same way as moths. The caterpillars have large heads, constricted 'necks' and smooth bodies, tapering towards the tail. They feed on grasses and related plants, and usually pupate in a silken web. Unlike other butterflies, the adults do not have clubbed antennae.

Papilionidae
This worldwide family of some 600 large and colourful species, including the Swallowtails and Apollos, is represented by only eleven species in Europe of which only one occurs in Britain. Most of the others are tropical species, including the spectacular Birdwing butterflies of south-eastern Asia. The caterpillars are often spiny or have fleshy protuberances. A characteristic of these caterpillars is the presence on the thorax of a forked glandular organ which can be expanded when the caterpillar is disturbed.

Pieridae
The Whites and Yellows belong to this large, worldwide family of butterflies, most of which are tropical. The pigments of many of these butterflies are interesting as they are derived from uric acid waste products deposited in the scales. The caterpillars are covered with short, fine hairs but have a generally smooth appearance. Their pupae are angular in shape and are held in an upright position by a girdle of silk around the middle.

Lycaenidae
The butterflies of this family are generally rather small and often jewel-like, with metallic scales. They include the Blues, Coppers and Hairstreaks which represent some of Europe's most colourful and attractive butterflies. The caterpillars are woodlouse-like in shape with the head retracted into the thorax and some possess 'honey glands' which are attractive to ants. Pupae of Lycaenidae are smooth and round.

Riodinidae
Sometimes known as the Nemeobiidae this family of mainly tropical butterflies, popularly known as Metalmarks, is closely related to the Lycaenidae. There is only one European species, the Duke of Burgundy Fritillary. Despite its superficial similarity to true fritillaries of the family Nymphalidae, it may easily be distinguished by its rapid, zigzag flight. The caterpillars are similar to those of the Lycaenidae although some tropical species are very hairy, an unusual feature in butterfly caterpillars. The pupae are rounded and hairy.

Libytheidae
Butterflies of this family are sometimes known as Snout butterflies because of their long palpi which project in front of the head. There is only one representative of this small family in Europe, the Nettle Tree Butterfly. The angular wings are very distinctively shaped and resemble dead leaves. Males have only two pairs of functional legs while females have the full complement of six.

Nymphalidae
Many European species belong to this large and diverse family of colourful butterflies which includes the Fritillaries, Emperors, Admirals and Tortoiseshells. They are sometimes referred to as Brush-footed butterflies because in both sexes the non-functional front pair of legs is reduced in size and often covered with tufts of hair-like scales. The caterpillars are generally covered with spines although some are modified in other ways, with horn-like projections on the head and tail. The pupae are mostly angular in shape and many have golden or silver metallic spots.

Satyridae

This group of butterflies which is considered by some to be a subfamily of the Nymphalidae includes the Browns and Ringlets. Although predominantly brown with distinctive eye-spots, there are exceptions in such species as the Marbled Whites. These may be distinguished from the Whites of the family Pieridae by the reduction of the first pair of legs. The caterpillars of Satyridae are distinguished from those of the Nymphalidae by having a pair of tail-like projections at the end of the body and by feeding exclusively on grasses and related plants. The pupae are rounded and without angular projections.

Danaidae

Another group sometimes regarded as a subfamily of the Nymphalidae, these butterflies are mainly tropical and are represented by only two species in Europe. These are the Monarch which is an occasional vagrant from North America, and the Plain Tiger, *Danaus chrysippus* Linnaeus, which occurs in the Canary Islands and sometimes reaches Greece and Italy. Both caterpillars and adult butterflies are poisonous and have bright warning colours.

Lasiocampidae

Although the greatest concentration of these moths occurs in the tropics, a number of species are found in Europe, including the Eggars, Lappets and Lackeys. They are generally large-bodied, robust, nocturnal insects which have a laboured flight. Their caterpillars are very hairy and in some species these hairs have irritant properties. Some live in communal webs or nests and may cause serious defoliation of trees and shrubs. The pupae are formed within tough cocoons, the egg-shaped nature of certain cocoons giving rise to the term 'Eggar'.

Saturniidae

This is a family of large moths that includes the Emperor Moths. Many members of this family have large eye-spots in the middle of the hindwings and the males have feathery antennae. They do not have developed mouthparts and so are not able to feed in the adult stage. The caterpillars are large and usually armed with stout hairs or pointed spines. They pupate in large, tough silken cocoons and some Chinese and Indian species are used for the commercial production of Tussore Silk.

Endromidae

This small family which is probably related to the Lasiocampidae includes only one European species, the Kentish Glory.

Limacodidae

Although primarily tropical and subtropical in its distribution, this family has two representatives in Europe, the Festoon, and the Triangle, *Heterogenea asella* Denis & Schiffermüller. They are related to the Zygaenidae although they show little superficial similarity in the adult stage. The caterpillars, however, are even more slug-like than those of the Zygaenidae and some tropical species have curious fleshy protuberances like arms and legs, while others are armed with stinging hairs. Fortunately the two European species are quite harmless.

Sesiidae

The appropriately named Clearwing Moths belong to this large worldwide family. Although the wings may be fully scaled on emergence from the pupa, most of the scales are shed during the first flight, leaving large areas where the veins show clearly. Many of these moths are excellent mimics of bees and wasps, even having banded bodies and flying with the same rapid buzzing flight. Their caterpillars are mostly wood-borers and some are pests of fruit trees and bushes.

Pyralidae

Few members of this very large family of small moths are commonly known although many are pests of stored foods and field crops. They are generally fairly delicate moths with rather long legs but can only be positively distinguished from most other small moths by the arrangement of the wing veins. Their caterpillars are small, smooth and seldom brightly coloured.

Pterophoridae

This is probably the most easily recognised family of small moths, due to the remarkable division of the wings into feathery plumes, which have given rise to the common name, Plume Moths. There are a large number of European species but many are difficult to identify without specialist knowledge. They are very delicate and have a weak fluttering flight. Their caterpillars are covered with tufts of fine hairs.

Adelidae

Sometimes regarded as a subfamily of the Incurvariidae, a large family of metallic-coloured 'micro-moths', the Adelidae are recognisable by the long antennae of the males which may be as much as six times the length of the body. For this reason, they are often called Long-horn Moths. They have a dancing, hovering flight and may sometimes be seen in large swarms. Their small caterpillars live in portable cases constructed from leaf fragments.

Tineidae

The Clothes Moths belong to this large family of 'micro-moths'. The moths may often be recognised by the raised hair-like scales on the head and the characteristic resting position with the wings steeply sloped over the body in a tent-like manner. Many tineid moths are reluctant to fly and will scuttle away rapidly on their long legs. The caterpillars or grubs of some species construct portable cases from food particles or debris.

Yponomeutidae

This diverse worldwide family of small moths includes many brilliantly coloured species which are confined mainly to the tropics. There are many European species, including the well known Small Ermine Moths. The caterpillars of some members of this family are gregarious and live in large communal webs.

Oecophoridae

Another large and diverse worldwide family of small moths with many representatives in Europe. Many of the species found in temperate regions are rather dull in coloration and have rounded wing-tips. A characteristic of many of these moths is that they are rather flattened in appearance and are sometimes called 'Flat-bodies'. Many of their small caterpillars are detritus feeders.

Tortricidae

The characteristic shape of many of these small moths when at rest gives rise to the popular name 'Bell moths'. There are many European representatives of this large worldwide family, with over 300 species in Britain. A number are pests of orchard and field crops.

Behaviour

Despite the fact that the Lepidoptera are one of the most extensively studied groups of insects, relatively little is known about their behaviour and detailed biology. While the life cycles and foodplants are known for all British butterflies, those of some European species are still only partly known and in the case of moths there are a great many gaps in our knowledge. We know very little indeed about courtship, mating, territorial behaviour and patterns of migration.

Flight

Flight patterns are an aspect of behaviour that can easily be studied. Butterflies exhibit a wide range of flight types, including the whirring flight of the Skippers, the slow fluttering flight of the Wood White and the rapid soaring flight of the Purple Emperor and the Two-tailed Pasha. Moths show an even greater diversity of flight types ranging from the dancing flight of the Long-horned Moth to the rapid and powerful flight of the Convolvulus Hawk-moth. The photographs of these insects show that they are specially modified for their particular mode of flight. Some Lepidoptera, such as the Hornet Moth, have evolved a flight pattern that mimics those of harmful or distasteful insects.

The importance of flight patterns can only be understood by watching insects in their natural habitats and seeing how they behave. Some relatively slow-flying species make use of air currents by flying up into the wind and allowing themselves to be

Chalkhill Blues *Lysandra coridon* courting

carried along. Some, such as the Common Clothes Moth, are very reluctant to fly at all and usually scuttle along on their long legs.

Many Lepidoptera are capable of aerobatic feats when attempting to escape from flying predators. A sparrow trying to catch a butterfly will soon realise how effectively they can manoeuvre. Many moths can detect the presence of bats and will swerve and dive erratically to avoid attack. Most hawk-moths do not settle to feed but hover in front of flowers while probing for nectar.

Butterflies and moths may have to warm themselves up before they can take off in flight. Butterflies do so by using their wings as miniature solar panels which absorb the rays of the sun even on quite cold days. This is one of the reasons that few butterflies are seen flying in dull weather. Many moths on the other hand are night fliers and cannot make use of the sun's heat. They warm themselves up by rapidly vibrating their wings.

Courtship

If a pair of butterflies is closely watched when courting, a distinct ritual of flight manoeuvres may be seen. Following this the two insects may settle on the ground and the male may circle around the female. During this 'courtship dance' the wings of both butterflies often come into close contact or the female may stroke the wings of the male with her antennae. In some species these movements are known to be connected with the release of sex attractant scents, called pheremones, from glands on the wings of the male. It is probable that many moths have equivalent courtship rituals although these would be difficult to observe as they mostly take place at night. Many female moths are mated as soon as they emerge from the pupa.

Prior to the final stages of mating, many female butterflies and moths are capable of attracting males by releasing their own pheremones. Unlike male pheremones which seem designed to operate at close quarters, those of the female are capable of attracting mates over quite long distances, up to several kilometres. Strangely female pheremones do not seem to be detectable by humans although some male pheremones may be recognised as flower-like or fruity scents.

Territorial behaviour

Associated with courtship and mating are the various patterns of territorial behaviour displayed by some male butterflies. The Purple Emperor male patrols his territory regularly, flying above the tree tops, and is frequently seen circling around isolated mature oak trees that mark the boundaries of his domain. The Speckled Wood is less ambitious in his territorial holdings but will fiercely defend his patch of sunlit woodland from other males in mock aerial battles.

Bath Whites *Pontia daplidice* mating

Green-veined Whites *Pieris napi* drinking

Feeding

While the feeding habits of adult butterflies have been widely observed, those of adult moths are less well known as much of this activity takes place at night. Many moths are attracted to flowers in gardens and those plants that release their scent at night, such as the tobacco plant (*Nicotiana*) and honeysuckle (*Lonicera*), are visited by a number of species including large migrant hawk-moths. Butterflies seem to be attracted to most flowers that produce a good supply of nectar but different butterfly species appear to have different flower preferences. Studies on the behaviour of the Silver Y moth in Austria have shown that it is attracted to flowers both by colour and by scent. Like other nectar-feeding insects, Lepidoptera are important pollinators of flowers.

Food

Flowers are the main food source of adult Lepidoptera although a wide range of other food supplies is exploited by certain species. The sap flowing from wounds in tree trunks attracts both butterflies and moths, as does the sugary secretion of aphids, known as honeydew, which often coats the leaves of trees in summer. In autumn overripe or rotting fruit is particularly popular with butterflies such as the Camberwell Beauty and the Red Admiral. The Death's Head Hawk-moth was notorious for invading old-fashioned beehives to steal honey but is unable to get into those of modern design.

Some butterflies, such as the Purple Emperors, are attracted to dead animals or to dung from which they suck up nutrient fluids. Other butterflies obtain such nutrients in a less obvious way by drinking from pools or puddles which have been contaminated by the excreta of animals. Many species, particularly in the warmer regions of southern Europe, gather at muddy puddles or on damp earth to drink. It is probable that some are able to absorb important mineral salts in this way.

Caterpillars also show a wide range of feeding habits. The first meal that many caterpillars eat is the empty egg shell from which they have hatched although some do not seem to require this and simply chew a hole large enough to escape, while others proceed to devour any other eggs that have not yet hatched. Cannibalism is quite common in some species, particularly in the early instars, and is often the result of overcrowding or lack of sufficient foodplant. By reduction of the number of individuals an adequate food supply is ensured for the survivors. Some species such as the Dun Bar will attack a wide range of caterpillars which seem to form an essential part of their diet.

Gregarious behaviour

Some caterpillars, particularly those that are distasteful to birds, are gregarious. The caterpillars of the Pine and Oak Processionary moths not only rest in communal silken nests but move to their feeding grounds in an impressive 'procession'. Some caterpillars even wave their bodies about in unison when threatened by enemies.

Resting

The resting habits of Lepidoptera are quite varied and sometimes give a clue to their identification. Skippers are quite unlike other butterflies in the way they hold their wings when at rest. Similarly the Poplar Hawk-moth is the only European hawk-moth to rest with its forewings pushed in front of its hindwings. The Great Banded Grayling and Woodland Grayling butterflies rest on tree trunks and are very well camouflaged while the closely related Grayling butterfly rests on the ground, tilting to one side in order to reduce the shadow cast by its wings.

A great many moths conceal themselves in crevices, under bark or amongst foliage by day and similarly butterflies hide away at night. A number of butterflies roost on grass stems and many blues and skippers may be found clinging to the flower heads in the evening.

Hibernation

Hibernation is a fascinating phenomenon in European butterflies and moths and may occur at any stage of the life history according to the species. Butterflies that hibernate through the winter in the adult stage, such as the Brimstone, the Peacock and the Small Tortoiseshell, hide themselves away in sheltered positions, often in hollow tree trunks or old outbuildings, and remain inactive until the first warm days of spring. Sometimes a warm spell in winter will induce a few to take to the wing but it is not known if these survive to go back into hibernation. Hibernating butterflies are sometimes found in houses, clinging to the curtains or ceiling of an unheated room. It is best to leave them undisturbed although if they become active they may be moved to an outside shed.

Many caterpillars hibernate although some will recommence feeding on mild winter days. The factors that trigger hibernation are probably a critical combination of day length, temperature and condition of food supply. Some Lepidoptera overwinter in the egg or pupa stage and often show remarkable resistance to climatic extremes. Most overwintering eggs are timed to hatch at the same time that the buds begin to burst, thus ensuring an immediate supply of fresh young leaves for food.

Migration

Some of our most attractive butterflies are migrants, including the Painted Lady, the Red Admiral and the Clouded Yellow. These are all natives of southern Europe or North Africa that travel northwards each year, some reaching as far as northern Finland and Iceland. There is seldom any return flight although some species produce a second generation, examples of which have been seen to fly southwards in late summer. In certain valleys of Switzerland, butterfly movements in both directions have been observed, suggesting an outward and return migration.

The purpose of migration in Lepidoptera is not certain, especially as there does not appear to be a significant return flight. It is possible that such movements prevent excessive build-ups of population in the south and provide a means of dispersal which allows the species to become established in new areas when climatic or other environmental changes take place.

Monarch butterfly

The Monarch butterfly which is a rare visitor to Britain is a remarkable migrant in its native North America. Each autumn these butterflies move southwards in vast numbers to their overwintering quarters in Florida and other southern parts of the USA. In the following spring they disperse and begin to move northwards again, reaching southern Canada in early June. Those Monarchs that have been found in the British Isles have all arrived in the autumn at about the time that the great southward migration is taking place in America and it is believed that these have been blown off course and managed to cross the Atlantic. However the Monarch is now established in the Canary Islands and it is possible that some European examples could have originated there.

Migrant moths

Probably the best known moth migrants are hawk-moths. These powerful insects can travel rapidly over long distances. The pretty little Humming-bird Hawk-moth, although one of the smaller and more delicate members of the family, is a regular migrant to the British Isles, arriving in early summer from its native southern Europe and North Africa. Moths of other families are also known to migrate, probably the most common example being the Silver Y moth, a common species in the Mediterranean region where it occurs throughout the year making northward migrations each spring and summer. The beautiful Crimson-speckled moth is a remarkable migrant and, as a result, is extremely widely distributed in Africa, Asia and Australia. It is common throughout the Mediterranean region and migrates into Central Europe each year, occasionally reaching as far north as Britain. This moth has been recorded far out at sea, on one occasion in a position nine hundred miles south-west of the Cape Verde Islands and over four hundred miles from South America.

Oleander Hawk-moth *Daphnis nerii* a migrant to Europe

Attraction to light

One aspect of the behaviour of Lepidoptera which must have been noticed by everyone at some time in their life is the attraction of moths to light. One of the most simple and probably most acceptable explanations of this phenomenon is that moths navigate by maintaining themselves at a fixed angle to the light of the moon but that on moonless or cloudy nights they will 'home in' on any bright light source, flying towards it in a spiral.

Habitats

One of the factors that makes insects as a group so successful is their ability to adapt to a wide range of living conditions. Butterflies and moths are found practically everywhere in the world, from the hottest parts of the tropics to well within the Arctic Circle, and varying degrees of tolerance to extremes of temperature and humidity play an important part in determining their distribution. While some Lepidoptera feed on a large range of plants and so tend to be widespread, others are restricted to one or two food plants and their range is governed by availability of food.

Most families of butterflies and moths are more strongly represented in tropical regions than they are in the temperate zones of Britain and Europe. There is a distinct decrease in the number of butterfly species as one travels north and the British fauna is relatively poor with only sixty or so species. Numbers also tend to be lower at high altitudes although alpine meadows are rich sources of butterflies and moths.

Parks and gardens

Lepidoptera commonly found in parks and gardens feed on weeds or cultivated plants related to those which grow wild in our meadows and hedgerows. The Small Tortoiseshell, the Peacock and related butterflies are attracted to such flowers as Buddleia, Michaelmas Daisy and Sedum. The Large and Small White butterflies have caterpillars which are pests but their attractive yellow relative the Brimstone is a welcome visitor in spring and is quite harmless. Gardens also provide a haven for a wide range of moths such as the Angle Shades, the Dot Moth, the Garden Carpet and the Garden Tiger. Although their caterpillars will all feed on garden plants, they seldom cause serious damage. The only species that are serious pests are those with cutworm caterpillars. The striking caterpillar of the Elephant Hawk-moth is sometimes found on the foliage of garden Fuchsia but despite its startling appearance it is quite harmless and worth rearing in order to see the beautiful adult moth. Another attractive hawk-moth which sometimes may be seen hovering over flowers in parks and gardens is the Humming-bird Hawk.

The trees growing in parks and gardens and along the verges of suburban streets also support a considerable fauna of moths. Both the Poplar and Lime Hawk-moths are common in towns where suitable trees grow and may sometimes be seen flying to the lights of shop windows at night. The day-flying Vapourer Moth is commonly found in parks and city squares where it is often mistaken for a small brown butterfly. Its pretty little caterpillar is sometimes found in large numbers and may cause a nuisance because of its irritant hairs.

Small Tortoiseshell *Aglais urticae* and **Comma** *Polygonia c-album* on Michaelmas Daisy

Fields and hedgerows

While intensively cultivated agricultural land is very poor in Lepidoptera species except for a restricted range of pests, field margins and hedgerows that have not been subjected to spraying are rich in butterflies and moths. The Meadow Brown and Hedge Brown abound in such habitats, together with such attractive species as the Orange-tip, the Small Copper and various blues, whites and skippers, as well as the ubiquitous Small Tortoiseshell and its relatives. Moths of the families Noctuidae and Geometridae frequently abound in such places, hiding by day low down in the hedgerow or beneath foliage on the ground. The Cinnabar is a common moth of field margins where its caterpillars feed on the foliage of ragwort. Lucerne and clover fields are attractive to Clouded Yellow butterflies in many parts of Europe and in some years considerable numbers may be seen in coastal regions of England. The Large White Plume Moth is associated with agricultural land where it feeds as a caterpillar on bindweed.

Downland

Chalk downland is an important habitat for Lepidoptera, particularly the blue butterflies such as the Chalkhill Blue and the Adonis Blue, and is also the home of such species as the Marbled White and the Silver-spotted Skipper. Many moth species will also be found including burnet moths, grass moths, the Mother Shipton and the Burnet Companion. Chalk quarries are similarly rich in these species and often provide a sheltered and sunny habitat. Mediterranean 'maquis' or scrubland is a rich source of butterflies and moths, particularly in limestone areas where the abundant and diverse flora provides food for a wide range of species.

Woodland

While few Lepidoptera are seen in dense woodland with little ground cover, butterflies and moths will be found wherever there is a clearing or path so that light is admitted. Many fritillary butterflies are closely associated with woodlands where their caterpillars feed on the foliage of violets. The attractive White Admiral is another woodland species, its caterpillars feeding on honeysuckle leaves, particularly where they twine around the trunks of trees and trail from the branches. Probably the most magnificent of woodland butterflies are the Purple Emperor and Lesser Purple Emperor, whose caterpillars feed on sallows and poplars. The handsome Great Banded Grayling is another species of European woodlands, the butterfly often resting on the trunks of trees where it is well camouflaged. In contrast the delicate little Wood White may be seen fluttering through woodlands where tuberous pea, the caterpillar's foodplant, grows. Probably the most common woodland butterfly in Britain is the Speckled Wood, a wonderfully camouflaged species whose brown and yellow wings blend superbly with the dappled sunlight in which it settles. Many moths are associated with woodlands and their caterpillars may be found on the foliage of trees or on the undergrowth of scrub and herbage. The Buff-tip is a typical example, its caterpillars feeding gregariously on the foliage of oak, sallow and many other deciduous trees. The attractive little Green Oak Tortrix is an extremely common and widespread species, occurring throughout Europe and sometimes causing damage when its caterpillars completely strip the foliage from areas of oak woodland.

Some species are confined to particular types of woodland, examples being the Barred Hook-tip, the Lobster Moth and the Tau Emperor, all of which are most frequently found in beech woods. Coniferous forests have their own distinctive fauna, including such species as the Pine Hawk-moth, the Pine Processionary, the Pine-tree Lappet and the rare Spanish Moon Moth. The caterpillars of the Black Arches moth will feed on the foliage of both deciduous and coniferous trees and are found in all types of forest.

Clearing in oak woodland, New Forest, England

Orchards

Many woodland and hedgerow Lepidoptera are found in orchards and some are regarded as pests. Both the Large Tortoiseshell and the Black-veined White butterfly were at one time orchard pests but have become scarce in many areas and no longer cause significant damage. An attractive butterfly which does not occur in Britain but is a visitor to many European orchards is the Scarce Swallowtail, another species that has been declining in numbers in recent years. Other butterfly visitors are the vanessids which come in the autumn to feed on fallen fruit. The Camberwell Beauty is a good example although it is only an occasional visitor to Britain. In southern Europe the most spectacular orchard moth is the splendid Great Peacock, whose striking caterpillar sometimes feeds on the foliage of fruit trees and is occasionally a minor pest. Other common moths of orchards which at times are serious pests are the Winter Moth, the Mottled Umber, the Lackey and the Codling Moth. The large Lappet moth was at one time an occasional pest in British orchards but is less common now and mainly confined to hedgerows.

Mountains

Mountains may seem to provide a rather hostile habitat for Lepidoptera but many species are completely confined to such areas. The handsome Apollo butterfly is a truly montane species, its caterpillar feeding on the succulent leaves of stonecrop (*Sedum*) which grows among the rocks. Many butterflies of the genus *Erebia* are confined to mountain habitats and are difficult to catch as they fly rapidly over rocks and scree. At high altitudes in the British Isles where the climate is particularly harsh only one butterfly is found, the Mountain Ringlet. Many moths have also adapted to mountain habitats although they are not so well known as the butterflies. Alpine meadows are frequently rich in flowers and have an abundant fauna of butterflies and moths, many of which also occur at lower altitudes.

Heath and moorland

Heath and moorland provide habitats for a number of interesting butterflies and moths, including the Small Heath, the Silver-studded Blue, the Emperor Moth, the Fox Moth, the Antler Moth, the Common Heath and the True Lover's Knot. Their caterpillars feed on heather or coarse grasses. The Large Heath is a butterfly of wet moorlands but it also occurs in lowland marshes and bogs.

Habitat of the **Large Heath** *Coenonympha tullia* in Cumbria, England

Wetland

Other examples of wetland butterflies are the Marsh Fritillary, the Lesser Marbled Fritillary, the Large Copper, the Purple-edged Copper and the British subspecies of the Swallowtail. Many moths are also associated with wetlands, including the Scarlet Tiger whose caterpillars feed mainly on comfrey (*Symphytum*), and the Common Wainscot which belongs to a group of species associated with coarse grasses growing in marshy places. Some moths, while not living in bogs and marshes, simply require damp conditions in order to thrive. Examples are the Chimney Sweeper which frequents damp ditches and many of the footman moths, whose caterpillars feed on algae and lichens in humid habitats. The caterpillars of the Brown China-mark moth feed on pondweeds and are semi-aquatic.

Brittany coast, France

Coastal regions

Coastal habitats are favoured by many butterflies and moths and are often good places for observing incoming migrant species. In England the Glanville Fritillary only occurs on the undercliffs of the Isle of Wight where frequent landslips provide ideal conditions for growth of the foodplant. The Lulworth Skipper is restricted to the cliffs of southern Dorset, centred around Lulworth Cove. Coastal sandhills provide a habitat for many species of moths, including the Grass Eggar and the Wormwood. Coastal areas of Mediterranean Europe are famous for some of the more exotic butterflies such as the Spanish Festoon and the Two-tailed Pasha.

Habitat preferences

Some species are unusual in that they have different habitat preferences in different parts of their range. An example is the High Brown Fritillary which frequents woodlands in the northern parts of its range but in southern Europe is found on upland heaths. Some Lepidoptera have distinct subspecies which can be recognised by their habitat preferences. In Britain the Five-spot Burnet is a good example with ssp. *palustrella* occurring on chalk downland and ssp. *decreta* confined to marshland. The English subspecies of the Swallowtail butterfly, ssp. *britannicus*, is restricted to wet fenland but the continental ssp. *machaon* is found in meadows and on hillsides up to an altitude of 2000 metres.

Man-made environments

It is the extreme versatility of butterflies and moths that makes them such interesting objects of study. They are even ready to recolonise land which man has disturbed in various ways. Roadside verges have always been good places to see butterflies and moths but the embankments and verges of motorways are providing new habitats that are relatively undisturbed once established. Railway cuttings and embankments provide habitats for many species and disused railways sometimes provide delightful footpaths with an abundance of butterflies and moths.

Enemies and Diseases

It may at first seem strange that butterflies and moths lay such large numbers of eggs, sometimes amounting to several hundred, when all that is required to maintain the population is the production of two adult offspring. However when we come to look at the vast array of predators, parasites and diseases that assail them from the instant that the eggs are laid, it seems remarkable that any survive.

Large predators

Probably the most obvious enemies of Lepidoptera are birds as they are often seen to attack and eat butterflies in gardens and feed their young with beakfuls of caterpillars in the spring. Even unlikely species such as owls have been found with large numbers of cutworm caterpillars in their crops. Another unlikely consumer of caterpillars is the fox but examination of stomach contents show that these animals often eat large numbers of ground dwelling species when larger food is not available. Smaller mammals such as mice and shrews are believed to account for large numbers of Lepidoptera in both the caterpillar and pupa stage. Bats are among the major enemies of nocturnal moths, caught on the wing with remarkable skill.

Whitethroat with **Winter Moth** *Operophtera brumata* caterpillars

Small predators

Many insects are predators including dragonflies, robber flies, solitary wasps and beetles. Dragonflies and robber flies are powerful fliers and will attack butterflies and moths on the wing while most predatory wasps and beetles attack the caterpillar stage. Solitary wasps of the families Vespidae and Sphegidae sting their caterpillar prey to paralyse it before carrying it to their nest where it serves as a living food supply for their larvae. Ground beetles of the family Carabidae are important caterpillar predators and the large and handsome *Calosoma sycophanta* Linnaeus is known to be an important agent in the control of populations of the Gypsy Moth.

Crab spider eating **Small Pearl-bordered Fritillary** *Boloria selene*

Spiders are enemies of butterflies, moths and their caterpillars and the wings of Lepidoptera may often be found in spiders' webs. The sinister crab spiders which so successfully resemble flowers are particularly important as predators of butterflies. Sometimes a butterfly that seems to have remained motionless on a flower head for a long time will be found to have fallen victim to one of these lethal impostors.

Parasitic wasps

While this collection of foes may seem formidable, by far the most important class of enemies are the parasitic wasps and flies which account for countless millions of Lepidoptera every year. The parasitic wasps are often referred to collectively as 'Ichneumons' although many do not belong to the family Ichneumonidae. Some of these parasitic wasps have long egg-laying tubes or ovipositors which are capable of penetrating the skin of a caterpillar so that eggs can be laid within its body. These eggs hatch and the parasitic grubs develop inside the caterpillar's body without damaging any of the vital organs. When the grubs are fully developed they either eat their way out through the skin or remain inside until the caterpillar pupates and then pupate themselves. In the former case the caterpillar dies and the parasitic grubs pupate alongside but in the latter case parasitic wasps emerge from the pupa of the butterfly or moth.

Many of the smaller species are unable to penetrate the skin with their ovipositors and have adopted other methods of attack. Some lay their eggs on the caterpillar's foodplant where they will be swallowed. Once inside the caterpillar's body the eggs rapidly hatch and the grubs take up their parasitic mode of life. Other species of parasitic wasps lay their eggs on the caterpillar's body where they hatch and the young grubs bore their way in, usually through the soft membranes between the segments.

Another strategy adopted by some wasps is to lay their eggs within the eggs of Lepidoptera. Some small species complete their development within the lepidopteran egg and emerge as adults before the egg can hatch, whereas others do not reach maturity until the caterpillar is full grown. Some wasps lay their eggs within the pupa, penetrating the cuticle while it is still soft. These eggs develop into adults before the butterfly or moth is due to emerge.

Probably the best known parasitic wasp is *Apanteles glomeratus* Linnaeus which belongs to the family Braconidae. It is an important parasite of the Large White butterfly and is believed to be responsible for controlling the size of populations of this serious pest. The grubs which emerge from the moribund caterpillar spin a distinctive mass of sulphur yellow cocoons alongside the body. A closely related species, *Apanteles zygaenorum* Marshall, is a common parasite of burnet moths.

Parasitic flies

Parasitic flies of the family Tachinidae are also important controllers of butterfly and moth populations. They attack caterpillars in similar ways to parasitic wasps although they do not have long ovipositors and are unable to reach those that are concealed in tunnels or leaf rolls. The grubs feed within the caterpillar's body and usually bore their way out to pupate. They may be distinguished at this stage from wasps by the fact that they pupate in smooth, oval puparia consisting of the hardened larval skin which encases the pupa. The puparium is often distinctly patterned and it is sometimes possible to recognise the species at this stage.

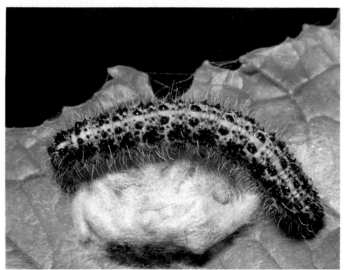

Large White *Pieris brassicae* caterpillar with cocoon mass of *Apanteles* parasite

Mites

A group of parasites about which relatively little is known are the mites. Red mites are sometimes seen on the bodies and wings of butterflies, particularly of the family Satyridae, and also on moths. These are the larval stages of mites of the families Erythraeidae and Trombidiidae which become free-living predators in their later stages. They attach themselves to Lepidoptera on which they feed until engorged and then drop off, apparently causing little harm to the host. Other less obvious mite parasites lodge themselves under the head behind the coiled proboscis or even within the tympanal organ (ear) of many moths of the family Noctuidae. Other species of mite doubtlessly use butterflies and moths as a means of transport, clinging to their bodies without actually feeding. As Dr Treat says in his fascinating book on mites of butterflies and moths, it is often difficult to distinguish the hitch-hiker from the hijacker!

Fungi

Fungi may be regarded as lying somewhere between parasites and pathogens (disease-causing viruses and bacteria) and are sometimes important controllers of insect populations. The most spectacular fungus that attacks caterpillars while they are hibernating belongs to the genus *Cordyceps*. The caterpillar is attacked while below ground and the fungal mycelium extends throughout the insect's tissues, finally sending up a fruiting body on a long stem which pushes out through the soil surface. The shrivelled and hardened caterpillar with the long fruiting body attached is a curious sight. In some places these are known as 'vegetable caterpillars' and in China they are ground up and used for medicinal purposes.

Diseases

Anyone who has reared large numbers of caterpillars will have experienced at some time the devastating effects of bacterial or viral infections. Bacterial infections are the most common form of insect disease and the cause of many deaths. Infected caterpillars become lethargic and then cease to feed, sometimes becoming blackened and discharging fluids in the final stages of the disease. Dead caterpillars rapidly blacken and become soft and shapeless. The best known pathogen of Lepidoptera is *Bacillus thuringiensis* Berliner which can now be artificially cultured for use as a biological insecticide.

Viruses

Virus diseases are also of great importance in the Lepidoptera although seldom found in other groups of insects. The initial symptoms are similar to those of bacterial infections but caterpillars do not change colour and often weaken and fall from the foodplant before dying. The use of viruses as control agents for pest species is also being investigated.

Transmission of disease

Transfer of disease is often by contact with the excreta of diseased caterpillars. It is believed that some of these diseases may be disseminated by birds and other predators that eat infected caterpillars and void viable disease spores in their droppings without themselves being affected. Most diseases are spread by air and water-borne spores, however, and conditions of stress may be required before they can take a hold.

A number of caterpillars attacked by these pathogens do not die but are weakened and carry the infection through to another generation.

Survival

Although it may seem surprising from this account that any butterflies or moths should survive at all, all of these predators, parasites and diseases rely on the ultimate survival of their host species for their own existence. They are thus maintained in a delicate balance that fluctuates from season to season and year to year.

Defence Systems

Poisonous hairs

Unlike some other insects, such as bees and wasps, butterflies and moths are unable to sting or bite although some have the ability to make their attackers feel distinctly uncomfortable. The nearest weapon to a sting is possessed by some caterpillars, particularly those of the Brown-tail and Processionary moths. These carry numerous barbed hairs equipped with irritant poison, and anyone unfortunate enough to have come into contact with them will know that they can cause an extremely painful nettle-rash on sensitive skins. Even hairy caterpillars such as those of the Garden Tiger which are possibly not poisonous may cause some irritation and would certainly make an unpleasant mouthful for most birds or small mammals. It is also likely that dense hairs afford some protection from parasitic wasps and flies, the caterpillars' worst enemies.

The Brown-tail Moth utilises the poisonous caterpillar hairs as a means of protection in all of its stages. When the caterpillar pupates, the cast skin remains within the cocoon and the female moth, on emergence, picks up the hairs on her 'brown-tail'. On laying her eggs she transfers caterpillar hairs onto the surface of the sticky egg mass, thus completing the cycle of protection. When threatened both male and female moths display their 'brown-tails' although it is only the female that carries poison hairs. The male therefore gains protection by resembling his poisonous partner, an interesting case of mimicry.

Distasteful species

Many Lepidoptera gain protection from being distasteful or even poisonous. Some caterpillars eat plants containing poisons that are not harmful to themselves but give protection from enemies by making them unpalatable. Others, such as those of the Burnet Moths, apparently manufacture their own poisons which are effective against all but the most determined of predators. One thing that most distasteful insects have in common is a conspicuous colour pattern, usually of red or yellow contrasted with black or white, that immediately advertises their unpalatability. Many are gregarious and so maximise the effect of their warning colours. An example may be seen in the brightly banded caterpillars of the Cinnabar Moth which feed together in companies on ragwort plants.

Mimicry

Some species that are not poisonous have developed similar colour patterns to those that are, and so gain protection. Mimicry of this sort is most evident in the tropics where there is a much greater abundance of both individuals and species. Some of the most interesting mimics to occur in Europe are the Clearwing moths and certain hawk-moths that resemble bees and wasps. The Hornet Clearwing is a superb example of an insect mimicking another of a different order. The transparent wings of this moth combined with its striped abdomen and buzzing flight make it very difficult to distinguish from a hornet at a distance and only the expert would be prepared to take a closer look!

The Lobster Moth has one of the most unusual caterpillars of all European moths. Its long legs and strangely shaped body make it look extremely spider-like while newly hatched caterpillars look just like ants. Coupled with this curious form is the ability to squirt a jet of formic acid at any predator that becomes too curious. This weapon is shared by caterpillars of the related Puss Moth which also give a most impressive display when threatened by an enemy. They puff up the front end of the body and wave their whip-like tails over their heads in a menacing manner like miniature dragons.

Flash coloration

Some Lepidoptera make use of 'flash coloration' to disconcert certain enemies. This is nicely illustrated by the Red Underwing moth which usually rests on tree trunks with its brightly coloured hindwings covered by the inconspicuous brown forewings. If the moth is disturbed it flicks forward its forewings to reveal the red hindwings as a brilliant flash of warning colour. The combination of bright and dull colours also serves to confuse enemies which pursue their prey in flight. Colours are often arranged so that they are visible while in flight but become concealed as soon as the insect lands so that it blends into the background quite suddenly and 'disappears'

Butterflies often use bright upperside wing colours to signal to their mates, whereas the underside of the wings is camouflaged. Thus in the Orange-tip butterfly the uppersides of the males have bright orange wing-tips while the undersides are patterned with green and white and merge with the surrounding foliage when the butterfly comes to rest with its wings closed over its back.

Eye-spots

Eye-spots are widely used by Lepidoptera as a protective device. Many species use brilliant eye-spots to scare or confuse birds and other predators. The caterpillar of the Elephant Hawk-moth possesses eye-spots on the sides of its thorax which do not seem very impressive at first encounter. However when it is disturbed the

caterpillar withdraws its head into the thorax which becomes swollen and distended to form a large false head with enormous eyes on either side. Many have likened this caterpillar to a small snake; its menacing appearance may be sufficient to frighten predators.

Another use of eye-spots is to divert the attention of predators away from the most vulnerable part of the insect's body. The eye-spots of many butterflies and some moths are placed towards the edges of the wings and form false targets for birds and small animals, such as lizards, aiming for the kill. Specimens are frequently found with pieces bitten out of the wings in these areas but, while this may be disfiguring, it does not seem to be a serious inconvenience to the insect. Some Hairstreak butterflies have small eye-spots and tails at the extremeties of the hindwings. When at rest these butterflies appear to have a head at the wrong end of the body with the small tails looking like antennae. This not only diverts the attacker but also enables the butterfly to fly off in an unexpected direction.

Camouflage

Most of the defence systems so far described have involved conspicuous markings or behaviour that either warn or confuse potential predators. Probably the most universal defence system to be found in the Lepidoptera is that of camouflage. 'Looper' or 'stick' caterpillars of the family Geometridae not only look like twigs or stems in colour and shape but also hold themselves at an angle from the main stem in such a way that they are almost impossible to detect until they move. Even fine details such as small buds and leaf scars are simulated by the caterpillar's patterning and structure. The space between the claspers which grip the stem is often furnished with fine hairs which break up any shadow cast by the body and make the join between plant and insect almost invisible. The avoidance of tell-tale shadows cast by the body is one of the tricks of camouflage. Caterpillars achieve this by counter shading so that the upper surface which is in the light is darker in colour than the under surface which is in shadow, making the whole insect appear as an evenly coloured, flat surface. Caterpillars such as those of the Poplar Hawk-moth which rest upside down on stems have this light and dark pattern reversed to maintain the counter-shading effect.'

The wings of many moths are patterned to blend with the bark of tree trunks on which they rest. These markings often continue over both fore- and hindwings and further serve to break up the shape of the insect. Some species can cope with a colour change in their background. In rural areas the most commonly found examples of the Peppered Moth are whitish, peppered finely with black, a useful camouflage on pale tree trunks bearing patches of lichen. In industrial areas however where smoke and soot have polluted the atmosphere and tree trunks are dark, the commonest form of this moth is almost black and blends extremely well with its background.

Orange-tip *Anthocharis cardamines* showing bright wing tips

Orange-tip *Anthocharis cardamines* at rest with wing tips concealed

Comma *Polygonia c-album* resembling dead leaf

Many Lepidoptera achieve their camouflage by resembling inanimate objects. Wing shape can play an important part in this form of camouflage. The Comma butterfly has ragged edges to its wings and when at rest hangs from a plant stem in such a way that it strongly resembles a dead leaf.

Bird-dropping mimics of many types may be found among the Lepidoptera, including both caterpillars and adults. The forewings of the Chinese Character moth are patterned with grey and white to produce a very convincing effect when it is at rest on a leaf with its wings folded over its back. Caterpillars of the Comma butterfly and Alder Moth have similar colouring and add to the effect by curling their bodies into a characteristic bird-dropping shape when at rest. The Alder Moth caterpillar changes in its final instar to a remarkable creature banded with black and yellow and possesses large, paddle-shaped hairs. The reason for this change in the final stage is probably that the startling effect of this form would not be achieved by small caterpillars. Similar changes in different instars occur in caterpillars of the Emperor Moth. When very small they are black and rest on stems of heather but, as they grow, they become too large for this kind of concealment and so take on a broken green and black pattern which blends very well with heather foliage. Caterpillars that feed externally on pine needles are almost invariably patterned in longitudinal stripes of green, yellow and white, a most important camouflage as pine needles otherwise offer little concealment.

Cocoons and other devices

The pupa is a vulnerable stage in the life cycle as it is virtually immobile and easily damaged. Amongst pupae that remain exposed, a few, such as those of the Magpie Moth, are distasteful and possess warning coloration but many rely on some form of camouflage for protection. The pupa of the Large White butterfly is one of those that can be adapted in colour to match its background. It has been proved that the colour of the pupa is influenced by colours perceived by the caterpillar prior to pupation. A great many pupae are concealed underground or beneath bark or dead foliage, and these are usually black or brown in colour. Many pupae are protected by an additional shelter of silk spun by the caterpillar and known as a cocoon. The most famous cocoons are those of the silkworms of commerce, *Bombyx mori* Linnaeus, each being composed of an unbroken thread of some 500 metres in length. Some cocoons, such as those of the Puss Moth, are made of silk combined with fragments of wood or other materials and are so tough that the emerging moth has to use special softening chemicals in order to break its way out. The Emperor Moth cocoon is armed with a ring of outward-pointing spines at its mouth, allowing the moth to emerge easily but preventing the entrance of enemies.

Some caterpillars construct shelters, often of leaves spun together with silk, and some gregarious species produce a communal protective web. Silk also provides a useful escape ladder for caterpillars when attacked. The caterpillar drops on a silken thread and sometimes spins round rapidly so that it becomes almost invisible. It can remain suspended for some time but climbs back to its feeding place when danger has passed.

Sound

One unexpected factor that plays an important role in some aspects of defence is sound. A number of pupae are capable of producing audible squeaking noises which appear to have a deterrent effect on predators. However, a more sophisticated use of sound is found in moths of the family Arctiidae. Most of these are night-flying moths which are distasteful but unable to make use of the devices of warning coloration. Instead they produce a distinctive, high-pitched sound which is audible to bats, their chief enemies, who associate this particular noise with a distasteful insect and do not attack. Other palatable night-flying moths have a highly tuned sense of hearing that enables them to dodge the attacks of bats. This is because bats navigate by a system of radar, using series of high-pitched squeaks that bounce back to them from surrounding objects. Although most of these sounds are inaudible to the human ear, moths are able to respond to these high frequencies. A similar sensitivity to particular sound frequencies may be found in many caterpillars which start to twitch at the sound of the high-pitched whine of parasitic wasps in flight. This seems to be a defensive action to prevent the parasites from landing to lay eggs on the caterpillar's body.

Escape

One of the most basic defence systems is that of running away when threatened with danger. Many Lepidoptera can fly and dodge quite rapidly; others drop to the ground and scuttle away into hiding, often a surer method of escaping from birds. The caterpillar of the White Ermine moth usually curls into a tight ball when first disturbed but after a few seconds will run off at amazing speed, hence its scientific name *lubricipeda* meaning fleet-footed.

Defence from disease and climatic extremes is largely a matter of physiological adaptation which may develop quite rapidly. An indication of this may be seen in the case of certain pest species that have developed resistance to insecticides within a few years. In spite of these defence systems, mortality in Lepidoptera is still very high but the balance is redressed by the large number of young produced by those that survive to maturity.

Butterflies and Moths as Pests

Pest species are usually those that feed naturally on wild plants closely related to cultivated varieties on which they can flourish equally well. With the intensification of agricultural methods and the building up of extensive monocultures where one particular crop is grown over a wide area, ideal conditions are provided for pests to become established. Devastating damage can be caused by such pests in the tropics and subtropics where entire crops may be destroyed, sometimes causing subsequent famine or economic disaster.

Cutworms

Most pest damage is caused by caterpillars although in tropical regions some moths of the family Noctuidae are capable of damaging fruits by piercing them with their specially modified probosces in order to suck the juices. Some of the most injurious caterpillar pests feed at the bases of young plants, cutting them off at ground level so that they fall over and die. These caterpillars are appropriately called 'cutworms' and mostly belong to the family Noctuidae, typical European examples being the Turnip Moth and the Garden Dart. Similar damage is sometimes caused by the caterpillars of the Common Swift and the Ghost Moth which are primarily root feeders and are particularly likely to attack crops grown on freshly ploughed grassland. Many cutworms may also feed on roots, and caterpillars of the Turnip Moth are frequently found in hollowed-out roots of swede and turnip as well as in potato tubers. Caterpillars of the Antler Moth sometimes reach plague proportions and destroy large areas of upland grazing.

Leaf-feeders

Probably the most common form of damage caused by butterflies and moths is defoliation as the great majority of species are leaf feeders. The Large and Small White butterflies are probably the most familiar examples of this type of pest and are important ravagers of cabbage and many related plants. When large populations of these species build up they can reduce a field of cabbages to skeletons in a relatively short time. Such large scale attacks are usually followed by a dramatic decrease in population size of these butterflies following a build-up of their parasites. While Large White caterpillars are easily seen on the foodplant, those of the Small White usually feed concealed within the hearts of cabbages and are not detected until considerable damage has been caused. This is also the case in caterpillars of the Cabbage Moth which often occur in similar situations but seldom cause extensive damage.

Forest and orchard pests

An important group of defoliators is that which feeds on forest trees and may cause serious reductions in timber yields. The amount of damage caused is often difficult to assess as trees that have suffered extensive attack may appear to have recovered even though their vigour is reduced and subsequently they become more prone to diseases and fungal infection. The small caterpillars of the Oak Tortrix may occur in such numbers that trees are completely denuded of foliage and entire areas of woodland appear to have been affected by a premature autumn although a second flush of foliage replaces the eaten leaves and little permanent damage is apparent. An important group of defoliators of fruit trees are known as 'Winter Moths' and include caterpillars of the Winter Moth, the Mottled Umber and the March Moth. All three species hatch in the spring and feed on the newly opening leaf and flower buds, sometimes causing a serious reduction in fruit yield. The distinctive caterpillars of the Magpie Moth are pests of blackcurrants, redcurrants and gooseberries and are particularly damaging in gardens and allotments.

Conifer pests

Coniferous forests have a number of serious moth pests, one of the most important and interesting being the Pine Processionary Moth. It causes extensive damage in Mediterranean Europe and the poisonous hairs of the caterpillars are a hazard to those who are involved in control measures. In Britain the most serious pest of coniferous forests has until recent times been the Bordered White moth whose caterpillar, the notorious 'Pine Looper', feeds on the needles and causes extensive damage. However, another species, the Pine Beauty, has recently caused concern after devastating new conifer plantations in Scotland. This species is a well-known pest in continental Europe.

Gypsy Moth

The Gypsy Moth which is a pest of deciduous trees in Europe was at one time quite common in England but in the mid nineteenth century became rare and died out. Almost simultaneously this moth was accidentally introduced to North America and became an extremely serious forest pest there.

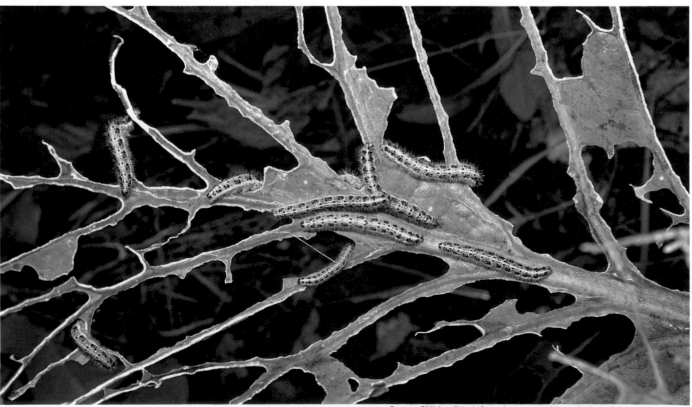

Large White *Pieris brassicae* caterpillars skeletonising cabbage leaf

Oaks defoliated by **Green Oak Tortrix** *Tortrix viridana*

Woodborers

Other pests of trees are those that bore into the wood, the most important being those belonging to the family Cossidae. The largest and most serious European pest in this group is the Goat Moth whose large, evil-smelling caterpillars may so seriously damage a tree that it dies. Caterpillars of the smaller Leopard Moth are much more common that the Goat Moth in many regions and feed in the branches, weakening them to such an extent that they may snap off. Caterpillars of many clearwing moths, such as the Hornet Clearwing, also bore into wood but seldom cause damage of economic importance. Parallel forms of damage may occur in herbaceous plants caused by stem borers such as the caterpillars of the Rosy Rustic moth which can be serious pests of potatoes, tomatoes and chrysanthemums.

Fruit and seed eaters

The fruits and seeds of plants are also attacked by caterpillars and these may cause serious reduction in crop yields. The caterpillar of the Scarce Bordered Straw moth, although seldom found in Britain, is a serious pest of tomatoes, maize and other crops in southern Europe and of cotton in Africa. Caterpillars of this widespread pest are variously known as the Tomatoworm, the Bollworm or the Corn Earworm. Many caterpillars of microlepidoptera are also pests of economic importance, an example being the Pea Moth. Its grub-like caterpillars are concealed within the pods and are the well known pea maggots. Caterpillars of the Codling moth which are the familiar apple maggots are an equally serious pest and rigorous control methods are applied to keep them in check.

Bright-line Brown-eye *Lacanobia oleracea* caterpillar in tomato

Clothes moth

Probably the best known of all moth pests is the clothes moth, a member of the family Tineidae. The Common Clothes Moth has a small white grub-like caterpillar which feeds on a wide range of substances of animal origin and readily attacks wool, felt, feathers and fur. In some regions this once exceedingly common pest seems to be on the decrease, probably due to the increasing use of man-made fibres on which the caterpillars are unable to feed. They also seem to require a fairly high humidity and are less likely to thrive in dry, centrally heated homes. Another domestic pest which is often more common than the clothes moth is the Brown House-moth, a member of the family Oecophoridae. This cosmopolitan pest will feed on all manner of substances of both plant and animal origin and frequently breeds in birds' and wasps' nests in the lofts of houses. The grub-like caterpillars will feed in dust and debris behind skirting boards and between floorboards and can cause serious damage to carpets and furnishings, particularly in damp conditions.

Control

Methods of control are continuously changing to meet the needs of present day society. As we have seen in the case of the Gypsy Moth, the status of a pest may change dramatically over the years so that the need for control disappears altogether. The caterpillars of the Black-veined White were at one time considered to be an orchard pest in England but this species is now extinct in the British Isles and is rapidly declining in many parts of Europe. Conversely many pine-feeding species have become more of a problem following the extensive afforestation that has taken place in recent years.

Insecticides

The use of insecticidal sprays is a controversial subject and it has been proved in many instances that in the long term these have caused more harm than good. Chemical insecticides are likely to be harmful to man and we have seen quite recently that severe restrictions have been placed on the use of DDT, a chemical that was at one time considered to be safe. A number of other insecticides have also been banned or restricted in use. In Britain insecticides that are regarded as safe are now marked with a government seal of approval but even these should be used with caution and strictly in accordance with manufacturers' instructions.

Many insects have built up resistance to insecticides and in some cases indiscriminate spraying has upset the balance of nature paving the way for new pest species to become established. These sprays may also kill bees and other beneficial insects and have an indirect effect on the birds and mammals that feed on them.

Biological methods

Methods of biological control have recently been proving extremely effective without serious disturbance to other wildlife. A simple method of biological control is to encourage predators such as insectivorous birds by providing plentiful nest boxes in woodland areas. Even more basic are adaptations of agricultural procedures to prevent the build up of pests by rotation of crops, use of resistant plant strains and thorough cleaning of the land.

Among the more sophisticated methods of control is the use of insect viruses and bacteria which may be sprayed from the air and will only affect the insects that are causing the damage. It has proved particularly successful in controlling forest pests such as the Pine Processionary Moth.

The powerful effects of sex attractant scents or pheremones have been used in two ways to control pest Lepidoptera. In some instances, particularly in the case of the Gypsy Moth in North America, pheremones have been used to trap males or have been released in such quantities that the males become confused and fail to find mates. In Britain and parts of continental Europe pheremone traps are used to monitor the population levels of specific pests such as the Pea Moth. In this way the critical time for applying control sprays may be accurately calculated.

Advice to gardeners

For the gardener or allotment holder who is faced with a bewildering array of products for killing pests the best way to control caterpillars is to hand pick them but where this is not possible the use of a non-persistent, plant-based insecticide is preferable to a powerful all-purpose chemical spray. Cleanliness in the garden is also important as weeds will often harbour insect pests that will later attack cultivated plants.

Collecting and Study

Collecting butterflies and moths is a long-established and popular hobby which has come under considerable criticism from conservationists in recent years. In the seventeenth and eighteenth centuries collectors were regarded as eccentrics and often as objects of fun but by the mid nineteenth century collecting had become respectable and continued to be so throughout the Victorian and Edwardian eras. Collecting Lepidoptera is today sometimes likened to the pursuit of collecting birds' eggs, an activity that is now prohibited by law in Britain. This analogy is not valid, however, as birds and insects have totally different population dynamics. One only has to consider that birds lay a small number of eggs, all in one nest, while Lepidoptera may lay several hundred eggs distributed singly or in small batches over a wide area. This does not mean that indiscriminate collecting is acceptable and the individual should think carefully before killing large numbers of these beautiful creatures. Our fauna of butterflies and moths is under threat and it is difficult to persuade farmers, foresters and developers to cooperate in conservation programmes if entomologists are still seen to be collecting insects in large numbers.

Why collect?

While most European butterflies and many of the larger moths are fairly easy to recognise in the field, it is often impossible to make accurate records of certain groups without capturing specimens and making a small reference collection. An example of the confusion that can arise may be seen in the case of the Copper Underwings which were considered to be represented by a single species in the British Isles but have only recently been discovered to consist of two species, the Copper Underwing and Svensson's Copper Underwing. All early records are now in doubt unless the specimens to which they refer can be examined.

The following section on collecting equipment is provided not only for those who wish to make a reference collection but also for those who wish to study insects more closely and possibly to rear them.

Nets

The basic net consists of a cotton or nylon net bag fixed to a hoop of cane or metal that in turn is attached to a short, strong handle. Butterfly collectors generally choose black or dark green nets as these are less conspicuous during the day, while moth collectors who frequently work at dusk often prefer a white net in which their captures may be more easily seen. One of the most popular nets is known as the kite net because of the shape of the supporting ring. The more simple round ring nets are easily collapsible for storage but are possibly less efficient for catching fast-flying species. The net bag should be rounded at the bottom so that specimens cannot become trapped and damaged and long enough to fold over the mouth of the net to close it.

Hunting butterflies in the Julian Alps, Yugoslavia

The technique of using a butterfly net is only acquired after considerable practice and requires a knowledge of the way different species fly. The basic technique is to make a smooth and rapid sweep of the net, rotating the wrist at the end of the stroke in order to close the mouth of the net and prevent the escape of any captives. Too strong a stroke with the net may damage a specimen you may later want to release. Care should also be taken to avoid brambles and sharp twigs which are likely to tear the net bag. Some lepidopterists carry a small repair kit for such emergencies. Once a specimen has been captured it should be transferred to a transparent pill box or similar container within the net bag, after which it may be examined at leisure. Live specimens should not be confined in small boxes for long periods and should never be exposed to bright sunlight.

Collecting caterpillars with a beating tray

Beating trays

The more robust sweep net which has a stout ring and heavy material bag is sometimes useful for sweeping through foliage to collect caterpillars. Although this can be quite productive, especially in meadows towards dusk when many caterpillars climb the plant stems to feed, it is often difficult to find out which foodplants the caterpillars have been swept from. A more efficient 'caterpillar net' is the beating tray. In its simplest form this is an upturned umbrella held under trees or bushes while the foliage is 'beaten' with a stick. The term beating is an unfortunate one as it implies causing damage to the plant. The correct technique is to tap the branches sharply to dislodge feeding or resting caterpillars. Any more violent activity tends to make the caterpillars cling more tightly, as they do in windy weather. Many forms of beating tray exist but probably the best design consists of a rectangular white sheet stretched over a cane frame which can be folded when not in use.

Searching

A less efficient but most rewarding method of collecting all stages of Lepidoptera is by careful searching in suitable habitats. The experienced lepidopterist looks for sunny sheltered places where butterflies and moths will rest and sun themselves. He will also look for signs of caterpillar feeding, such as webbed and eaten leaves, droppings, dying foliage and distorted flower heads. The undersides of leaves and twigs are good places to look for egg batches and pupae may be found by digging at the roots of the foodplant. A good knowledge of plants is a great help to the lepidopterist and will often lead to the discovery of species that would otherwise be very difficult to find.

Sugaring

It was in the mid nineteenth century that the famous British lepidopterist Edward Doubleday discovered the principle of sugaring for moths when he noticed that they were attracted to empty sugar casks in the back yard of his grocer's shop. The technique consists of painting bands of sugar mixture on tree trunks and other suitable surfaces at dusk and visiting them at regular intervals during the night to capture the moths that have been attracted. Recipes for 'sugar' have a certain magic of their own and most practitioners like to experiment with different mixtures. The basic ingredients are raw sugar or molasses mixed with beer which are then boiled together to make a sticky treacle. Just before use a small quantity of rum can be added as an additional attractant. The moths that are most readily attracted to sugar are those of the family Noctuidae and the majority are common species. However, this is a fascinating and exciting method of collecting and sometimes produces the unexpected rarity.

Light traps

The phenomenon of the attraction of moths to light is well known and has been employed by collectors for a long time. This method of collecting was revolutionised in the late 1940s by the invention of the mercury vapour trap. This uses an ultra-violet emitting mercury vapour lamp which is much more attractive to moths than ordinary tungsten light. The conventional trap consists of a circular drum fitted at the top with a conical perspex or plastic collar, in the centre of which is seated the bulb surrounded by a series of vanes which deflect the moths into the chamber below. The trap should contain plenty of broken egg cartons or other material which will provide shelter for the captured moths and prevent them from damaging each other.

Light traps should be examined early in the morning and those specimens not required should be placed in a large covered box where they can remain until released in the evening. All too often collectors have liberated the contents of their trap in the morning only to find that birds have snapped them all up in a few minutes. Birds soon locate the site of a light trap and will wait nearby in the prospect of a feast.

A more instructive and often more exciting way to collect moths at night is to suspend a lamp over a white sheet spread on the ground and to examine and capture the moths that arrive. In this way it is possible to catch species that avoid being caught in traps and also to gain some appreciation of how different species fly at different times of night. Slow-flying species such as some geometrid moths sometimes settle at the periphery of the lighted area and should be carefully watched for.

A word of warning should be given regarding mercury vapour lights as the ultra-violet emission is damaging to the eyes if protective glasses are not worn. Another danger is that the bulb gets very hot and may explode if a few drops of rain fall on it, so it should be carefully protected. A wide range of lamps are now used in light traps including 'black lights' which emit ultra-violet light only and small actinic fluorescent tubes which have a low power consumption. The old-fashioned petrol or paraffin hurricane lamp can also be very effective and is particularly useful in out-of-the-way places where an electrical power source is not available. Even a lighted room with the window left open will attract quite large numbers of moths under favourable conditions. Warm, humid nights when the sky is overcast are always the most productive and sites that are sheltered but in fairly close proximity to woodland or other dense vegetation are likely to give the best results.

Assembling

One of the most novel ways of collecting is by assembling. This is achieved by imprisoning the female of a species known to emit a powerfully attractive scent in an open mesh cage and waiting for the males to approach. Suitable moths for this method are the Vapourer, the Emperor moth, the Kentish Glory and some moths of the family Lasiocampidae.

Collecting caterpillars

Equipment for collecting caterpillars has already been described but the techniques are rather different from those involving adult Lepidoptera which are either released or killed shortly after capture. Caterpillars should be kept in labelled containers lined with absorbent paper to prevent condensation. It is better to have a large number of small containers than a few large ones as one of the prime objects should be to avoid overcrowding. Caterpillars from one foodplant only should be kept in each container and it is a good idea to avoid mixing large specimens with small. A careful lookout should be kept for potential cannibals, particularly the notorious caterpillar of the Dun Bar.

Rearing

One of the most fascinating methods of studying butterflies and moths is to rear them. In this way it is possible to observe the complete life cycle and to obtain perfect specimens. Many butterflies and moths can be persuaded to lay eggs in captivity although butterflies usually require warmth, sunlight and a source of nectar before they will oblige. Moths generally are much easier to deal with and some females will readily lay in the box in which they are captured. Fresh cut foodplant should be provided as soon as the caterpillars hatch and this should be replenished as soon as it shows signs of wilting. Some species will only thrive on growing foliage and the only way to achieve this when they feed on the foliage of trees or shrubs is to 'sleeve' the caterpillars on a living branch. This is achieved by enveloping a branch of the foodplant with a large tube of muslin or nylon mesh tied at both ends.

Handle small caterpillars with a soft paint brush as they are very delicate. Droppings should be removed regularly and the paper lining replaced as soon as it becomes soiled. Cleanliness is of the utmost importance in rearing caterpillars, together with a plentiful supply of foodplant and the avoidance of overcrowding.

As the caterpillars grow, all but the smallest species are best transferred to a cage with a mesh lid or front to provide ventilation. The cylinder cage, consisting of a ring of Perspex or plastic fitted onto a metal or plastic base and capped with a wire mesh lid, is a very popular design suitable for most butterflies or moths. In these cages it is often possible to use potted plants or sprays of foliage in a small container of water. If the latter method is used, care should be taken to plug the mouth of the water container tightly to prevent caterpillars from drowning themselves.

Problems

If disease strikes, the only hope is to isolate sickly specimens and transfer the others to a clean container. Unfortunately it is often too late once symptoms begin to show and the entire brood is frequently lost. The risk of infection can be reduced by avoiding overcrowding and extremes of temperature and humidity. Little can be done to avoid parasitism by wasps and flies but when parasites emerge these should be carefully recorded as an important aspect of the species' biology.

Read as much as possible about the habits of the species being reared in order to find out its favourite foodplants, method of feeding, place and manner of pupation, whether it is likely to attack its fellows and whether it hibernates as a caterpillar, pupa or adult. It is probably a good idea to start by rearing caterpillars found in the spring as these generally feed up quite quickly and pupate to produce butterflies or moths in the summer. Most autumn caterpillars either hibernate or overwinter in the pupa stage to produce adults in the following spring and are much more difficult to deal with. Generally the best procedure with overwintering pupae is to place them in a sealed tin to retain moisture and to store them in an unheated but generally frost-free outhouse. Overwintering caterpillars are even more difficult and are usually best kept out of doors in a sheltered place.

Provision of a suitable pupation site is very important and may vary from a twig or branch from which the pupa will be suspended to a layer of peat or soil in which the pupa will be buried. When the adults are about to emerge, the pupae should be transferred to a reasonably large cage provided with plant stems or strips of rough paper to which the emerging adults can cling while expanding their wings.

Preparing specimens

When Lepidoptera are required as cabinet specimens they must first be killed. This is abhorrent to many people but where it is necessary it should be done rapidly so that the insect does not damage itself. The traditional killing jar contained lumps of potassium cyanide covered by a layer of plaster of paris and was known as a cyanide jar. A number of safer killing agents are now more frequently used, the most popular being ethyl acetate, a highly volatile fluid which may be poured in small quantities onto a pad of cotton wool or onto the plaster of paris base of a specially designed jar. The vapour of this fluid will rapidly immobilise an insect and kill it after about twenty minutes. Other killing agents are .880 ammonia or carbon tetrachloride. Great care should be exercised in the use of all of these chemicals as they can be harmful if inhaled in any quantity.

Setting

When the specimen has been killed it is necessary to render it soft so that it can be successfully spread or 'set'. After a butterfly or moth dies *rigor mortis* sets in for a few hours and it is usually advisable to keep the specimen in a damp atmosphere to prevent desiccation until the muscles become relaxed again. This is usually achieved in a 'relaxing box' which is an airtight container lined with damp cotton wool, blotting paper or sand to which a few crystals of thymol or other mould-inhibiting chemical have been added. The specimens should be supported above this lining, preferably on a grid of perforated zinc or similar material, so that they are suspended in a humid atmosphere without coming into direct contact with the water. Such boxes can also be used to soften old dried specimens although this can take several days.

When the specimen is relaxed it is ready to be pinned and set. The best entomological pins are made of stainless steel and come in a wide range of sizes. The largest pin that will pass through the thorax without causing damage should be used. This should be pushed through the centre of the thorax so that it comes out between the legs. The specimen should now be pinned onto a setting board which consists of a strip of cork, or similar material, with a central groove to accommodate the insect's body. Once the specimen is pinned in position with its body resting in the groove, its wings may be gently spread into position. This is achieved by manoeuvering the wings with a mounted needle which is hooked carefully behind the leading wing vein and pushed forwards. Strips of translucent setting paper are pinned in position over the wings to hold them in place until they are dry. The antennae and abdomen are then manipulated into the correct position and held in place with pins. When setting is complete the specimen must be left until it is completely dry before removing it from the board. This may take from a few weeks to several months depending on the size of the specimen and conditions of temperature and humidity.

Labelling

Keep the data-labels associated with each specimen. These are eventually pinned under the specimen and remain with it permanently. The most important data to record are the place of capture, the date, any biological information such as foodplant, and the collector's name. It is important to give a full locality reference and many collectors include a complete map reference. A notebook should be kept for recording details about the type of locality, weather conditions and other relevant information that would not fit on the small specimen labels.

Storage

Set insects are normally stored in cork-lined wooden drawers with glass lids and housed in a cabinet. Individual cork-lined boxes known as storeboxes are much cheaper but do not have glass lids and must be opened in order to see the specimens inside. It is possible to improvise storage for insect collections but it is essential that this should be reasonably pest-proof or the specimens will soon be destroyed. Museum or Carpet Beetles of the genus *Anthrenus* are the most serious attackers of insect collections and their hairy grubs will soon reduce a drawer of butterflies or moths to dust. Crystals of naphthalene or paradichlorbenzene have been used to deter these pests although the latter chemical is extremely poisonous and should not be used. Both of these substances evaporate quite quickly and should be replenished every year. Many drawers and storeboxes have special 'camphor cells' for this purpose but any small container may be pinned in place to hold the crystals.

Studying

Today many entomologists prefer to do their collecting with a camera and this is becoming increasingly popular with the advent of the modern 35mm single lens reflex camera. Stalking insects with a camera can be very exciting and is a good way of observing behaviour patterns. The resulting pictures may also prove to be much more attractive than regimented rows of dead insects on pins.

For those who have the artistic ability, sketching butterflies and moths is a useful alternative to photographs. So little is known about the feeding, courtship and mating habits of even the most common butterflies that there is room for anyone to make an original contribution by making detailed notes of what they see.

While some people may prefer to work in isolation, most will wish to share their enthusiasm and observations and this may be achieved by joining societies at local, national or even international level. Many countries including Britain are operating recording schemes for mapping the distribution of the insect fauna and will welcome assistance from competent amateurs. Other organisations, such as the British Butterfly Conservation Society, are conducting butterfly surveys to monitor numbers of species and individuals in various localities and assistance with these projects is urgently required.

Conservation

Habitats

It is not possible to conserve a particular species of butterfly or moth in isolation, as each is an integral part of an interdependent natural complex of plants and animals. It is essential to look towards habitat conservation where the entire community of plants, insects, birds, mammals, other living organisms and the land on which they live can exist together. By the same token it should be regarded as a serious warning of the state of our environment when we notice that certain species are declining in numbers or even becoming extinct.

Some people may argue that conservation is not necessary and will point to the large areas of open countryside and forest that remain. They may ask what difference it will make if a few rare species become extinct and why we should stand in the way of agricultural improvements and road and housing developments. The facts are that even common species are likely to be affected in the near future. Today, particularly in the British Isles, there are enormous pressures on land use and natural habitats are being destroyed at an alarming rate. While we cannot stand in the way of progress, there is a grave danger that our quality of life may be seriously affected by the destruction of our countryside.

Habitat of the **Lulworth Skipper** *Thymelicus acteon* Dorset, England

Old meadowland, habitat of many butterflies and moths

Habitat destruction

Today there are not as many butterflies as there used to be and it is important that we should try to discover the reasons why. Many farmland habitats have been destroyed or seriously damaged by modern agricultural methods. Land drainage has ruined many fine wetlands and in the British Isles was responsible for the extinction of the Large Copper. Other races of this butterfly are under similar threat in continental Europe. The destruction of hedgerows or their replacement by wire fences has destroyed a most important insect habitat in many areas and those that remain are often spoiled by the use of mechanical hedge trimmers or by spraying with insecticides and herbicides. The damage caused by these poisons is sometimes quite unintentional as spray drift from agricultural land can be quite lethal to nearby populations of butterflies and moths.

A less obvious threat to insect life is the improvement of grasslands by the use of fertilisers which stimulate the growth of grasses important for animal grazing at the expense of other plants that are important as food for Lepidoptera. The introduction of myxomatosis to the British Isles has had a serious and long-lasting effect on the flora of our grasslands, as the reduction in rabbit grazing has resulted in large areas becoming overgrown with scrub. It is believed that this was a very important factor in the extinction of the Large Blue in England. This butterfly is reliant on certain species of ant for the completion of its life cycle and these ants require close cropped, low-growing vegetation which soon becomes overgrown without rabbit grazing.

Forest insects

Our forest insects are endangered by commercial conifer plantations that are gradually replacing our deciduous hardwoods. Fortunately a more enlightened attitude is being adopted in some regions where conifer forests are planted with mixed hardwoods around the margins or where new areas of mixed woodland are being established. The increase of conifers has benefited some species whose caterpillars feed on their foliage, and some are becoming serious pests. The afforestation of large areas of mountain and upland slopes is also destroying insect habitats both in Britain and in Europe.

Pollution

Apart from the danger from chemical sprays, another pollution problem is that of 'acid rain' caused by atmospheric pollution which may drift long distances from industrial regions into the surrounding countryside. There has been a considerable decline in

Conifer plantation, New Forest, England

butterfly populations in those areas of Europe that are situated to the north and east of major industrial regions; situations that are liable to be affected by atmospheric pollution drifting on the prevailing south-westerly winds. That industrial pollution has an effect on Lepidoptera populations has been proved by Dr Kettlewell's studies of industrial melanism.

27

Urban development

In some parts of Europe urban development has caused the widespread destruction of habitats, sometimes quite unnecessarily. The development of tourist resources has had a devastating effect on natural habitats, particularly in coastal and mountain resorts. As mentioned earlier, however, there are unexpected benefits from man's activities, as in motorway developments where the extensive verges and embankments provide a useful environment for many insects. Such highways also have the advantage that they relieve the traffic pressure on country roads where the hedgerow fauna subsequently benefits.

Collectors

One of the least significant factors in the decline of insect populations, although one receiving a great deal of publicity, is the activity of insect collectors. There is no proven case of populations of butterflies or moths being destroyed by collectors although it is generally accepted that serious damage could be caused to populations of rare species by a greedy collector. Fortunately most lepidopterists are concerned to preserve the insects in which they are interested.

Organisations in Britain

In Britain the major entomological societies responding to the initiative of the Royal Entomological Society of London have established the Joint Committee for the Conservation of British Insects. This council works in conjunction with such bodies as the Forestry Commission, the Ministry of Agriculture and the Nature Conservancy Council and has set out A Code For Insect Collecting which, if adopted throughout Europe, would pave the way for future cooperation in conservation activities.

The British Butterfly Conservation Society was established in 1968 and now has a membership of over two thousand. Membership of such a body will keep you in touch with others who feel the same way about protecting our butterfly fauna and may enable you to participate in study schemes to provide vital information for professional conservationists.

Legislation

Many European countries have legislated to protect certain rare and endangered insects, mainly butterflies, by prohibiting their collection. This type of legislation is, however, very difficult to enforce and does nothing to prevent the major source of danger, that of habitat destruction. The establishment of nature reserves that are managed for the benefit of wildlife is one positive means of rectifying the situation. In Britain, where relatively few species are protected by law, probably more is being done than anywhere else in Europe to attack these problems by the setting up of nature reserves and in some cases by compensating farmers for adopting 'less efficient' farming practices where an endangered species is known to occur. In order to establish which species are already endangered or likely to be at risk in the near future, studies are being carried out throughout Europe and a series of 'Red Data Books' are being prepared to list those species that may require protection.

How we can help

It is difficult to suggest what we as individuals can do to support these activities although perhaps the most important aim should be to encourage an awareness of wildlife and the need for its conservation. Many people like to make their own contribution by maintaining their gardens as miniature nature reserves by establishing nectar-bearing flowers for butterflies and moths, by avoiding extensive use of weedkillers and persistent insecticides and if possible leaving a corner undisturbed, where wild plants such as nettles, docks and bramble can provide food and shelter for insects. Some even endeavour to persuade local farmers and landowners to leave patches of undisturbed vegetation as wildlife reservoirs or to spare hedges that might otherwise be lost for ever.

Collectors need not feel guilty about their activities if they follow the conservation code, particularly if they involve themselves in the activities of conservation bodies and help to provide some of the urgently needed data on insect habitats and populations. One of the activities in which many entomologists have been able to play an

important part is the European Invertebrate Survey which operates an extensive mapping scheme to record the distribution of butterflies, moths and other invertebrates. The information gathered by this survey may prove to be of vital importance in future conservation studies.

Further Reading

A Field Guide to the Butterflies of Britain and Europe by L. G. Higgins and N. D. Riley (Collins, 1980)

South's British Butterflies by T. G. Howarth (Warne, 1973)

Moths of the British Isles by R. South (Warne, 1961), two volumes

The Moths and Butterflies of Great Britain and Ireland by J. Heath *et al.* (Curwen, 1976, 1979), further volumes to be published

The Observer's Book of Caterpillars by D. J. Carter (Warne, 1979)

Atlas des Lépidoptères de France by F. Le Cerf and C. Herbulot (Boubée, 1963-71), three volumes

Guide des Papillons Nocturnes d'Europe et d'Afrique du Nord by P.-C. Rougeot and P. Viette (Delachaux et Niestlé, 1978)

Mariposas de la Peninsula Ibérica by M. R. Gómez-Bustillo and F. Fernández-Rubio (Ministerio de Agricultura, Madrid, 1974-79), further volumes to be published

Die Schmetterlinge Mitteleuropas by W. Forster and T. Wohlfahrt (Keller, 1954-74)

Butterfly Watching by P. Whalley (Severn House, 1980)

Butterflies by E. B. Ford (Collins, 1977)

Moths by E. B. Ford (Collins, 1972)

Studying Insects by R. L. E. Ford (Warne, 1973)

British Butterfly Wallcharts by Joyce Bee (British Museum [Natural History] 1980-81)

Protected Species

The following is a list of butterflies and moths illustrated in this book which are protected by law in certain parts of Europe. Further legislation is likely in the near future and more species may be added to the protected list. In some regions there is a total ban on collecting and care should be taken to check with the authorities before visiting an unfamiliar area.

Species	Countries where protected
Adonis Blue	France
Alcon Blue	France
Apollo	Austria, Czechoslovakia, Finland France, Germany, Poland
Camberwell Beauty	Austria
Chequered Skipper	UK
Heath Fritillary	UK
Large Blue	UK
Large Copper	France, Netherlands
Large Heath	France
Marsh Fritillary	Netherlands
Moorland Clouded Yellow	France
Poplar Admiral	Austria
Purple Emperor	Austria
Swallowtail	Austria, UK
Scarce Swallowtail	Austria, Czechoslovakia, Luxembourg, Poland
Spanish Festoon	France
Spanish Moon Moth	France

Plants for a Butterfly Garden

The flowers of the following garden plants are all attractive to either butterflies or moths. The 'top ten' plants are asterisked and these are probably the best species to grow where space is limited. Times of flowering are given.

Ageratum	*Ageratum houstonianum*	summer
Alyssum	*Alyssum maritimum*	summer – autumn
Arabis	*Arabis albida*	spring
★ Aubretia	*Aubretia deltoidea*	spring
★ Buddleia	*Buddleia* spp.	summer – autumn
Candytuft	*Iberis umbellata*	summer
Catmint	*Calamintha nepetoides*	summer
Cornflower	*Centaurea cyanus*	summer
Cosmea	*Cosmos bipinnatus*	summer – autumn
Erigeron	*Erigeron* spp.	summer – autumn
French Marigold	*Tagetes patula*	summer
Golden Rod	*Solidago canadensis*	summer – autumn
Heather	*Calluna & Erica* spp.	spring – autumn
Hebe	*Hebe speciosa*	summer
Helenium	*Helenium autumnale*	summer
Heliotrope	*Heliotropium peruvianum*	summer
★ Honesty	*Lunaria* spp.	spring – summer
Honeysuckle	*Lonicera* spp.	summer
★ Ice Plant	*Sedum spectabile*	autumn
Laurel (Common)	*Prunus laurocerasus*	summer
Laurustinus	*Viburnum tinus*	summer
★ Lavender	*Lavandula* spp.	summer
Lilac	*Syringa vulgaris*	summer
Marjoram	*Origanum vulgare*	summer
★ Michaelmas Daisy	*Aster novae belgii*	autumn
Mignonette	*Reseda odorata*	summer – autumn
Phlox	*Phlox* spp.	spring – summer
Polyanthus	*Primula polyanthus*	spring
Red Hot Poker	*Kniphofia uvaria*	summer
Scabious	*Scabiosa* spp.	summer – autumn
Shasta Daisy	*Chrysanthemum maximum*	summer
Siberian Wallflower	*Cheiranthus allionii*	summer
★ Sweet Rocket	*Hesperis matronalis*	spring – summer
Sweet William	*Dianthus barbatus*	spring – summer
Thrift	*Armeria maritima*	summer
★ Tobacco Plant	*Nicotiana alata*	summer – autumn
★ Valerian	*Centranthus* spp.	summer
Verbena	*Verbena* spp.	summer
Wallflower	*Cheiranthus cheiri*	spring
★ Yellow Alyssum	*Alyssum saxatile*	spring

Small Tortoiseshell *Aglais urticae* Royal Horticultural Society Gardens

Glossary

abdomen the hindmost of the three main body divisions.
antennae paired sensory organs on the head, acting as 'feelers'.
claspers sucker-like false legs on the abdomen of a caterpillar.
cocoon the protective outer casing of the pupa, constructed by the caterpillar.
coniferous applying to cone-bearing trees (i.e. pines and their relatives).
cuticle the outer skin of an insect.
deciduous applying to trees that shed their leaves annually.
double-brooded having two generations a year.
Fennoscandia Scandinavia and Finland.
gregarious living together in a group.
habitat the type of locality in which a species naturally lives.
honeydew the sugary secretion of aphids.
instar a stage in the caterpillar's life between one moult and the next.
leguminous belonging to the pea family, Leguminosae.
Lepidoptera butterflies and moths.
local occurring in restricted localities.

locally common local but plentiful in suitable situations.
palpi paired sensory 'taste organs' situated close to the mouth.
proboscis the tubular sucking tongue of Lepidoptera.
pupa the 'chrysalis' stage between caterpillar and adult.
pupate to change into a pupa.
race see subspecies.
single-brooded having one generation a year.
skipper butterfly of the family Hesperiidae.
subspecies or **race** a division of species based on differences in appearance, structure or behaviour, usually associated with geographical isolation.
thorax the second of the three main body divisions, situated between head and abdomen.
umbellifers plants of the carrot and parsnip family, Umbelliferae.
Vanessids the Red Admiral and closely related butterflies of the family Nymphalidae.
venation the arrangement of the wing veins.

δ

♀

δ △

♀ △

Heteropterus morpheus

Carterocephalus palaemon

△

δ

♀

δ △

Thymelicus sylvestris

♀ △

δ △

Thymelicus lineola

♀ △

Large Chequered Skipper *Heteropterus morpheus* Pallas, family Hesperiidae. The only butterfly which occurs in the Channel Islands (Jersey) but nowhere else in the British Isles. Its distribution extends through southern and central Europe to western and central Asia. It is widespread and locally common, occurring in marshy meadows in northern Europe and on hillsides in the south. The caterpillar has a brown head and the body is greyish-white with a dark line along the back and white lines on the sides. It feeds on grasses such as false-brome (*Brachypodium*) and purple moor-grass (*Molinia caerulea*), spinning a grass blade to form a protective tube in which it overwinters. The butterfly flies from June to August in meadows and forest clearings. It is distinctively marked, showing very little geographical variation, and is unlikely to be confused with any other species.

Chequered Skipper *Carterocephalus palaemon* Pallas, family Hesperiidae. At one time this butterfly occurred locally in a number of counties in central England but now appears to be extinct there, and in the British Isles occurs only in western Inverness. It is widespread but local in north-eastern and central Europe, usually occurring in open woodland. The caterpillar is pale green at first but becomes pale yellowish-brown with pinkish-brown stripes when full grown. It feeds on various grasses, particularly false-brome (*Brachypodium*) and brome (*Bromus*), spinning the edges of a blade together to form a protective tubular shelter. When full grown, after hibernating on the foodplant through the winter, it pupates in a cocoon formed by spinning blades of grass together. The butterfly flies from May to July and lays its eggs singly on grass blades. The life-span of this very active butterfly is two to three weeks.

Small Skipper *Thymelicus sylvestris* Poda, family Hesperiidae. A widespread species in England and Wales as far north as Yorkshire but it does not occur in Scotland or Ireland. It is found throughout Europe with the exception of Scandinavia, occurring up to 2000 metres in lush meadows, woodland margins and waste land. The caterpillar has a dark green head and the body is yellowish-green with a dark line along the back and a pale yellow line along each side. It feeds in spring on various grasses such as false-brome (*Brachypodium*) and Yorkshire fog (*Holcus lanatus*), constructing a shelter by spinning the edges of a grass blade together with silk. When full grown it pupates in a cocoon spun between grass blades. The butterfly is on the wing in June and July and has a characteristic buzzing flight.

Essex Skipper *Thymelicus lineola* Ochsenheimer, family Hesperiidae. First recognised as a separate species in the British Isles in 1888, this butterfly occurs in many southern counties of England as well as in Essex and is locally common. It is widespread in southern and central Europe and occurs in parts of Scandinavia. The usual habitat is on grassy hillsides and meadows up to 2000 metres. The caterpillar has a brown head and its body is green with a dark line along the back and yellow lines on each side. It feeds on various coarse grasses such as false-brome (*Brachypodium*) and common couch (*Agropyron repens*) in spring. When full grown in early summer it pupates within a cocoon spun between grass blades. The butterfly emerges after about three weeks and is often found flying in company with the Small Skipper. These two species are very similar but may be distinguished by the fact that in the Essex Skipper the underside of the tip of the antenna is black.

Lifesize

Specimens on 'set' plates are uppersides unless otherwise indicated. Where the sexes are similar in appearance, only one is figured. Abbreviations and symbols used in the captions: δ male ♀ female △ underside aest. summer form f. form ssp. subspecies var. variety vern. spring form.

Essex Skipper *Thymelicus lineola* feeding

Large Chequered Skipper *Heteropterus morpheus*

Small Skipper *Thymelicus sylvestris* at rest

Chequered Skipper *Carterocephalus palaemon*

31

♂

♀

♂ △

♀ △

Thymelicus acteon

♂

♀

♂ △

♀ △

Hesperia comma

♂

♀

♂ △

♀ △

Ochlodes venata

Lulworth Skipper *Thymelicus acteon*
Rottemburg, family Hesperiidae. This local
butterfly is widespread in western and central
Europe but does not occur in Scandinavia. In
Britain it is only found in a few localities along
the coast of Dorset and Devon. It was first
discovered in Lulworth Cove from which it takes
its common name. It occurs in meadows and on
dry hill and mountain slopes up to about 2000
metres. The caterpillar is green with a darker line
on the back and a pale yellow stripe along the
sides. It feeds on brome (*Bromus*) and
false-brome (*Brachypodium*), spinning the edges
of a grass blade together to form a tubular
shelter. When full grown the caterpillar pupates
amongst grass blades which are spun together
with silk. The butterfly is on the wing in late
spring or summer according to the locality
although individual specimens only live for
about a fortnight. It darts about with a rapid
flight and is attracted to flowers, particularly
those of rest-harrow (*Ononis repens*).

Silver-spotted Skipper *Hesperia comma*
Linnaeus, family Hesperiidae. This is a
widespread but local butterfly throughout
central, southern and northern Europe. In the
British Isles it is confined to the chalk hills of
southern England. It may be found in dry
meadows and grassy hillsides, usually on
calcareous soils up to 2500 metres. The
caterpillar has a black head and the body is olive
green speckled with black. It feeds on sheep's
fescue (*Festuca ovina*) and other grasses such as
hair grass (*Aira*), making a tubular shelter from a
spun grass blade. When full grown it pupates in a
cocoon spun amongst the foodplant close to the
ground. The butterfly emerges from the pupa
after about ten days and may be found in July and
August. It flies close to the ground and is
particularly attracted to the flowers of
low-growing thistles (*Cirsium* spp.). This
butterfly may be distinguished from the Large
Skipper by the silvery spots on the underside of
the wings.

Large Skipper *Ochlodes venata* Bremer and
Grey, family Hesperiidae. This widespread and
common Skipper occurs throughout Europe and
its range extends across northern Asia to China
and Japan. In the British Isles it is confined to
England, Wales and the Channel Islands. It
occurs up to 2000 metres on hillsides, forest
margins, waste land and similar grassy places,
often in coastal areas. The caterpillar has a large
blackish-brown head and a bluish-green body
with a dark line down the back and a yellow
stripe along each side. It feeds on various grasses,
including false-brome (*Brachypodium*) and
cock's-foot (*Dactylis glomerata*), sheltering inside
a tube spun from grass blades. When full grown
in pupates in a cocoon spun amongst grass
blades, the adult emerging after about three
weeks. The butterfly is a strong flier and in warm
weather is restless, constantly alighting on
foliage and flying off again. It is on the wing from
June to August according to locality. Although
this species is single-brooded in northern
Europe, it may have up to three broods in the
south.

Lifesize

Silver-spotted Skipper *Hesperia comma*

Lulworth Skipper *Thymelicus acteon* feeding

Large Skipper *Ochlodes venata*

Erynnis tages

♂   ♀

♂ △   ♀ △

Carcharodus alceae

△

Pyrgus malvae

△

Lifesize

Grizzled Skipper *Pyrgus malvae* caterpillar

Mallow Skipper *Carcharodus alceae*

Dingy Skipper *Erynnis tages* Linnaeus, family Hesperiidae. This common butterfly is widespread in central and southern Europe and occurs in southern Scandinavia. It is widely distributed and often common in chalk and limestone areas of the British Isles although it is rather local in Scotland and Ireland. Habitats range from roadsides and railway embankments to heaths and forest margins up to 2000 metres. The caterpillar has a brown head and a yellowish-green body with a dark line along the back and a faint pale line along each side. It feeds on the foliage of birdsfoot-trefoil (*Lotus corniculatus*) and other members of the pea family (i.e. *Hippocrepis* and *Coronilla*), spinning leaflets together to form a shelter. When full grown it spins a cocoon on the foodplant in which it overwinters before pupating in the spring. The butterfly is on the wing from May to June or later and in southern Europe it may produce two broods a year. The butterflies often bask on bare ground with their wings spread open.

Mallow Skipper *Carcharodus alceae* Esper, family Hesperiidae. Although widespread in central and southern Europe and North Africa, this butterfly does not occur north of France and southern Germany. It does not occur in the British Isles although two specimens were captured in Surrey in 1923. It frequents flowery hillsides and other areas where its foodplants occur up to 1500 metres. The caterpillar has a black head and a greyish-green body with a darker line along the back and a pale stripe along each side. Behind the head is a black collar with large yellow spots. It feeds on mallow (*Malva*), hollyhock (*Althea*) and ketmia (*Hibiscus*), sheltering in a folded leaf. The butterfly may be found from April to August according to the area. In lowland areas this butterfly may have two or even three broods a year, while at higher altitudes it has only one.

Grizzled Skipper *Pyrgus malvae* Linnaeus, family Hesperiidae. Although widespread throughout Europe, this species is absent from northern Scandinavia, Scotland, Ireland and northern England. It is common in southern England, particularly on chalk downlands, and in continental Europe occurs from sea level to 2000 metres in fields, bogs, forest clearings and roadsides. The caterpillar has a black head and the body is purplish-brown on the upperside and green below. It feeds on wild strawberry (*Fragaria*), cinquefoil (*Potentilla*), mallow (*Malva*) and agrimony (*Agrimonia*), concealing itself in the shelter of a rolled leaf. When full grown it pupates in a cocoon spun at the base of the foodplant. The butterfly may be seen from April to August according to locality. There are normally two broods a year in the south and one in the north. The butterfly has a rapid darting flight and is fond of basking in the sun on bare earth with wings outspread.

Grizzled Skipper *Pyrgus malvae*

Dingy Skippers *Erynnis tages* mating

Dingy Skipper *Erynnis tages* at rest

Grizzled Skipper *Pyrgus malvae*

Papilio machaon

Iphiclides podalirius

Swallowtail *Papilio machaon*

Swallowtail *Papilio machaon* Linnaeus, family
Papilionidae. This large butterfly is widely
distributed throughout Europe and also occurs
in North Africa. In the British Isles it is confined
to the fens of Norfolk, Suffolk and Cambridge.
British specimens belong to a distinct race which
has been named subspecies *britannicus* Seitz. It is
a smaller and darker form than the continental
race and is weaker in flight. Occasional
specimens recorded along the south coast of
England belong to the larger continental race and
are evidently migrants. In Europe, this butterfly
occurs in meadows and on flowery hillsides up to
2000 metres. The distinctive caterpillar is green
with orange-spotted black bands. It feeds on the
foliage of fennel (*Foeniculum vulgare*), hog's
fennel (*Peucedanum officinale*), wild carrot
(*Daucus carota*) and other umbellifers. The pupa
is attached to a silk pad spun on the foodplant or
other surrounding herbage, often on reed stems.
This stage may last from two weeks to six months
according to the brood and locality. In northern
regions the butterfly is single-brooded, whereas
in the south it may have two or three broods in a
year. The butterfly may be found from April
until August, individual specimens living for
about three to four weeks.

Scarce Swallowtail *Iphiclides podalirius* Scopoli,
family Papilionidae. The common name of this
butterfly is misleading as it is widespread and
sometimes common in central and southern
Europe. It is essentially a lowland species, often
associated with orchards, but in the Alps it
occurs up to 1600 metres. The term 'scarce'
refers to its occurrence in the British Isles where
it was at one time believed to be a rare resident.
Recent records in Britain have been attributed to
accidental introductions. The caterpillar of this
butterfly is green with red spots along yellow
diagonal lines. It is rather flat and slug-like in
appearance but merges successfully with the
leaves on which it feeds. The foodplants are
blackthorn (*Prunus spinosa*), cherry (*P. cerasus*)
and other species of *Prunus*. The full grown
caterpillar usually pupates on a branch of the
foodplant. Pupae produced in the summer are
usually green, while those in the autumn which
hibernate through the winter are yellow or
brown. North of the Alps this species produces
only one generation a year and butterflies fly
from May to July, while in southern Europe
there are two broods and butterflies are on the
wing from May to June and July to August.

⁴/₅ lifesize

Swallowtail *Papilio machaon*

Scarce Swallowtail *Iphiclides podalirius* at rest

Scarce Swallowtail *Iphiclides podalirius* feeding

37

♂   ♀

♂ △

♀ △

Zerynthia rumina

Parnassius apollo

Lifesize

Spanish Festoon *Zerynthia rumina* Linnaeus, family Papilionidae. This butterfly is confined to the south-west of Europe and occurs in Spain, Portugal and southern France. It also occurs in North Africa where it is represented by a distinct subspecies (ssp. *ornatior* Blachier). Variation in wing pattern is considerable and a number of races and forms have been described. It occurs in rough uncultivated places and on hillsides and mountains up to 1500 metres, particularly in coastal areas. The caterpillar is grey or reddish-grey with six rows of reddish-brown spines along the body. It feeds on various species of birthwort (*Aristolochia*). The butterfly flies on stony slopes and may be found from February to May depending on locality and altitude. This species is single-brooded throughout its range. The closely allied Southern Festoon *Zerynthia polyxena* Denis & Schiffermüller which occurs in southern and south-eastern Europe may be distinguished by the lack of red markings on the forewing.

Apollo *Parnassius apollo* Linnaeus, family Papilionidae. This magnificent mountain butterfly is widespread in Europe occurring at altitudes from 750 to 2000 metres, but in Scandinavia it is found at much lower altitudes. It is very variable and a great number of subspecies and local races have been described. In the Sierra Nevada of Spain, a subspecies occurs (ssp. *nevadensis* Oberthur) which has the normal red rings on the hindwings replaced by orange-yellow. This butterfly has from time to time been reported from the British Isles, usually from the Scottish Highlands, but it is unlikely that it has occurred there naturally in recent times. The caterpillar is velvety-black with a line of red spots along each side. It feeds on the fleshy leaves of stonecrop (*Sedum*) but is only active in sunny weather. When full grown the caterpillar pupates in a loose cocoon on the ground, often under rocks. The pupal stage lasts for about a week and butterflies are on the wing in July and August, frequently showing a preference for damp areas such as the margins of streams. The flight is rather heavy with a slow wing-beat. In a number of regions collecting this butterfly is prohibited by law.

Spanish Festoon *Zerynthia rumina*

Apollo *Parnassius apollo*

39

Leptidea sinapis

Colias palaeno

Colias hyale

Wood White *Leptidea sinapis* Linnaeus, family Pieridae. This frail-looking butterfly occurs locally throughout most of Europe from sea level to 1900 metres but is absent from the Dutch-German coast of the North Sea. In the British Isles it is confined to southern parts of England, Wales and Ireland. It is most usually found in woodland rides and clearings, but in south Devon it occurs along the undercliffs of the coast. The caterpillar is yellowish-green with a dark line along the back and a bright yellow line along each side. It feeds on the foliage of a number of leguminous plants, including tuberous pea (*Lathyrus tuberosus*) and birdsfoot trefoil (*Lotus corniculatus*). The pupa is attached to a stem of the foodplant and resembles a withered leaf. The butterfly has a slow fluttering flight and is on the wing in spring and summer. There are two or more broods a year, according to locality.

Moorland Clouded Yellow *Colias palaeno* Linnaeus, family Pieridae. The range of this butterfly extends through central Europe and Scandinavia to Siberia and Japan. The only record from the British Isles is of a single specimen captured in Sussex but this was most probably an accidental introduction. Its usual habitat is boggy moorland, damp meadows and marshes although in the Alps it occurs up to 2500 metres. The caterpillar is deep green with a bright yellow stripe along each side. It feeds on the foliage of bog whortleberry (*Vaccinium uliginosum*) and hibernates through the winter. Butterflies are on the wing in June and July and there is only one generation a year. As in the other Clouded Yellows the flight of this species is typically strong although it is only active in the warmest part of the day. Drainage and peat cutting have severely restricted the habitat of this butterfly in some areas and have sometimes resulted in the extinction of a colony.

Pale Clouded Yellow *Colias hyale* Linnaeus, family Pieridae. The range of this migratory species extends through central Europe to southern Russia. It sometimes appears in large numbers on the North Sea coasts of the Netherlands and Germany and in some years it occurs along the south coast of England. This butterfly is usually found in or near fields of lucerne or clover and while in many areas it is a lowland species, in the Alps it is found up to 2000 metres. The caterpillar is deep green with a broken red and orange line along each side. It feeds on the foliage of clover (*Trifolium*), lucerne (*Medicago*) and vetches (*Vicia* and *Coronilla*). The full grown caterpillar pupates on a stem of the foodplant and the butterfly emerges after about seventeen days. Butterflies are on the wing from May to June and from August to September in two broods. This species does not survive the winter in the British Isles.

Lifesize

Moorland Clouded Yellow *Colias palaeno*

Pale Clouded Yellow *Colias hyale* feeding

Wood White *Leptidea sinapis* caterpillar

Wood White *Leptidea sinapis*

41

♂

♀

♂ △

♀ △

Colias australis

♂

♀

♂ △

♀ △

♀ var.

♀ var. △

Colias croceus

Berger's Clouded Yellow *Colias australis* Verity,
family Pieridae. This butterfly was not
recognised as a distinct species in central Europe
until as recently as 1947. It occurs throughout
central and southern Europe and is recorded as
an occasional migrant in southern England. The
preferred habitat seems to be rough,
uncultivated slopes and rocky ground. The
caterpillar is deep green with two yellow stripes
down the back and a yellow stripe along each
side, margined with black spots. It feeds on the
foliage of horseshoe vetch (*Hippocrepis comosa*)
and crown vetch (*Coronilla varia*). The butterfly
is on the wing from May to June and August to
September in two broods with a third generation
in southern areas. Although clearly different in
the caterpillar stage and in general biology, it is
often extremely difficult to distinguish this
butterfly from the Pale Clouded Yellow. Berger's
Clouded Yellow can generally be recognised by
its brighter colour, less extensive black marking
on the forewing and a more brilliant orange spot
on the hindwing.

Clouded Yellow *Colias croceus* caterpillar

Lifesize

Clouded Yellow *Colias croceus* pupa

Clouded Yellow *Colias croceus* Geoffroy, family Pieridae. The distribution of this species extends over most of Europe. It remains in southern Europe and North Africa during the winter but in spring migrates northwards as far as the British Isles, southern Scandinavia and northern Germany. In the British Isles it is most frequently found along the south coast of England. The caterpillar is deep green with a yellow band along each side marked with red streaks. It feeds on the foliage of lucerne (*Medicago*), clover (*Trifolium*), vetch (*Vicia*) and other leguminous plants. The full grown caterpillar pupates on a plant stem and the butterfly emerges after about eighteen days. There are two generations in the north and a succession of broods further south so that the butterflies are on the wing from April to September, according to the locality. This species shows considerable variation and a common form of the female (f. *helice*) is almost white.

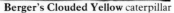

Berger's Clouded Yellow caterpillar

Berger's Clouded Yellow *Colias australis* at rest

Clouded Yellow *Colias croceus* at rest

43

Gonepteryx rhamni

Gonepteryx cleopatra

⁴/₅ lifesize

Brimstone *Gonepteryx rhamni* Linnaeus, family Pieridae. This butterfly is widely distributed throughout Europe with the exception of northern Scandinavia. In the British Isles it is found in England, Wales and Ireland, but becomes less common further north and is absent from Scotland. It occurs up to 2000 metres on open ground and in light woodland. The caterpillar is bluish-green with a pale line low down along each side. It feeds on buckthorn

Brimstone *Gonepteryx rhamni* emerging from pupa

(*Rhamnus catharticus*) and alder buckthorn (*Frangula alnus*) and when full grown pupates on the foodplant. The enlarged, green wing-cases of the pupa resemble a curled leaf. The butterfly is on the wing from July to September and after hibernation from as early as February until June. This species is single-brooded but individual specimens may live for more than ten months. It is a common sight in gardens and has been well known since the mid seventeenth century. It seems quite probable that its yellow colour gave rise to the name butter-coloured fly which has since been contracted to 'butterfly'.

Cleopatra *Gonepteryx cleopatra* Linnaeus, family Pieridae. This is a southern European species occurring in Spain, Portugal, Italy and southern France and also in North Africa and the Canary Islands. It has been recorded several times from the British Isles but these occurrences are almost certainly accidental as the species is not a migrant. It occurs in lowland meadows and open woodland and also in open scrub on mountain slopes up to 2000 metres. The caterpillar is similar to that of the Brimstone but more bluish and has a stronger line along the side. It feeds on the foliage of various species of buckthorn (*Rhamnus*). Butterflies are on the wing from March to June and later in August and September, according to the locality. This is a single-brooded species and butterflies hibernate through the winter. Males of the Cleopatra are easily recognised by the vivid orange flush on the forewings but females are very similar to those of the Brimstone, although they may be distinguished by a faint orange streak on the underside of the forewing.

Brimstone *Gonepteryx rhamni* feeding

Cleopatra *Gonepteryx cleopatra* feeding

Aporia crataegi

♂

♀

♂ △

♀ △

Pieris brassicae

⁴/₅ lifesize

Large White *Pieris brassicae* pupa

Black-veined White *Aporia crataegi* Linnaeus, family Pieridae. This distinctive species is found throughout central and southern Europe and occurs as far north as Scandinavia. The preferred habitat is open country with hedgerows or orchards. It was at one time a relatively common butterfly in England and Wales but by the mid nineteenth century its numbers had begun to decline and it became extinct by 1925. It also used to be a serious orchard pest in parts of central Europe but is now much scarcer. The caterpillar is reddish-brown above with black stripes along the back and sides, underneath it is grey. It feeds on the foliage of hawthorn (*Crataegus*), blackthorn (*Prunus spinosa*) and various fruit trees. Caterpillars hibernate through the winter in a communal nest of silk and emerge in the spring to complete their feeding and growth. The full grown caterpillar pupates on the foodplant and the butterfly emerges after about three weeks. It is on the wing from May to July and is often found in clover and lucerne fields.

Large White *Pieris brassicae* Linnaeus, family Pieridae. The range of this extremely common and well-known butterfly extends throughout Europe, with the exception of northern Scandinavia, to North Africa and the Himalaya Mountains. It is common in the British Isles, the native population often being increased by migrants from continental Europe. The greyish-green caterpillar is spotted with black and has a yellow line down the back and along each side. It feeds on cabbage (*Brassica*) and related plants and also on garden 'nasturtium' (*Tropaeolum*), often completely stripping plants of their foliage. It is a serious pest of field crops but is often controlled by parasitic wasps. Full grown caterpillars pupate either on the foodplant or on nearby fences or walls. Overwintering pupae are often found under window sills and the eaves of houses. Butterflies are on the wing from April to May and from July to August in two or sometimes three broods. They are fond of visiting flowers and are common in gardens and the margins of cultivated fields.

Black-veined Whites *Aporia crataegi* mating

Large White *Pieris brassicae* feeding

Large White *Pieris brassicae* feeding

Pieris rapae

Pieris napi

Small White *Pieris rapae* pupa

Small White *Pieris rapae* caterpillar

Small White *Pieris rapae* Linnaeus, family Pieridae. The range of this species in Europe is the same as that of the Large White but it also extends across Siberia to Japan. It is one of the commonest butterflies in the British Isles although it seldom occurs in the Outer Hebrides and the Shetlands. This species is also well known in Australia, New Zealand and North America where it is an introduced pest. The caterpillar is bluish-green with a yellowish line down the back and a row of yellow spots along each side. It feeds on cabbage (*Brassica*) and related plants and also on garden mignonette (*Reseda*) and 'nasturtium' (*Tropaeolum*). Full grown caterpillars either pupate on the foodplant in which case they are green or on nearby fences or walls when they are brown or greyish to blend with the background. Butterflies may be found from March to July with one or two generations in the north and up to four generations in southern Europe. Caterpillars of this butterfly often occur as pests together with those of the Large White although they seldom cause such extensive damage.

Green-veined White *Pieris napi* Linnaeus, family Pieridae. This butterfly occurs throughout Europe excluding the extreme north and its range extends to North Africa, across Siberia to Japan and also to North America. In the British Isles it is found almost everywhere. It occurs in meadows, woodland margins and damp places from sea level up to an altitude of 1500 metres. The caterpillar is green with a darker line down the back and a row of small yellow spots along each side. It feeds on hedge mustard (*Sisymbrium officinale*), garlic mustard (*Alliaria petiolata*) and other plants of the family Cruciferae. Pupation takes place either on the foodplant or on some other suitable support such as a fence, the colour of the pupa varying to blend with its background. This is one of the first butterflies to be seen in the spring and may be found from March to August, according to locality. In the British Isles the first specimens usually emerge from the pupa in April and there are two broods a year.

Lifesize

Green-veined Whites *Pieris napi* mating

Small White *Pieris rapae* feeding

Small White *Pieris rapae* feeding

Pontia daplidice

Anthocharis cardamines

Lifesize

Orange-tip *Anthocharis cardamines* pupa

Bath White *Pontia daplidice* Linnaeus, family Pieridae. This butterfly is a resident of southern Europe and North Africa but is a strong and regular migrant to most other parts of Europe, occasional specimens occurring in England, the Netherlands and West Germany. The common name is derived from one of the earliest British specimens which was taken in Bath, Somerset, at the close of the eighteenth century. Its usual habitat is rough uncultivated land on dry, sandy soils from sea level up to 2000 metres. The caterpillar has a yellow head dotted with black and the body is bluish-grey with shining black spots and yellow lines along the back and sides. It feeds on the foliage of mignonette (*Reseda*), rock cress (*Arabis*), mustard (*Sinapis alba*) and other plants of the family Cruciferae. Butterflies may be found from February to September in two or more broods according to locality. They are strongly attracted to clover and lucerne fields.

Orange-tip *Anthocharis cardamines* Linnaeus, family Pieridae. This butterfly occurs throughout Europe with the exception of southern Spain, northern Scotland and northern Scandinavia and Finland. Its range extends eastwards across temperate Asia to China and Japan. The usual habitats are along hedgerows, in meadows and in woodland clearings, mainly in damp areas which have a rich flora. It may be found at altitudes above 2000 metres in the Alps. The caterpillar is pale bluish-green above and dark green below with a white band along each side. It feeds on the seedpods of garlic mustard (*Alliaria petiolata*), hedge mustard (*Sisymbrium officinale*), lady's smock (*Cardamine pratensis*) and related plants. The full grown caterpillar leaves the foodplant to pupate amongst the herbage where it remains for up to eleven months before the butterfly emerges. Butterflies are on the wing for about two months between April and May according to locality.

Bath White *Pontia daplidice*

Bath White *Pontia daplidice*

Orange-tip *Anthocharis cardamines*

Brown Hairstreak *Thecla betulae* at rest

Purple Hairstreak *Quercusia quercus* caterpillar

Callophrys rubi

Thecla betulae

Quercusia quercus

Lifesize

Green Hairstreak *Callophrys rubi* Linnaeus, family Lycaenidae. This widespread butterfly occurs throughout Europe and its range extends into Siberia. In the British Isles it occurs almost everywhere with the exception of the Orkneys and Shetlands. It is common in hedgerows, woodland margins and boggy heathland. The caterpillar is bright green with a darker line along the back and yellow oblique stripes on the sides. It feeds on a wide range of different plants including furze (*Ulex*), bramble (*Rubus*) and buckthorn (*Rhamnus*), eating the developing fruits. The full grown caterpillar pupates at the base of the plant under a loose web and the butterfly emerges some eight months later in the following spring. The pupa is capable of producing a remarkable squeaking sound if disturbed. Butterflies are on the wing from March to July, according to locality, but do not usually appear in the British Isles before late April. They fly rapidly for short distances and are very difficult to detect when at rest with the wings closed.

Brown Hairstreak *Thecla betulae* Linnaeus, family Lycaenidae. This butterfly occurs widely in central and southern Europe, ranging from southern Scandinavia to northern Italy. In the British Isles it is confined to the southern and midland counties of England, Wales and a few localities in western Ireland. It is a woodland species of retiring habits and, although not rare, is seldom seen. The caterpillar has a brown head and the body is bright green with wedge-shaped yellow markings on the back and a yellow line low down on each side. It feeds on the foliage of blackthorn (*Prunus spinosa*), plum (*Prunus domestica*) and birch (*Betula*). When full grown the caterpillar turns a reddish-purple colour before pupating on or under the leaves of the foodplant. Butterflies may be found from July to early October, according to locality. Although their usual habit is to fly high up amongst trees, they may occasionally be found feeding on bramble blossom.

Green Hairstreak *Callophrys rubi* at rest

Brown Hairstreak *Thecla betulae*

Purple Hairstreak *Quercusia quercus*

Purple Hairstreak *Quercusia quercus* Linnaeus, family Lycaenidae. This butterfly occurs throughout most of western Europe with the exception of northern Scandinavia and Finland. In the British Isles it is widespread in England, Wales and parts of western Scotland but local and scarce in Ireland. It occurs in oak woodland up to an altitude of about 1700 metres. There is a distinct race (ssp. *ibericas* Staudinger) occurring in Spain, Portugal and North Africa which has a very pale underside and reduced markings. The caterpillar is reddish-brown with a black line down the back and a series of dark brown, oblique lines along each side. It feeds on the young foliage of oak (*Quercus*) and sometimes, but rarely, ash (*Fraxinus*), sallow (*Salix*) and sweet chestnut (*Castanea sativa*). Pupation takes place beneath a few strands of silk spun over a leaf or on the tree trunk. Butterflies may be found in July and August but they usually fly high up in the trees and are most frequently seen when they come down to feed on the honeydew deposited by aphids.

Nordmannia ilicis

Strymonidia w-album

Strymonidia pruni

Lifesize

Ilex Hairstreak *Nordmannia ilicis* at rest

Ilex Hairstreak *Nordmannia ilicis* Esper, family Lycaenidae. Although this butterfly is widespread and common in southern and central Europe, it does not occur in southern Spain or in the British Isles and is only recorded from southern parts of Scandinavia. Its habitat is usually rough, hilly country where scrub oak grows, up to an altitude of about 1700 metres. The caterpillar has a black head and a pale green body with a darker line down the back and a row of oblique dark green stripes along each side. It feeds on the foliage of various species of oak (*Quercus*) but shows a preference for the low-growing forms. Caterpillars overwinter on the undersides of leaves and complete their growth in the following spring. Butterflies are on the wing in June and July but like many other Hairstreaks they are difficult to find because of their retiring habits.

White-letter Hairstreak *Strymonidia w-album* Knoch, family Lycaenidae. This butterfly is widespread in southern and central Europe, including southern Scandinavia, but is absent from Spain and Portugal and very scarce in the Netherlands. In the British Isles it is confined to southern and central England, Wales and the Channel Islands. It may be found in woodland rides and forest margins where elm trees grow. The caterpillar has a black head and its body is yellowish-green with a row of diagonal dark green stripes along each side. It feeds on the blossom, buds and young foliage of wych elm (*Ulmus glabra*) and English elm (*Ulmus procera*). The pupa is usually attached to a leaf or twig. Butterflies are on the wing in June and July, usually flying in the treetops, but sometimes descending to feed on flowers of bramble (*Rubus*) and privet (*Ligustrum*). Both the scientific and common names of this species refer to the white w-shaped marking on the underside of the hindwing.

Black Hairstreak *Strymonidia pruni* Linnaeus, family Lycaenidae. This is a widespread but local species in central Europe although it is more common in eastern Europe. It is absent from

White-letter Hairstreak *Strymonidia w-album* feeding

Black Hairstreak *Strymonidia pruni* caterpillar

most of southern Europe, western France and the Netherlands and only occurs in the extreme south of Scandinavia. In the British Isles it is confined to a few localities in England and is very scarce. It is a butterfly of light woodlands where there are blackthorn thickets. The caterpillar has a pale brown head and a yellowish-green body with a double reddish-purple line along the back. It feeds on buds and developing leaves of blackthorn (*Prunus spinosa*), plum (*Prunus domestica*) and related plants. The pupa is attached to a leaf or stem and bears a remarkable resemblance to a bird dropping. The butterfly is on the wing in June and July and may be seen feeding at honeydew or on the flowers of bramble (*Rubus*) and other shrubs.

Black Hairstreak *Strymonidia pruni*

55

Lycaena phlaeas

Lycaena dispar

♂ △   ♀ △

Heodes tityrus

♂   ♀

♂ △   ♀ △

Lifesize

Small Copper *Lycaena phlaeas* at rest

Small Copper *Lycaena phlaeas* caterpillar

Small Copper *Lycaena phlaeas* Linnaeus, family Lycaenidae. This common and widespread species occurs throughout Europe, its range extending to North Africa and across temperate Asia to Japan. In the British Isles it is found almost everywhere and in Ireland occurs as a separate subspecies *hibernica* Goodson which is more brightly marked on the underside. Its habitats are meadows, roadsides, downland and hillsides from sea level up to 2000 metres. The caterpillar is dark green, sometimes with a pink stripe down the back and one along each side. It feeds on various species of dock and sorrel (*Rumex*) and also knotgrass (*Polygonum*), the autumn brood overwintering on the foodplant. Pupation takes place on a stem or leaf and the butterfly emerges after about a month. There are usually two or three broods a year and butterflies may be seen at any time between May and September. The arctic subspecies *polaris* Courvoisier is single-brooded and on the wing in June and July.

Large Copper *Lycaena dispar* Haworth, family Lycaenidae. This beautiful species occurs locally in widely scattered colonies throughout central Europe. Butterflies from the Netherlands belong to ssp. *batavus* Oberthür, while those from the rest of Europe belong to ssp. *rutilus* Werneberg. The Large Copper became extinct in the British Isles in the mid nineteenth century but a colony of the Dutch subspecies has been established in Wood Walton Fen, Huntingdon, and survives under careful management. This is a butterfly of marshes and fens and is constantly under threat from drainage and cultivation. The caterpillar is bright green and merges very successfully with its foodplants, great water dock (*Rumex hydrolapathum*) and Scottish water dock (*Rumex aquaticus*). Caterpillars exude a sweet substance attractive to ants which tend them and offer some protection from their enemies. Butterflies of ssp. *batavus* are single-brooded and fly in June and July while those of ssp. *rutilus* are double-brooded and are on the wing from May to June and August to September.

Sooty Copper *Heodes tityrus* Poda, family Lycaenidae. This butterfly is found locally in many parts of central and southern Europe. It does not occur in southern Spain and is absent from the British Isles and from Scandinavia with the exception of eastern Denmark. Its habitats are meadows and forest clearings mostly in lowlands but sometimes up to 1700 metres. The alpine subspecies *subalpinus* Speyer occurs in mountain meadows, usually at an altitude of 1300 to 2000 metres. The caterpillar is bright green or sometimes purplish and spotted with white. It feeds on leaves of dock (*Rumex*) on which it overwinters, pupating in the following spring. The lowland race has two broods a year and is on the wing from April to May and August to September, while the alpine subspecies is single-brooded and flies in June and July.

Large Copper *Lycaena dispar* at rest

Small Copper *Lycaena phlaeas* at rest

Large Copper *Lycaena dispar* feeding

Heodes alciphron

Palaeochrysophanus hippothoe

Lampides boeticus

Lifesize

Purple-shot Copper *Heodes alciphron* ssp. *gordius* at rest

Purple-edged Copper *Palaeochrysophanus hippothoe* Linnaeus, family Lycaenidae. This is a widespread but local species in western and northern Europe, its range extending into Siberia. It does not occur in the British Isles or the Netherlands although there is some evidence to suggest that it may have occurred in Britain in the seventeenth and eighteenth centuries. There are a number of described subspecies in which the extent of the purple colouring and the intensity of markings vary. Its habitats range from damp meadows and bogs in the lowlands to sub-alpine pastures up to an altitude of 2300 metres. The caterpillar has a brown head and a deep green body with a darker line along the back and a white line along each side. It feeds on dock (*Rumex*) and knotgrass (*Polygonum*), overwintering and feeding again in the spring. Butterflies are on the wing from June to August, according to locality, and there is one generation a year. It seems that populations have been on the decline in recent years, possibly due to drainage of the habitat.

Long-tailed Blue *Lampides boeticus* Linnaeus, family Lycaenidae. Although mainly a species of the tropics and subtropics, ranging from Africa to the Pacific Islands, this butterfly is resident in southern Europe and migrates to many other parts of Europe as far north as the Netherlands and Germany. Its occurrence in the British Isles is quite rare and almost always confined to southern England. The habitats are rough, uncultivated places up to an altitude of about 2000 metres. Caterpillars vary in colour from bright green to reddish-brown, with a darker line down the back and oblique stripes along the sides. They feed on the seedpods of a wide range of leguminous plants, especially bladder senna (*Colutea*) and in the tropics are sometimes pests of peas (*Pisum*) and related crops. In southern Europe butterflies are on the wing throughout spring and summer in a succession of broods but migrants do not usually reach the British Isles until summer or autumn.

Purple-shot Copper *Heodes alciphron* Rottemburg, family Lycaenidae. The range of this fine butterfly extends across much of western Europe to Asia Minor and Iran. It does not occur in the British Isles, the Netherlands, Belgium or Fennoscandia. The northern subspecies *alciphron* occurs in lowland meadows, while the southern subspecies *gordius* Sulzer flies in sub-alpine pastures up to 2000 metres. The

caterpillar is bright green with dark lines along the back and sides. It feeds on dock (*Rumex*) and overwinters on the foodplant before pupating below ground in the spring. Specimens of the northern subspecies are on the wing in June and July, while in southern Europe the flight period is from June to August. The butterflies fly in warm dry meadowland and are attracted to the blossoms of bramble and thyme.

Purple-edged Copper

Long-tailed Blue *Lampides boeticus* caterpillar

Long-tailed Blue *Lampides boeticus* feeding

Purple-edged Copper *Palaeochrysophanus hippothoe*

59

Cupido minimus

Everes argiades

Plebejus argus

Lifesize

Small Blue *Cupido minimus*

Short-tailed Blue *Everes argiades* Pallas, family Lycaenidae. Although widespread in central and southern Europe, this butterfly is not found in central and southern Spain and is generally absent from north-west Europe, although occasional vagrant specimens occur in the Netherlands, northern Germany and the British Isles. The first capture of this rare migrant in the British Isles was on Bloxworth Heath, Dorset, in 1885 and because of this it is sometimes known as the Bloxworth Blue. The usual habitats are rough pastures and heaths, often in damp situations and sometimes up to an altitude of 500 metres. The caterpillar has a shining black head and the body is pale green with a darker stripe down the back and oblique stripes along each side. It feeds on the developing seeds and leaves of various leguminous plants, particularly of medick (*Medicago*) and birdsfoot-trefoil (*Lotus*), and overwinters on the foodplant. Pupation takes place in the spring and butterflies emerge after about two weeks. They are on the wing from April to September with two or more broods in a year.

Silver-studded Blue *Plebejus argus* Linnaeus, family Lycaenidae. The range of this butterfly extends over most of Europe with the exception of northern Fennoscandia. There are distinct races in the higher Alps (ssp. *aegidion* Meisner) and Spain (ssp. *hypochionus* Rambur). In the British Isles it is confined to England, Wales and the Channel Islands but is common in suitable localities. The habitats for this species are usually sandy heaths and hillsides with poor soils such as chalk downland. The caterpillar is either pale green with purple and pinkish stripes or olive green with reddish stripes. It feeds on the flowers and foliage of gorse (*Ulex europaeus*), birdsfoot-trefoil (*Lotus*), broom (*Cytisus*), ling (*Calluna*) and a number of other plants. Pupation takes place low down on the foodplant and the butterfly emerges after about eighteen days. Butterflies are on the wing from May to August, according to locality, with one brood a year in the north and two in the south.

Small Blue *Cupido minimus* Fuessly, family Lycaenidae. This little butterfly is widespread and common throughout most of Europe, but is absent from the southern part of the Iberian peninsula, the Netherlands and parts of northern Germany and Scandinavia. In the British Isles it is locally common, especially in southern England, and often occurs in small isolated colonies. The usual habitats are dry uncultivated downland slopes and meadows, often on chalk or limestone, although in some areas butterflies are found on coastal sandhills. The caterpillar has a black head and the body varies in colour from pale brown to yellow with pinkish markings along the back and sides. It feeds on the developing seeds of kidney vetch (*Anthyllis vulneraria*) and related plants and overwinters in the calyx of a dead flower. Pupation takes place in the following spring, usually on a grass stem. Butterflies may be found from April until September, according to the locality and altitude.

Silver-studded Blues *Plebejus argus* at rest

Small Blue *Cupido minimus*

Silver-studded Blue *Plebejus argus* feeding

♂ ♀

♂ △ ♀ △

Lycaeides idas

△

Aricia agestis

△

Aricia artaxerxes

♂ ♀

♂ △ ♀ △

Polyommatus icarus

Idas Blue *Lycaeides idas* Linnaeus, family Lycaenidae. The precise distribution of this butterfly is uncertain due to confusion with a closely related species, Reverdin's Blue *Lycaeides argyrognomon* Bergstrasser which, although generally larger, is impossible to distinguish with certainty by external features. The Idas Blue is widespread in Europe but is absent from the British Isles and parts of the Iberian Peninsula. Its habitats are dry sandy heaths and hillsides up to about 1500 metres. The caterpillar is green and marked with red and brown and feeds on various leguminous plants. It is associated with ants which carry the caterpillars to their nest where they overwinter and eventually pupate. Butterflies are on the wing from June to August with one brood in the north and two in the south. The Silver-studded Blue is very similar, but distinguished by the presence of a spine on the foreleg.

Brown Argus *Aricia agestis* Denis & Schiffermüller, family Lycaenidae. This butterfly is found in most parts of central and southern Europe but is absent from Spain, Portugal and Fennoscandia. In the British Isles it is widespread in the southern half of England and in Wales but is replaced by the Northern Brown Argus in northern England and Scotland. The usual habitats are chalk downlands and sandy heaths. The caterpillar has a black head and the body is green with purplish lines along the back and sides. It feeds on the foliage of rock rose (*Helianthemum*), stork's bill (*Erodium*) and cranesbill (*Geranium*). Caterpillars of the later brood overwinter and pupate at the base of the foodplant in the following spring. Butterflies may be found between April and August, according to locality. Usually double-brooded but in southern Europe there are three generations a year.

Northern Brown Argus *Aricia artaxerxes* Fabricius, family Lycaenidae. Formerly regarded as a subspecies of the Brown Argus, this butterfly is found in central and northern Europe, its distribution being uncertain due to difficulties of identification. In the British Isles it is found in northern England and Scotland. Specimens from northern England are regarded as a distinct race (ssp. *salmacis* Fabricius) while those from continental Europe belong to ssp. *allous* Geyer. The green caterpillar is more slender than that of the Brown Argus and the side stripes are white. It feeds on the foliage of rock rose (*Helianthemum*) and stork's bill (*Erodium*), hibernating through the winter and completing its growth in the following spring. Butterflies are on the wing from June to August, according to locality. Some races of Northern Brown Argus and Brown Argus are very difficult to separate but in the British Isles, the former species may be distinguished by the presence of a white spot on the upperside of each forewing.

Common Blue *Polyommatus icarus* Rottemburg, family Lycaenidae. This widespread and common butterfly is found from North Africa to the Arctic. In the British Isles it occurs almost everywhere, specimens from Ireland being regarded as a distinct race (ssp. *mariscolore* Kane). Habitats for this species include lowland meadows and hillsides up to an altitude of about 2000 metres. The caterpillar has a black head and the body is bright green with a darker line down the back and a whitish stripe along each side. It feeds on the flowers and foliage of birdsfoot-trefoil (*Lotus corniculatus*), rest harrow (*Ononis spinosa*), clover (*Trifolium*) and related plants. Caterpillars of the autumn brood hibernate through the winter. Pupation takes place at the base of the foodplant under a few strands of silk. Butterflies may be found April to September. In the north only one brood but further south up to three broods a year.

Lifesize

Idas Blue *Lycaeides idas*

Common Blue *Polyommatus icarus* at rest

Brown Argus *Aricia agestis*

Brown Argus *Aricia agestis*

Common Blue *Polyommatus icarus* settling

Lysandra coridon

Lysandra bellargus

Cyaniris semiargus

Lifesize

Chalkhill Blue *Lysandra coridon* Poda, family Lycaenidae. This butterfly occurs throughout most of Europe with the exception of Scandinavia and some southern parts of Spain and Italy. In the British Isles it is confined to southern England where it appears to be getting scarcer due to the effects of agriculture on many downland habitats. This species is found in meadows and on hillsides on chalk or limestone soils. The markings of this attractive butterfly are extremely variable and a great many forms have been named. The caterpillar has a glossy black head and the body is green with bright yellow stripes. It feeds on horseshoe vetch (*Hippocrepis comosa*) and other leguminous plants, overwintering on the foodplant before completing its growth in the following spring. This is one of the caterpillars which secretes a honey-like fluid attractive to ants. Pupation takes place on the ground amongst the roots. Butterflies may be seen in July and August.

Adonis Blue *Lysandra bellargus* Rottemburg, family Lycaenidae. This beautiful butterfly is widespread, occurring from southern Europe northwards to the Baltic coast. In the British Isles it is confined to southern England where it is found locally on chalk downlands. This species often occurs in the same localities as the Chalkhill Blue and on rare occasions hybrids between these two species have been found. The caterpillar is deep green with orange-yellow longitudinal stripes and possesses a 'honey-gland' which is attractive to ants. It feeds on the foliage of horseshoe vetch (*Hippocrepis comosa*) and related plants and when full grown pupates on the ground in a flimsy cocoon of silk and earth. There are two broods and caterpillars of the second generation overwinter on the foodplant before completing their growth in the following spring. Butterflies may be found in May and June and again from July until September, according to locality.

Mazarine Blue *Cyaniris semiargus* Rottemburg, family Lycaenidae. This butterfly is widespread and common throughout Europe with the exception of southern Spain and northern Fennoscandia. In the early nineteenth century it occurred locally in many parts of England and Wales but by the beginning of the present century it became extinct as a resident species. Subsequent records for the British Isles are rare migrants. Habitats are rough uncultivated fields and alpine meadows up to 2000 metres. The caterpillar is green with darker lines on the back and sides and a shining black head. It feeds on the flowers, seeds and foliage of thrift (*Armeria maritima*), kidney vetch (*Anthyllis vulneraria*), clover (*Trifolium*) and related plants, overwintering while still small amongst dead flower heads. Pupation takes place on the foodplant in late spring and butterflies emerge after about seventeen days. Butterflies are on the wing from June to August, according to altitude, and may be seen drinking from puddles or damp patches of earth. This species is single-brooded.

Adonis Blue *Lysandra bellargus*

Chalkhill Blue *Lysandra coridon* feeding

Adonis Blue *Lysandra bellargus* ♀

Mazarine Blue *Cyaniris semiargus* settling

Glaucopsyche alexis

Celastrina argiolus

Lifesize

Holly Blue caterpillar

Green Underside Blue *Glaucopsyche alexis* Poda, family Lycaenidae. Although this butterfly is widespread in southern and central Europe and occurs in parts of Scandinavia, it becomes scarcer in the northern part of its range and is absent from the British Isles, the Netherlands and Denmark. Its distribution in the Iberian Peninsula is restricted to the Pyrenees and Sierra Nevada. This species may be found in meadows and woodland clearings at low elevations and also occurs on hills and mountain slopes up to 1300 metres. The caterpillar is green or brownish with a darker line along the back and black diagonal stripes along the sides. It feeds on milk vetch (*Astragalus*), broom (*Cytisus*) and other legumes, overwintering on the foodplant. This species is single-brooded and butterflies may be found in April and May.

Holly Blue *Celastrina argiolus* Linnaeus, family Lycaenidae. This widely distributed butterfly occurs throughout Europe with the exception of northern Fennoscandia and its range extends across Siberia to Japan. It is also widespread in North America. In the British Isles it occurs almost everywhere except in northern Scotland. Habitats range from woodland clearings to hedgerows and gardens. The caterpillars have several colour forms varying from yellowish-green with pale lines to brownish-green with yellow stripes and purplish-red markings. They feed on the buds, flowers, berries and young leaves of various shrubs, particularly holly (*Ilex*) in spring and ivy (*Hedera helix*) in autumn. Pupation usually takes place on the foodplant. This species is double-brooded and butterflies are on the wing from April to May and from July to August. They are seldom attracted to flowers but may be seen drinking from puddles or feeding on carrion or the sap of damaged trees.

Green Underside Blue *Glaucopsyche alexis*

Holly Blue *Celastrina argiolus*

Holly Blue *Celastrina argiolus* caterpillar

67

♂

♀

♂ △

♀ △

Maculinea alcon

♂

♀

♂ △

♀ △

Maculinea arion

Lifesize

Large Blue *Maculinea arion*

Large Blue caterpillar tended by ants

Large Blue *Maculinea arion* Linnaeus, family Lycaenidae. This interesting species is widespread in central and southern Europe although in Spain it is only found in the central mountains. In the British Isles it used to occur locally in the south-west of England but has gradually disappeared from each locality and now unfortunately appears to be extinct. The caterpillar is dull pink at first and merges successfully with the flower buds of thyme (*Thymus serpyllum*) on which it feeds. After its third moult, the caterpillar wanders away from the foodplant until it is found by ants which are attracted by the secretions of its 'honey-gland'. It is then carried to the nest where it becomes brownish-white in colour and feeds on the ant larvae. In the following spring the full grown caterpillar pupates in the nest and the butterfly emerges after about three weeks. Butterflies are on the wing from June to August and may be seen flying on dry sandy hills where the foodplant grows.

Alcon Blue *Maculinea alcon* Denis & Schiffermüller, family Lycaenidae. The distribution of this species is very similar to that of the Large Blue although it has never been recorded from the British Isles. It is most common in Germany but occurs locally thoughout most of central and southern Europe. Habitats range from damp meadows and moorland to dry sandy hillsides. This butterfly occurs from near sea level up to 1000 metres, while the alpine subspecies *rebeli* Hirschke is found at an altitude of 1300 to 2000 metres. The caterpillar is green or reddish-brown and feeds inside the flowers of gentians (*Gentiana*) for about two month before leaving the foodplant to be picked up by ants in a similar manner to the Large Blue. It overwinters in the ants' nest, feeding on their larvae and pupae, and remains there to pupate in the spring. There is one brood a year and butterflies may be seen in July and August.

Large Blue *Maculinea arion*

Alcon Blue *Maculinea alcon*

69

Hamearis lucina

Libythea celtis

Lifesize

Duke of Burgundy Fritillary *Hamearis lucina*
Linnaeus, family Riodinidae. This species
occurs throughout central and southern Europe
with the exception of southern parts of Spain and
Italy. Although at one time found in
Scandinavia, it no longer occurs there. In the
British Isles it is widely distributed but local in
England, occurring mostly in the south. This is a
woodland butterfly usually of the lowlands but
sometimes occurring up to 1300 metres. The
caterpillar is brown with black and white hairs
and dark lines along the back and sides. It feeds
on the foliage of cowslip (*Primula veris*) and
primrose (*Primula vulgaris*) and frequently rests
on the underside of a leaf. Pupation takes place
on the foodplant. This species is single-brooded
in the north and double-brooded in the south
with butterflies on the wing from May to June
and August, according to locality.

Nettle-tree Butterfly *Libythea celtis* Laicharting,
family Libytheidae. This unusually shaped
butterfly occurs in southern Europe and parts of
North Africa, its range extending eastwards to
southern Siberia and Japan. Although this
species is generally confined to areas below 500
metres where the foodplant grows, in late
summer specimens may be found at much higher
altitudes. The caterpillar has a brown head and a
green body with a white line down the back and a
pink line along each side. It feeds on nettle-tree
(*Celtis australis*). Butterflies emerge from the
pupa in June and are active until September.
They then go into hibernation until the following
spring when mating and egg laying take place.

Duke of Burgundy Fritillary *Hamearis lucina*

Duke of Burgundy Fritillary pupa

Nettle-tree Butterfly *Libythea celtis* at rest

Duke of Burgundy Fritillary *Hamearis lucina*

Nettle-tree Butterfly *Libythea celtis*

Two-tailed Pasha *Charaxes jasius* Linnaeus, family Nymphalidae. This striking butterfly occurs along the Mediterranean coasts of Europe and North Africa. It is generally rather scarce and local but is quite common in parts of western Italy and the Mediterranean islands. It is found mainly in coastal areas and occurs on dry hills up to 800 metres. The caterpillar is green with a yellow stripe along each side and two blue-centred, eye-like spots on the back. The head is green with four reddish horns. It feeds on strawberry tree (*Arbutus unedo*). The pupa is bluish-green, rather rounded and is usually attached to a twig. This species is double brooded and butterflies are on the wing in May and June and again in August and September. They have a powerful sailing flight and generally rest high on the trees although they will descend to feed on rotting fruit.

Poplar Admiral *Limenitis populi* Linnaeus, family Nymphalidae. This species is widespread in central and northern Europe, but is very scarce in the extreme west and absent from northern Fennoscandia. It does not occur in the British Isles. The preferred habitats are open woodland and forest clearings, generally in damp situations, from sea level up to about 1000 metres. The caterpillar is green with darker spots and two rows of spines along the back, the first pair being extra long and projecting forward over the head. It feeds on the foliage of aspen (*Populus tremula*) and poplars (*Populus*), overwintering on a twig of the foodplant and completing its growth in the following spring. The brownish-yellow pupa is attached to a leaf and the butterfly emerges after a fortnight. Butterflies are on the wing in June and July and generally fly high about the tree tops although in the morning they may be found feeding on dung or carrion.

White Admiral *Ladoga camilla* Linnaeus, family Nymphalidae. The range of this butterfly extends through central Europe eastwards across southern Siberia to China and Japan. In the British Isles it is restricted to southern and eastern England where it is sometimes quite abundant. This is a woodland species preferring damp situations and occurring both in the lowlands and at altitudes up to 1500 metres in the Alps. The caterpillar is green with a purplish-red underside and two rows of brown spines along the back. It feeds on the foliage of honeysuckle (*Lonicera*) and overwinters inside a shelter formed by folding the edges of a leaf together with silk. The unusual pupa which is green and brown with two small horns on its head is attached to a leaf. Butterflies are on the wing in June and July and may be seen feeding at bramble (*Rubus*) blossom. This species may be distinguished from the closely related Southern White Admiral (*Ladoga reducta* Staudinger) by the double row of black spots on the underside of the hindwing.

Charaxes jasius

Limenitis populi

Ladoga camilla

⁴/₅ lifesize

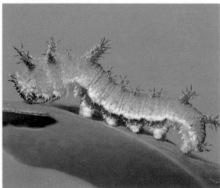

White Admiral *Ladoga camilla* caterpillar

Two-tailed Pasha *Charaxes jasius*

White Admiral *Ladoga camilla*

White Admiral *Ladoga camilla* feeding

Poplar Admiral *Limenitis populi* freshly emerged from pupa

Purple Emperor *Apatura iris* Linnaeus, family
Nymphalidae. The range of this widespread
butterfly extends through central Europe
eastwards across temperate Asia to Japan. It does
not occur in Scandinavia and in the British Isles
is generally confined to the southern counties of
England. This woodland butterfly is usually
found in lowland areas although it does rarely
occur at altitudes above 1000 metres. The
slug-like caterpillar has diagonal yellow stripes
along each side and the head has two red-tipped
horns which are pointed forward when at rest. It
feeds on the foliage of sallow and willow (*Salix*)
and overwinters on the foodplant attached to a
branch. Pupation takes place under a leaf and the
butterfly emerges after about a fortnight.
Butterflies may be found in July and August in
woodland rides and clearings where they are
often attracted to carrion and dung. They usually
fly high in the treetops and often patrol around
solitary oaks (*Quercus*).

Lesser Purple Emperor *Apatura ilia* Denis &
Schiffermüller, family Nymphalidae. This
butterfly is similar to the Purple Emperor both in
appearance and distribution although its range is
slightly more southern in Europe. There is
considerable geographical variation and a
number of subspecies have been described. It
does not occur in the British Isles, the
Netherlands or north-western Germany. It is a
woodland species but generally occurs in damp
places or by streams where the foodplants grow.
The slug-like caterpillar is green with red and
yellow diagonal stripes along the sides and
branched horns on the head. It feeds on the
foliage of poplar (*Populus*), aspen (*Populus
tremula*), sallow and willow (*Salix*). There is one
generation a year in the north and two in the
south with butterflies on the wing from May to
June and August to September, according to
locality. This species may be distinguished from
the Purple Emperor by the presence of a
red-ringed black spot on each forewing.

Purple Emperor *Apatura iris* eggs

⁴/₅ lifesize

Lesser Purple Emperor *Apatura ilia* drinking

Purple Emperor *Apatura iris* about to fly

Purple Emperor *Apatura iris* caterpillar

Lesser Purple Emperor *Apatura ilia* drinking

Vanessa atalanta

Cynthia cardui

Aglais urticae

Nymphalis polychloros

Red Admiral *Vanessa atalanta* Linnaeus, family Nymphalidae. This migrant species occurs throughout Europe, its distribution extending into North Africa and eastwards across temperate Asia to China and Japan. It is a regular and common visitor to the British Isles, spring arrivals producing a second generation in late summer, but does not normally survive the winter. This butterfly also occurs in North America. It may be found almost anywhere from sea level up to about 2000 metres but is attracted to woodlands, orchards and gardens. The caterpillar varies in colour from black to greenish-grey, with a yellow line along the sides and with the upper surface covered with rows of spines. It feeds on nettle (*Urtica*), spinning leaves together to make a tent-like shelter. The pupa is greyish-brown with metallic golden spots and is suspended upside down from a leaf. Butterflies are on the wing from May to October and are attracted to wild and garden flowers.

Painted Lady *Cynthia cardui* Linnaeus, family Nymphalidae. The distribution of this migrant species is almost worldwide with the exception of South America. There is a regular migration from North Africa and southern Europe northwards to Scandinavia and the British Isles and, except in the extreme north, these butterflies produce a second brood. However, the second generation does not normally survive the winter in regions north of the Alps. May be found almost anywhere, even above 2000 metres, but most usually occurs in open ground, fields and gardens. The caterpillar is grey or black with a yellow line down each side. It feeds on thistles (*Carduus*), burdock (*Arctium*) and other plants. The pupa is greyish-brown with metallic golden spots and is suspended from the foodplant. Butterflies are on the wing from April until October.

Small Tortoiseshell *Aglais urticae* Linnaeus, family Nymphalidae. This common and widespread butterfly occurs throughout Europe and its distribution extends across Siberia to Japan. It has been recorded from most parts of the British Isles and is often abundant. Butterflies may be found from sea level up to 3000 metres. They prefer situations such as fields, roadsides and gardens. The caterpillar is yellowish with dense black speckling and there are two yellow lines down the back and one along each side. The spines along the back and sides are black. The caterpillars feed together on nettle (*Urtica dioica*), spinning the terminal leaves together. When full grown they disperse and pupate suspended from some suitable support usually away from the foodplant. There are two generations a year except in the extreme north and butterflies are on the wing from March until October.

Large Tortoiseshell *Nymphalis polychloros* Linnaeus, family Nymphalidae. This butterfly is widespread in central and southern Europe but becomes more local further north and is absent from northern Fennoscandia. In the British Isles it used to be quite common and widespread but in recent years it has become scarce and is restricted to southern England and the Channel Islands. Woodland margins are the usual habitat and this species may be found up to 1700 metres. The caterpillar is black with a double yellowish-brown band down the back and similar markings along the sides. The spines along the back and sides are yellowish with black tips. Caterpillars feed together in an open web spun on the outer branches of elm (*Ulmus*), willow (*Salix*), poplar (*Populus*) and fruit trees. The pupa is golden brown and green with silver spots on the back and is suspended upside down. Butterflies may be found from June until September and again after hibernation in the following April and May.

⁴/₅ lifesize

Small Tortoiseshells *Aglais urticae* feeding

Painted Lady *Cynthia cardui* feeding

Large Tortoiseshell *Nymphalis polychloros*

Small Tortoiseshell *Aglais urticae* caterpillars

Large Tortoiseshell *Nymphalis polychloros*

77

Nymphalis antiopa

Inachis io

Polygonia c-album

Camberwell Beauty *Nymphalis antiopa*
Linnaeus, family Nymphalidae. This handsome
migrant species occurs throughout Europe with
the exception of southern Spain and the
Mediterranean islands. It also occurs in North
America where it is known as the Mourning
Cloak. Although this butterfly is generally a rare
visitor to the British Isles it sometimes occurs in
quite large numbers along the eastern seaboard
and its common name refers to the specimen
recorded in 1748 from Cool Arbour Lane in
Camberwell. The usual habitats are open
country and light woodlands, often among hills
and mountains. The caterpillar is black with a
series of red patches down the back and rows of
shining black spines along the back and sides. It
feeds on the foliage of sallow, willow (*Salix*),
birch (*Betula*) and elm (*Ulmus*). The caterpillars
feed gregariously beneath a silken web and do
not disperse until about to pupate. There is a
single generation each year flying from June until
late autumn and again in the spring, after
hibernation.

Peacock *Inachis io* Linnaeus, family
Nymphalidae. This common and distinctive
butterfly occurs throughout Europe with the
exception of northern Fennoscandia, its
distribution extending across temperate Asia to
Japan. It is widespread and sometimes abundant
in the British Isles although less common in
northern Scotland. This species may be found in
orchards, gardens and other places where flowers
abound. The caterpillar is black spotted with
white and has shining black spines along the back
and sides. The usual foodplant is nettle (*Urtica
dioica*) although caterpillars will sometimes feed
on hop (*Humulus*). They feed gregariously,
dispersing when full grown to pupate suspended
from tree trunks or other suitable supports.
There is one generation a year which flies from
July until late autumn and overwinters in such
places as outhouses and hollow trees before
reappearing in the following spring. If disturbed
while hibernating these butterflies can produce a
hissing sound by rubbing their wings together.

Comma *Polygonia c-album* Linnaeus, family
Nymphalidae. This butterfly occurs throughout
Europe with the exception of northern
Fennoscandia, its range extending eastwards
across Siberia to China and Japan. In the British
Isles this species seems to be increasing its range
in recent years after going into a decline during the
beginning of the century. It now occurs widely in
southern England and Wales and is sometimes
quite common. Usual habitats are woodland
clearings and hedgerows and at one time these
butterflies were particularly associated with hop
gardens. The caterpillar is black with a red band
along each side and a large white patch on the
rear part of the back which gives the appearance
of a bird dropping. There are rows of spines
along the back and sides. The usual foodplants
are nettle (*Urtica dioica*), hop (*Humulus*) and elm
(*Ulmus*). The pupa is usually suspended from the
foodplant. There are two generations a year and
butterflies are on the wing from May to June and
from August to September, those of the latter
brood hibernating and reappearing in the spring.

⁴/₅ lifesize

Comma *Polygonia c-album*

Camberwell Beauty *Nymphalis antiopa*

Comma *Polygonia c-album*

Peacock *Inachis io*

♂ vern.   ♀ vern.

♂ aest.   ♀ aest.

♂ △   ♀ △

Araschnia levana

Lifesize

Map *Araschnia levana* Linnaeus, family Nymphalidae. This interesting little butterfly occurs widely in central Europe and ranges eastwards as far as Japan. In the British Isles it was introduced into localities in Herefordshire and Monmouth in 1912 and may have established itself were it not for the action of one entomologist, who disagreed with the introduction of foreign species and deliberately exterminated the colonies by collecting. It is a woodland insect occurring in forest rides and clearings up to 1000 metres. The caterpillar is black, sometimes striped with brown and has rows of black or yellowish-brown spines along the back and sides. The foodplant is nettle (*Urtica dioica*) and caterpillars feed communally. Pupae of the second generation overwinter. Butterflies are on the wing from April to June and again in August and September. This species is particularly interesting because butterflies of the two broods are quite distinct in colour and patterning. Both forms are illustrated.

Map *Araschnia levana*

Map *Araschnia levana*

Pandoriana pandora

Boloria selene

Boloria euphrosyne

Cardinal *Pandoriana pandora* Denis &
Schiffermüller, family Nymphalidae. This is a
southern butterfly, occurring both in southern
Europe and North Africa although the occasional
specimen has occurred as far north as Poland. It
has never been recorded from the British Isles.
Habitats are meadows, woodland margins and
rough mountain slopes up to 2000 metres. The
caterpillar is brown with a broad black band
along the back streaked with bluish-grey. The
rows of spines along the back and sides are
brown. It feeds on the leaves of violets (*Viola*)
and occasionally rue (*Ruta*). The pupa is
greyish-green or brown with shining spots on the
back. Although there are two broods a year in
North Africa, this species is single-brooded in
Europe with butterflies on the wing in June and
July. This butterfly is easily distinguished from
the similar Silver-washed Fritillary by the
beautiful rosy-red colour of the underside of the
forewing.

Small Pearl-bordered Fritillary *Boloria selene*
Denis & Schiffermüller, family Nymphalidae.
This widely distributed butterfly occurs
throughout Europe except in the extreme south
and ranges eastwards across central Asia to
Korea. It also occurs in North America where it
is known as the Silver-bordered Fritillary. In the
British Isles it is widespread although absent
from Ireland. This is generally a woodland
butterfly but in some regions it frequents
moorlands and mountain sides up to 2400
metres. The caterpillar is reddish-brown with
small white spots. There are rows of yellowish
conical projections along the back and sides, each
with short black bristles. Violets (*Viola*) are the
foodplant and the caterpillar overwinters in a
curled up leaf before completing its growth in the
following spring. The pupa is brown with
metallic spots along the sides and is suspended
upside down from the foodplant. There is
usually one brood a year in the north and two in
the south with butterflies on the wing from June
to July and again in August.

Pearl-bordered Fritillary *Boloria euphrosyne*
Linnaeus, family Nymphalidae. This species
occurs widely throughout Europe with the
exception of southern Spain. In the British Isles
it is widespread but less common in the north and
in Ireland is restricted to Co. Clare. The usual
habitat is damp woodland, but butterflies may
also be found in meadows and on heathland up to
2000 metres. The caterpillar is black with a
greyish line along each side and rows of yellowish
spines along the back and sides. It feeds on the
foliage of violets (*Viola*), hibernating in a curled
up leaf through the winter. The greyish-brown
pupa is suspended upside down from the
foodplant. There is one brood a year in the north
and two in the south with butterflies on the wing
from April until August depending on locality.
This species may be distinguished from the
Small Pearl-bordered Fritillary by the orange-red
ground colour of the underside of the hindwing.

Cardinal *Pandoriana pandora* feeding

Small Pearl-bordered Fritillary *Boloria selene*

Small Pearl-bordered Fritillary *Boloria selene*

Argynnis lathonia

Argynnis niobe

. ♂

♀

♂ △   *Argynnis adippe*   ♀ △

Lifesize

Niobe Fritillary *Argynnis niobe*

High Brown Fritillary *Argynnis adippe* Denis &
Schiffermüller, family Nymphalidae. This
widespread butterfly occurs throughout Europe
with the exception of northern Fennoscandia, its
range extending to North Africa and eastwards to
Japan. It is a variable species and many
geographical races have been described. In the
British Isles it occurs widely in England and
Wales but becomes scarcer further north and is
absent from Scotland and Ireland. Habitats are
usually woodland rides and clearings although
southern races may be found on heathland and at
altitudes up to 3000 metres. The caterpillar is
black, heavily marked with yellowish-grey and
with a white line down the back. The rows of
spines along the back and sides are reddish-
brown. The foodplants are various species of
violet (*Viola*). Pupation takes place within the
shelter of spun leaves of the foodplant.
Butterflies are on the wing in June and July and
there is only one brood a year.

Niobe Fritillary *Argynnis niobe* Linnaeus, family
Nymphalidae. Although this species has a
similar distribution to the closely related High
Brown Fritillary, it does not occur in the British
Isles and its range does not extend so far to the
east. Habitats are usually woodland margins,
meadows and mountain pastures up to 2500
metres. The caterpillar is brown with a white line
down the back edged with black and rows of
reddish-brown spines along the back and sides.
It feeds on the foliage of violet (*Viola*) or more
rarely plantain (*Plantago*). The pupa stage lasts
for about four weeks. Butterflies are on the wing
in June and July and there is only one brood a
year. This species may be distinguished from the
High Brown Fritillary by its smaller size and the
presence of black veins on the underside of the
hindwing.

Queen of Spain Fritillary *Argynnis lathonia*
Linnaeus, family Nymphalidae. This butterfly is
a native of North Africa and southern Europe but
migrates north to most parts of Europe each year.
It is a scarce but regular migrant to the British
Isles, occurring mainly in south-eastern
England. The usual habitats are rough, dry open
ground, heathland and meadows up to 2500
metres. The caterpillar is black with minute
white dots and a broken yellowish-white stripe
along each side. There are six rows of black

spines along the back and sides. It feeds on the
foliage of violets (*Viola*). Pupation takes place on
the foodplant and the pupa which is brown with
shining metallic spots along the sides is
suspended upside down. This species is
single-brooded in the north but may have up to
three broods a year in the south. It flies from
March until late summer in the extreme south
but migrants usually arrive in central and
northern Europe in May and produce offspring
in late summer.

Queen of Spain Fritillary *Argynnis lathonia*

High Brown Fritillary *Argynnis adippe* drinking

Queen of Spain Fritillary *Argynnis lathonia*

High Brown Fritillary *Argynnis adippe*

♂   ♀

♂ △   Argynnis aglaja   ♀ △

♂   ♀

♂ △   Argynnis paphia   ♀ △

Brenthis ino   △

Dark Green Fritillary *Argynnis aglaja*

Silver-washed Fritillary *Argynnis paphia*

Silver-washed Fritillary caterpillar

Dark Green Fritillary *Argynnis aglaja* Linnaeus, family Nymphalidae. This widespread butterfly occurs throughout Europe and is represented in North Africa by a distinct race, ssp. *lyauteyi* Oberthür. In the British Isles it may be found almost everywhere and is locally common. The distinctly dark form occurring in the western isles of Scotland has been named ssp. *scotica* Watkins. Habitats range from woodland clearings to open hillsides and moorland up to altitudes of 3000 metres. The caterpillar is black with a yellowish-white stripe down the back and a row of red spots low down along each side. The rows of spines along the back and sides are black. Violets (*Viola*) are the usual foodplant. Pupation takes place on the foodplant and the pupa is suspended in a shelter of spun leaves. Butterflies are on the wing in June and July with only one generation a year.

Silver-washed Fritillary *Argynnis paphia* Linnaeus, family Nymphalidae. The range of

⁴/₅ lifesize

Dark Green Fritillary *Argynnis aglaja*

this butterfly extends through most of Europe eastwards through temperate Asia to Japan. It is absent from southern Spain and northern Fennoscandia. In the British Isles it occurs locally in southern England and Wales, becoming scarcer further north, while in Ireland it is generally more widespread. A beautiful dark form of the female (f. *valesina* Esper) occurs sporadically and in Britain is only found in the New Forest, Hampshire. This is a woodland insect occurring up to 1500 metres in clearings and forest rides. The caterpillar is black with yellow lines down the back and sides and six rows of black-tipped reddish-brown spines. It feeds on violet (*Viola*) and when full grown pupates on the foodplant suspended upside down. This species is single-brooded and butterflies are on the wing in July and August. They may often be seen feeding on bramble (*Rubus*) blossom.

Lesser Marbled Fritillary *Brenthis ino*
Rottemburg, family Nymphalidae. Although this butterfly has a scattered distribution in Europe it can be quite common in suitable localities. It occurs as far north as Scandinavia and extends southwards to south-eastern Europe but is absent from the British Isles, northern France and most of Spain and Italy. This is an insect of marshy meadows, peat bogs and damp open woodland and may occur up to 1600 metres. The caterpillar is yellowish-grey with a dark brown line down the back and a brown stripe along each side bordered with yellow. The six rows of spines along the back and sides are yellow. The foodplants are meadow-sweet (*Filipendula ulmaria*), goat's-beard (*Aruncus dioicus*) and related species. The caterpillar may be found in autumn and again in the following spring after hibernation. Butterflies are on the wing from June until August, depending on locality, and there is only one brood a year.

Lesser Marbled Fritillary *Brenthis ino* feeding

Eurodryas aurinia

Melitaea didyma

Lifesize

Marsh Fritillary *Eurodryas aurinia* caterpillars

Marsh Fritillary *Eurodryas aurinia* Rottemburg, family Nymphalidae. This variable butterfly occurs throughout most of Europe with the exception of the Alps and northern Fennoscandia although in Italy it is very scarce. In the British Isles it is widespread in the west but it has disappeared from a number of areas in recent years, often due to land drainage. In Ireland it is sometimes extremely abundant in suitable areas and caterpillar 'plagues' have been reported. This butterfly occurs both in damp marshy ground and on hillsides where the foodplant grows. The caterpillar is black with minute white dots and rows of short black spines along the back and sides. It feeds communally on the leaves of devil's bit scabious (*Scabiosa succisa*), plantain (*Plantago*) and related plants in a dense silken web. The caterpillar completes its growth after overwintering and pupates suspended upside down. Butterflies are on the wing from May to June but are sluggish in habit and seldom fly far.

Spotted Fritillary *Melitaea didyma* Esper, family Nymphalidae. This extremely variable species is widespread in Europe with the exception of northern Germany, the Netherlands, the British Isles and Scandinavia. Its range extends into North Africa and central Asia and there are many described subspecies. Habitats are meadows, woodland clearings and mountain slopes up to 1700 metres. This species always chooses warm sunny situations and may be quite abundant where it occurs. The caterpillar has a brown head and the body is bluish-grey with rows of reddish-brown spines along the back and sides. It feeds on plantain (*Plantago*), toadflax (*Linaria*) and speedwell (*Veronica*). Caterpillars of the autumn brood overwinter before completing their growth in the following spring. The pupa stage usually lasts about two weeks. There are from one to three generations a year according to locality and altitude and butterflies may be on the wing at any time between May and August.

Spotted Fritillary *Melitaea didyma*

Marsh Fritillary *Eurodryas aurinia*

Marsh Fritillaries *Eurodryas aurinia* mating

Melitaea cinxia

Mellicta athalia

Lifesize

Heath Fritillary *Mellicta athalia* caterpillar

Heath Fritillary *Mellicta athalia* pupa

Glanville Fritillary *Melitaea cinxia* Linnaeus, family Nymphalidae. The range of this butterfly extends throughout Europe, except for southern Spain and most of Fennoscandia, eastwards to Siberia. A distinct race (ssp. *atlantis* le Cerf) occurs in the mountains of Morocco. In the British Isles it is restricted to the Channel Islands and the Isle of Wight. This insect was named after Mrs Eleanor Glanville, who collected butterflies in the eighteenth century. Habitats are meadows, roadsides and rough uncultivated land. The caterpillar is black with white spots and a series of olive green conical warts along the back and sides each covered with black hairs. Caterpillars feed communally on plantain (*Plantago*) under a silken web in which they hibernate through the winter before completing their growth in the spring. The pupa is suspended upside down from the foodplant. There are two generations a year in the south and only one in the north with butterflies on the wing from May to June and August to September, according to locality.

Heath Fritillary *Mellicta athalia* Rottemburg, family Nymphalidae. This widespread and frequently common species occurs throughout Europe with the exception of southern Spain and its range extends eastwards to Japan. In the British Isles it is now restricted to a few colonies in southern England, although it was at one time more widespread and was also recorded in Ireland from Killarney. The common name is misleading as this is predominantly a woodland butterfly, although the Scandinavian subspecies *norvegica* Aurivillius occurs on moorland. The caterpillar is black, spotted with white and has rows of orange-yellow conical projections along the back and sides, each covered with black hairs. Caterpillars live communally under a web and hibernate on the foodplant before completing their growth in the following spring. Foodplants are cow-wheat (*Melampyrum*), foxglove (*Digitalis*) and plantain (*Plantago*). The pupa is suspended upside down from the foodplant. There are two broods a year in the south and one in the north with butterflies on the wing between June and September, according to locality.

Glanville Fritillary *Melitaea cinxia*

Heath Fritillary *Mellicta athalia* feeding

Heath Fritillary *Mellicta athalia* feeding

Glanville Fritillary *Melitaea cinxia* at rest

Pararge aegeria

Lasiommata megera

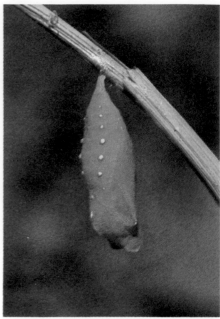

Wall *Lasiommata megera* pupa

Speckled Wood *Pararge aegeria* pupa

Lifesize

Speckled Wood *Pararge aegeria* Linnaeus, family Satyridae. This butterfly occurs throughout Europe except for the extreme north and is also found in North Africa. In the British Isles it is widespread in England, Wales and Ireland but local and less common in Scotland. As its name suggests, this is a woodland insect found in rides and clearings where its wing pattern blends well with the dappled lighting. The caterpillar is green with darker longitudinal stripes and is successfully camouflaged on its foodplants which are various grasses such as couch grass (*Agropyron repens*) and cock's foot (*Dactylis glomerata*). The pale green pupa is suspended from a grass stem. Autumn pupae overwinter but those of other generations produce butterflies within about a month. Two broods a year in the north but further south a succession of broods with butterflies on the wing from March until October.

Wall *Lasiommata megera* Linnaeus, family Satyridae. This butterfly is widespread in western Europe, occurring as far north as southern Scandinavia. Its range extends into North Africa and eastwards to central Asia. In the British Isles it is common in many areas although less abundant in the north. Habitats are roadsides, field margins, heathland and other dry open situations up to an altitude of 1700 metres. The caterpillar is pale green with scattered white spots and a series of white lines along the back and sides. It feeds on various grasses such as meadow grass (*Poa*) and cock's foot (*Dactylis glomerata*). The pupa is usually green with yellowish markings but sometimes blackish forms occur. Autumn pupae overwinter but those of the summer broods produce butterflies in about two weeks. There are usually two generations a year in central Europe and three in the south with butterflies on the wing from March until September, according to locality. They are fond of basking in the sun on walls and hedge banks.

Wall *Lasiommata megera* at rest

Speckled Wood *Pararge aegeria* at rest

Speckled Wood *Pararge aegeria*

Erebia epiphron

Erebia aethiops

♂

♀

♂ △

♀ △

Erebia ligea

Lifesize

Mountain Ringlet *Erebia epiphron*

completing its growth in the following spring. Pupation takes place low down among the grass stems and the butterfly emerges after about three weeks. Butterflies are on the wing from June until August, according to locality, flying only in sunshine and dropping to the ground as soon as the sun is obscured.

Scotch Argus *Erebia aethiops* Esper, family Satyridae. This is one of the most widely distributed European species of the genus *Erebia*, occurring in most central regions and parts of the south although absent from the Pyrenees and Scandinavia. In the British Isles it is found in many parts of Scotland but its range in northern England is now restricted to Cumbria although it was formerly more widespread. Habitats are damp meadows and woodland margins from lowlands up to 2000 metres. The caterpillar is pale yellowish-brown with a dark brown line down the back. It feeds on purple moor grass (*Molinia caerulea*), cock's foot (*Dactylis glomerata*) and other grasses. Pupation takes place in an open network cocoon on the ground and butterflies emerge after about a fortnight. The flight period is from July to September, according to locality, and, like the Mountain Ringlet, butterflies will only fly when the sun is shining.

Arran Brown *Erebia ligea* Linnaeus, family Satyridae. This is a butterfly of the uplands, occurring both in southern Europe and Scandinavia but is absent from the Pyrenees and much of central Europe. Its range extends eastwards to Japan. There have been a number of records from Scotland, one from the Isle of Arran from which this species takes its common name, but most of these are not substantiated. Habitats are light woodland and meadows from about 500 metres to 1500 metres and at lower altitudes in the north. The caterpillar is pale brown with a dark line along the back and feeds on various grasses such as finger-grass (*Digitaria*) and wood millet (*Milium*). Caterpillars often overwinter twice, taking two years to complete their growth. Pupation takes place on the ground and the pupa is brown. Butterflies may be found from late June until August.

Mountain Ringlet *Erebia epiphron* Knoch, family Satyridae. Like most of the Erebias this is a high altitude species occurring in most mountainous areas of Europe, with the exception of Fennoscandia, although it appears to be extinct in the Harz mountains of Germany from where it was originally described. In the British Isles it is found in Cumbria and highland Scotland but seems to have died out in Ireland. Habitats are wet grassy mountain slopes up to 2000 metres. The caterpillar is green with a darker line down the back and cream-coloured stripes along the sides. It feeds on grasses such as mat grass (*Nardus stricta*) and hibernates before

Scotch Argus *Erebia aethiops*

Arran Brown *Erebia ligea*

Scotch Argus *Erebia aethiops*

Erebia medusa

Melanargia galathea

Lifesize

Marbled White *Melanargia galathea* at rest

Marbled White *Melanargia galathea* caterpillar

Woodland Ringlet *Erebia medusa* Denis & Schiffermüller, family Satyridae. This butterfly is widespread in central and south-eastern Europe. A distinct race, ssp. *polaris* Staudinger, occurring in Scandinavia and north-west Germany, has been regarded as a separate species and is popularly known as the Arctic Woodland Ringlet. This species does not occur in the British Isles. Habitats are damp meadows, often near woodland, on mountain slopes up to 2500 metres. The caterpillar is either green or brownish with a black band down the back and pale stripes along the sides. It feeds on wood millet (*Milium*) and finger grass (*Digitaria*), taking two years to become fully grown. Pupation takes place on the ground and the pupa overwinters. Butterflies are on the wing in June and July, often seen flying near the tree line.

Marbled White *Melanargia galathea* Linnaeus, family Satyridae. This is the commonest and most widespread of a group of distinctly marked butterflies, distinguished from each other by minor differences in pattern, and occurring throughout central and southern Europe. In the British Isles it is quite widespread in England, particularly in the south, and also occurs in South Wales. Habitats are rough fields, downland and woodland margins from sea level up to 1700 metres. The caterpillar is either pale brown or yellowish-green with darker lines along the back and sides and has a brown head. It feeds on many types of grass, including cock's foot (*Dactylis*) and cat's-tail (*Phleum*), overwintering while still small and completing its growth in the following spring. Pupation takes place on the ground and butterflies emerge two to three weeks later. This species is single-brooded with butterflies on the wing in June and July. The flight is rather slow and flapping and individuals seldom wander far from the colony.

Marbled White *Melanargia galathea* feeding

Woodland Ringlet *Erebia medusa* at rest

Hipparchia semele

Hipparchia fagi

Grayling *Hipparchia semele* caterpillar

Grayling *Hipparchia semele* Linnaeus, family Satyridae. This widespread butterfly occurs throughout Europe with the exception of northern Fennoscandia. In the British Isles it is widely distributed, occurring particularly in coastal districts, and represented by a number of distinct races. In parts of southern Europe there is some confusion with the closely related Southern Grayling, *Hipparchia aristaeus* Bonelli which can only be reliably distinguished on internal structures. Habitats are cliffs, sand hills, heaths and open woodland. The caterpillar is pale yellowish-brown with darker stripes and feeds on hair grass (*Aira*) and many other grasses. It overwinters before completing its growth in the following spring and pupates just below the soil in a silk-lined chamber. Butterflies may be found from May until August, according to locality. They have a rapid flight and frequently settle on the ground with their wings closed and tilted to one side so that they merge with the background.

Woodland Grayling *Hipparchia fagi* Scopoli, family Satyridae. This butterfly occurs throughout central and southern Europe with the exception of central and southern Spain and Portugal. It is absent from northern Europe and the British Isles. As its name suggests, this is a woodland insect, occurring from the lowlands up to 1000 metres. The caterpillar is reddish-brown with narrow dark lines along the body and a blackish head. It feeds on various grasses, particularly species of *Holcus*, overwintering and completing its growth in the spring. Pupation takes place on the ground and the pupa is dark brown. There is one brood a year and butterflies are on the wing from June until August. They are locally quite common and may be found on tree trunks with their wings folded. This species may usually be distinguished from the closely related Rock Grayling, *Hipparchia alcyone* Denis & Schiffermüller by its larger size.

Lifesize

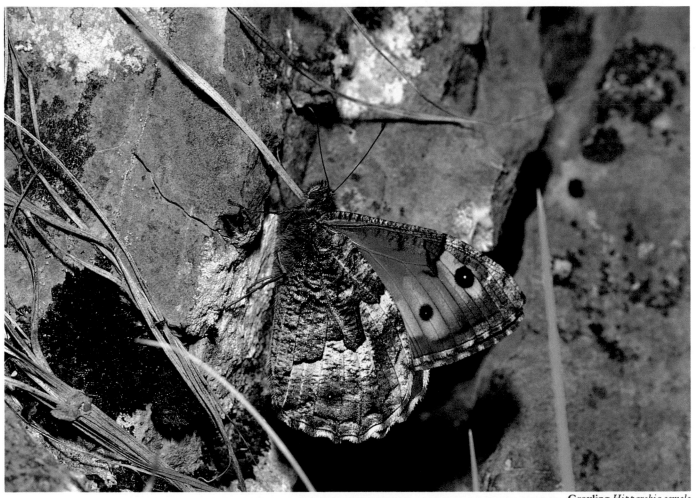

Grayling *Hipparchia semele*

Woodland Grayling *Hipparchia fagi* at rest

99

Minois dryas

Brintesia circe

Arethusana arethusa

Dryad *Minois dryas* Scopoli, family Satyridae. This rather large and distinctive brown butterfly occurs locally in a wide area of central and southern Europe although absent from southern Spain, most of Italy and northern Europe, including the British Isles. It occurs in light woodland and dry scrub on hill slopes up to an altitude of 1500 metres. The caterpillar is greyish-yellow with darker lines along the back and sides and has a brown head. It feeds on various grasses such as wild oat (*Avena*) and brome (*Bromus*) and overwinters on the foodplant before completing its growth in the following spring. The pupa is brown. There is only one generation a year and butterflies are on the wing from July until September, according to locality. The flight of this species is rather slow and clumsy and butterflies do not fly any great distance from the colony.

Great Banded Grayling or **Greater Wood Nymph** *Brintesia circe* Fabricius, family Satyridae. In western Europe this large and striking butterfly is mainly confined to central and southern regions but in the east it also occurs further north. It does not reach as far north as the Netherlands or the British Isles. This is an insect associated with open woodland, particularly where oak (*Quercus*) is plentiful, and occurs from low levels up to 1500 metres. The caterpillar is brown with a dark line down the middle of the back and yellowish-brown stripes on either side. It feeds on various species of grass such as brome (*Bromus*) and rye-grass (*Lolium*). The pupa is reddish-brown spotted with yellow. There is only one generation a year and butterflies are usually on the wing in June or July although sometimes as late as September. They frequently rest on tree trunks but fly off readily if disturbed.

False Grayling *Arethusana arethusa* Denis & Schiffermüller, family Satyridae. This butterfly is locally common in central and southern Europe, its range extending to North Africa and central Asia. It does not occur in northern Europe and has only once been recorded from the British Isles. The British record was only of a single specimen found in Surrey but in an area which seemed to provide a suitable habitat for the species to breed. This butterfly is found on dry heathland and grassy places on calcareous soils up to 1500 metres. The caterpillar is yellowish-brown or grey with a dark line down the back, bordered with red or yellow. It feeds on grasses, particularly fescues (*Festuca*), hibernating through the winter and completing its growth in the following spring. Pupation takes place on the ground. There is only one brood a year and butterflies are on the wing in July and August. They fly in rough places and frequently settle on the ground or on rocks.

⁴/₅ lifesize

Dryad *Minois dryas* feeding

Great Banded Grayling *Brintesia circe* at rest

Pyronia tithonus

Maniola jurtina

Coenonympha pamphilus

Lifesize

Meadow Brown *Maniola jurtina* pupa

its growth in spring after hibernation. The pupa is suspended from a grass stem and the butterfly emerges after about three weeks. Butterflies are on the wing in July and August and may be seen feeding at bramble (*Rubus*) blossom.

Meadow Brown *Maniola jurtina* Linnaeus, family Satyridae. This very common and widespread species occurs in all parts of Europe except for the extreme north and is also found in North Africa. In the British Isles it occurs almost everywhere and is represented by a number of named subspecies. Habitats are fields, roadsides and woodland margins from sea level up to 1800 metres. The caterpillar is yellowish-green with a darker line down the back and a narrow white stripe along each side. It feeds on various grasses but particularly meadow grass (*Poa*), overwintering before completing its growth in the following spring. The pale green pupa is suspended from a grass stem and produces a butterfly within about a month. There is only one brood a year but butterflies have a long flight period and may be seen from June through to September, according to locality and climate. This is one of the few species to fly both in dull weather and in sunshine.

Small Heath *Coenonympha pamphilus* Linnaeus, family Satyridae. This common little butterfly occurs almost everywhere in Europe except for the extreme north and its range extends into North Africa. It is widespread and often abundant in the British Isles. Habitats are meadows, heaths, roadsides and mountain slopes up to 1800 metres. The caterpillar is green with dark stripes along the back and sides. It feeds on various grasses but particularly on annual meadow grass (*Poa annua*), overwintering before completing its growth in spring. The pale green pupa is suspended upside down from a grass stem and produces a butterfly in about three weeks. While there is only one generation a year in northern regions, this species is more usually double-brooded and in the south there is a succession of broods. Butterflies are on the wing from May until October, according to locality, and have a slow fluttering flight above the foliage.

Gatekeeper or **Hedge Brown** *Pyronia tithonus* Linnaeus, family Satyridae. This is a widespread but local butterfly in central and southern Europe. It is absent from Scandinavia and southern Italy and only occurs on the southern slopes of the Alps. In the British Isles it is common in places, particularly in southern England and Wales and also occurs in Ireland. It was formerly recorded from Scotland but does not occur there now. Habitats are fields, hedgerows and open woodland mainly in lowlands but also in mountainous areas up to 900 metres. The caterpillar is yellowish-brown with a dark line down the back and pale lines along the sides. It feeds on various grasses particularly annual meadow grass (*Poa annua*), completing

Small Heath *Coenonympha pamphilus*

Meadow Brown *Maniola jurtina* caterpillar

Gatekeeper *Pyronia tithonus* feeding

Meadow Brown *Maniola jurtina* feeding

103

Coenonympha tullia

Coenonympha arcania

Aphantopus hyperantus

Pearly Heath *Coenonympha arcania*

Large Heath *Coenonympha tullia* Müller, family Satyridae. This interesting and variable species is widespread in central and northern Europe and occurs locally in parts of the south. Its range extends eastwards across temperate Asia and includes North Africa. In the British Isles it is found in northern parts of England and Wales and is widespread in Scotland and Ireland. There are many named races and subspecies, some with different habitat preferences. Habitats range from lowland marshes and bogs to moorlands and wet mountain meadows up to 2300 metres. The caterpillar is bright green with a dark green stripe down the back and two whitish lines along each side. It feeds on white beak-sedge (*Rhynchospora alba*) or cotton grass (*Eriophorum*), overwintering at the roots before completing its growth in the spring. The pupa is suspended from a grass stem and produces a butterfly within a month. Butterflies are on the wing in June and July.

Pearly Heath *Coenonympha arcania* Linnaeus, family Satyridae. This butterfly is widespread throughout Europe with the exception of southern Spain, northern Fennoscandia, the Netherlands and the British Isles. It may be found from the lowlands up to altitudes of 1800 metres and is most common in hill country. Habitats are woodland clearings, meadows and mountain slopes. The caterpillar is green with a darker line down the back and a yellow line along each side. The pointed tail is marked with red. It feeds on grasses such as melick (*Melica*) and overwinters before completing its growth in the following spring. There is normally only one brood a year although in some parts of southern Europe there may be a partial second generation. Butterflies are usually on the wing in June and July although those of the alpine subspecies *darwiniana* Staudinger fly from July until August.

Ringlet *Aphantopus hyperantus* Linnaeus, family Satyridae. This species occurs throughout most of Europe except for the extreme north and parts of the south such as peninsular Italy and most of Spain. It is widespread in the British Isles with the exception of northern Scotland and is particularly common in southern and western Ireland. Habitats are damp meadows, hedgerows and woodland margins from lowlands up to 1500 metres. The caterpillar is pale brown with a darker line down the back and white lines along

Lifesize

Large Heath *Coenonympha tullia* pupa

Large Heath *Coenonympha tullia*

the sides. It feeds on various grasses such as cock's foot (*Dactylis glomerata*) and meadow grass (*Poa*), overwintering while small and completing its growth in the spring. The pale brown pupa is suspended from a grass stem near to the ground and produces a butterfly in about two weeks. Butterflies are on the wing from June until August, according to locality, and may be found feeding at the flowers of bramble (*Rubus*).

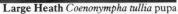

Ringlet *Aphantopus hyperantus*

Monarch or **Milkweed** *Danaus plexippus*
Linnaeus, family Danaidae. This magnificent
American migratory butterfly occurs from time
to time as a rare vagrant in Europe. There are a
number of specimens recorded from the British
Isles and it has been suggested that many of these
have travelled part or all of the way from America
on board ship, while others argue that the
butterfly is quite capable of crossing the Atlantic
with wind assistance. This butterfly first reached
the Canary Islands in the late nineteenth century
and has now become established so that some
European specimens may originate from there.
The distinctive black and yellow banded
caterpillar feeds on various kinds of milkweed
(*Asclepia*) and other related plants. It extracts
certain heart-poisons from the foodplant which
remain in its body throughout its transformation
to the butterfly stage and protect it from
predators. For this reason both the caterpillar
and butterfly are strongly patterned and readily
recognised. The pupa is bluish-green with
metallic golden spots and is suspended from the
foodplant. Seen in Britain in late summer or
autumn.

Danaus plexippus

Lifesize

Monarch *Danaus plexippus* pupa

Monarch *Danaus plexippus* caterpillar

Monarch *Danaus plexippus* feeding

Poecilocampa populi

♂   ♀

Malacosoma neustria

♂   ♀

Lasiocampa trifolii

♂

♀

Lasiocampa quercus

♂

♀

December Moth *Poecilocampa populi* Linnaeus, family Lasiocampidae. This moth is distributed widely throughout northern, central and southern Europe and is often quite common. In Britain it is widespread but less common in northern England and Scotland and is only recorded from scattered localities in Ireland. Habitats are woodlands, hedgerows and parkland. The caterpillar is pale brown heavily freckled with black and covered with hairs which are short on the back and longer on the sides. Behind the head is a reddish-brown mark divided by a white line. Caterpillars feed on the foliage of poplar (*Populus*), lime (*Tilia*), oak (*Quercus*) and other deciduous trees. The glossy brown pupa is protected by a silken cocoon spun amongst dead leaves or under loose bark. Moths emerge in late autumn or winter, and become active at dusk. On the wing from September to December.

Lackey *Malacosoma neustria* Linnaeus, family Lasiocampidae. A common species throughout most of Europe, its range extending into central Asia. Widespread in England and Wales but scarcer further north and absent from Scotland. Also occurs locally in Ireland. Habitats are woodlands, hedgerows, gardens and orchards. The hairy caterpillar is slate blue striped with red and black and with a white line down the middle of the back. Its head is blue with two round black spots which look like eyes. Caterpillars live gregariously in a silken tent spun over the foliage. Foodplants are hawthorn (*Crataegus*), blackthorn (*Prunus*) and many deciduous trees, including fruit trees. The blackish-brown pupa is surrounded by a double-walled oval cocoon which contains a fine yellow powder. Moths are on the wing in July and August, flying at night only.

Grass Eggar *Lasiocampa trifolii* Denis & Schiffermüller, family Lasiocampidae. The range of this moth extends through Europe from southern Fennoscandia to the Mediterranean. In the British Isles it occurs in the Channel Islands, the Scilly Isles and scattered coastal localities in England. Its habitats are coastal sand hills and heathland. The hairy caterpillar is dark grey with a series of velvety black bands around the body. The hairs along the back are reddish-brown, while those along the sides are greyish. Among the many foodplants of this species are birdsfoot-trefoil (*Lotus corniculatus*), clover (*Trifolium*), sea pink (*Armeria maritima*), sallow (*Salix*), heather (*Calluna*), bramble (*Rubus*) and various species of grass. Pupation takes place within an oval brown cocoon spun on the ground. On the wing in summer and autumn. They fly at night and are attracted to light.

Oak Eggar *Lasiocampa quercus* Linnaeus, family Lasiocampidae. This widespread moth is found throughout Europe and also occurs in North Africa and the Canary Islands, very variable with many named forms and subspecies. Found in many localities throughout the British Isles and northern specimens are assigned to ssp. *callunae* Palmer, the Northern Eggar. Habitats range from woodland to open heath and moorland. The caterpillar is dark brown with velvety black rings between the segments and a broken white stripe along each side. The body hairs are usually pale brown. Foodplants of this species include bramble (*Rubus*), blackthorn (*Prunus*), hawthorn (*Crataegus*) and heather (*Calluna*). Pupation takes place within a tough egg-shaped cocoon spun in a fragile web of silk among foliage near the ground. The biology of this species varies greatly. Moths may be on the wing in any month from spring to late summer.

Lifesize

Specimens on 'set' plates are uppersides unless otherwise indicated. Where the sexes are similar in appearance, only one is figured. Abbreviations and symbols used in the captions: ♂ male   ♀ female   △ underside   aest. summer form   f. form   ssp. subspecies   var. variety   vern. spring form.

Lackey *Malacosoma neustria* caterpillar

Lackey *Malacosoma neustria* at rest

Oak Eggar *Lasiocampa quercus* caterpillar

Oak Eggar *Lasiocampa quercus* pupa

Oak Eggar *Lasiocampa quercus*

Macrothylacia rubi

Dendrolimus pini

Philudoria potatoria

Gastropacha quercifolia

Lifesize

Fox Moth *Macrothylacia rubi* Linnaeus, family Lasiocampidae. The distribution of this species extends throughout Europe eastwards to central Asia. In the British Isles it is widespread and sometimes quite common. Habitats range from woodland margins and hedgerows to open heathland. The caterpillar is black with dense brown hairs and with shorter reddish-brown hairs down the back. These hairs are highly irritant. Foodplants of this species are heather (*Calluna*), bramble (*Rubus*), bog myrtle (*Myrica gale*) and bilberry (*Vaccinium*). The pupa is formed within a tubular silken cocoon spun amongst vegetation near the ground. Moths are on the wing in spring and early summer. The males fly actively by day and also at night, while females fly only at night.

Pine-tree Lappet *Dendrolimus pini* Linnaeus, family Lasiocampidae. This moth occurs in many parts of Europe, ranging from Scandinavia south to the Mediterranean and its distribution extends into North Africa. This species is quite variable, particularly in the southern part of its range and there are many named subspecies. It is not a resident in the British Isles although the occasional specimen has been recorded. The habitats of this moth are conifer forests and plantations and in more southern regions it is regarded as a pest. In the Alps it occurs up to an altitude of 1500 metres. The caterpillar is greyish-brown with reddish-brown hairs and two bluish patches on the back behind the head. It feeds on the needles of pine (*Pinus*), particularly Scots pine (*P. sylvestris*), and spruce (*Abies*). Moths are on the wing in summer; females do not seem to be very active and are seldom found.

Drinker *Philudoria potatoria* Linnaeus, family Lasiocampidae. This beautiful moth is found throughout Europe from Lapland to central Spain, and eastwards across Siberia to Japan; widespread and often quite common in Britain. Favoured habitats are damp fields, fens and moorland up to 1500 metres. The hairy caterpillar is bluish-grey with lines of yellowish dots along the back and patches of white and yellow hairs along the sides. There is a conspicuous tuft of hairs behind the head and another towards the tail. It feeds on various coarse grasses such as cock's foot (*Dactylis*) and couch (*Agropyron*). The caterpillar appears to have a high moisture requirement and is often seen drinking from drops of water on the foliage. From this habit it became known in the seventeenth century as the Drinker Caterpillar. Caterpillars overwinter, pupating the next spring in a boat-shaped cocoon attached to a grass stem. Moths are on the wing from June to August.

Lappet *Gastropacha quercifolia* Linnaeus, family Lasiocampidae. This widespread species is found from southern Fennoscandia to the Iberian Peninsula and its range extends eastwards to China and Japan. In the British Isles it is restricted to England, Wales and the Channel Islands but is locally quite common. It is found in woodlands, hedgerows and orchards. The caterpillar is brownish-grey with fleshy 'lappets' along the sides covered with long brown hairs. It feeds on the foliage of blackthorn (*Prunus*), hawthorn (*Crataegus*), sallow (*Salix*), apple (*Malus*) and related trees and is sometimes an orchard pest in southern Europe. Some caterpillars overwinter before completing their growth in the following spring. Pupation takes place in a greyish silken cocoon spun amongst twigs. In the north there is only one generation a year but further south there may be two broods and moths may be seen from May until August according to locality. When at rest the moth folds its wings in such a way that it resembles a bunch of dead leaves.

Drinker *Philudoria potatoria* caterpillar

Fox Moth *Macrothylacia rubi* caterpillar

Drinker *Philudoria potatoria* at rest

Lappet *Gastropacha quercifolia* at rest

♂

Saturnia pavonia

♀

Saturnia pavonia

Saturnia pyri

Emperor Moth *Saturnia pavonia* caterpillar

Emperor Moth *Saturnia pavonia* Linnaeus,
family Saturniidae. The range of this common
and widespread species extends from western
Europe to eastern Siberia. In the British Isles it is
widely distributed and often common. The
preferred habitats are generally heaths and
moorland up to 2000 metres although this species
is also found on waste ground and on the borders
of woodland. The distinctive caterpillar is green
with black spots or bands. It has a series of warts
along the back and sides which may be yellow,
pink or purplish in colour. It feeds on a wide
range of plants including bramble (*Rubus*),
heather (*Erica*), loosestrife (*Lythrum*) and sallow
(*Salix*). When full grown the caterpillar
constructs a tough silken cocoon amongst the
foodplant in which it pupates. Moths are on the
wing from March to July, according to locality.
The females fly only at night, but the males also
fly during the day.

Great Peacock *Saturnia pyri* Denis &
Schiffermüller, family Saturniidae. This is the
largest moth to be found in Europe. Its
distribution extends through the Iberian
Peninsula, south-western France, southern
Switzerland, Italy and the Mediterranean islands
to North Africa. It does not occur in the British
Isles. The usual habitats are orchards and open
countryside up to altitudes of 2000 metres. The
striking caterpillar is bright yellowish-green with
a series of raised blue warts along the back and
sides, each bearing a tuft of hairs. It feeds on the
foliage of various fruit trees and other deciduous
trees and is sometimes a minor orchard pest.
There is one brood a year, although caterpillars
have been known to take up to three years to
complete their development. Moths fly at night,
usually from March to June, but occasionally
also in late summer. This species is also known as
the Giant Emperor or Viennese Emperor.

⁴/₅ lifesize

Emperor Moth *Saturnia pavonia*

Emperor Moth *Saturnia pavonia* eggs

Emperor Moth *Saturnia pavonia* caterpillars hatching

113

♂

Aglia tau

♀

♂

Endromis versicolora

♀

Tau Emperor *Aglia tau* Linnaeus, family Saturniidae. The range of this moth extends from southern Fennoscandia to western France and the northern part of the Iberian Peninsula and also eastwards across temperate Asia to Japan. This species does not occur in the British Isles. It is a forest insect found particularly in beech woods and is found up to altitudes of 1600 metres. The green caterpillar has a series of oblique whitish lines along the sides and, in its early stages, possesses a number of red-branched spines along the back. It feeds on the foliage of beech (*Fagus*), birch (*Betula*), oak (*Quercus*) and a number of other deciduous trees. Pupation takes place in a silken cocoon amongst dry leaves on the ground. Moths are on the wing from March to June with males usually flying during the day and females by night. This moth rests with its wings over its back, like a butterfly, in which position it strongly resembles a dead leaf.

Spanish Moon Moth *Graellsia isabellae* Graëlls, family Saturniidae. Sadly this beautiful moth is scarce and local, occurring only in the mountains of central Spain and in parts of the French Alps. It has been extensively studied and collected and there are a number of named subspecies. It is an insect of pine forests and occurs up to 1800 metres. The caterpillar is green, banded with brown and white and feeds on the needles of various *Pinus* species. There is one brood a year and this overwinters in the pupa stage. Moths are on the wing from March to July, according to locality, and fly both during the day and at night. This is the only European Saturniid moth to possess tails on the hindwings and its unusual form and handsome colouring have made it the prey of many collectors. It is now, apparently, protected by law in some parts of France.

Kentish Glory *Endromis versicolora* Linnaeus, family Endromidae. This widespread moth occurs throughout western Europe, its range extending eastwards to Siberia. Unfortunately the range of this species has contracted in the British Isles and although it once occurred in Kent and other parts of southern and central England, it now appears to be restricted to northern Scotland. Habitats range from open forests to hilltops and moorland up to 2000 metres where birches (*Betula*) grow. The caterpillar is bright green with yellowish-white, oblique stripes along each side and a raised hump at the tail end. It feeds on the foliage of birch, alder (*Alnus*), lime (*Tilia*), hazel (*Corylus*), elm (*Ulmus*) and some other deciduous trees. According to climatic and other local conditions, caterpillars may take from one to four years to complete their development. Moths are on the wing from March to May, according to altitude. Males fly by day but females do not become active until the night.

Lifesize

Kentish Glory caterpillar

Tau Emperor caterpillar

Tau Emperor young caterpillar

♂

Graellsia isabellae

♀

Lifesize

Falcaria lacertinaria

♂   ♀

Drepana binaria

♂   ♀

Drepana cultraria

♂   ♀

Drepana falcataria

Cilix glaucata

Thyatira batis

Habrosyne pyritoides

Tethea ocularis

Lifesize

Peach Blossom *Thyatira batis* caterpillar

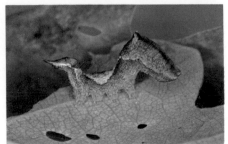

Oak Hook-tip *Drepana binaria* caterpillar

Scalloped Hook-tip *Falcaria lacertinaria* Linnaeus, family Drepanidae. This moth is common in Europe except for the extreme south and its range extends eastwards into central Asia. In the British Isles it is widespread but is less common in Scotland and northern England. Habitats are birch woods, heaths and commons. The caterpillar is pale brown, marked with darker brown and has two humps on the back behind the head and a further hump towards the tail. It feeds on the foliage of birch (*Betula*) and alder (*Alnus*). The full grown caterpillar spins an open silken cocoon amongst the foliage within which it pupates. There are two generations a year and caterpillars of the second generation overwinter. Moths are on the wing in May and June and again in late summer. They fly at night and rest on the foliage and twigs of trees by day when they resemble dead leaves.

Oak Hook-tip *Drepana binaria* Hufnagel, family Drepanidae. This is a widespread species occurring in many parts of central and southern Europe and also in North Africa and western Asia. In the British Isles it is widely distributed in England and Wales and also occurs in the Channel Islands. It occurs in woodlands where the foodplant grows. The caterpillar is pale brown with yellowish diamond-shaped markings along the back. There is a double-pointed hump on the back behind the head. It feeds on the foliage of oak (*Quercus*) and when full grown pupates in a silken cocoon spun between two leaves. There are two broods a year and moths are on the wing in spring and again in summer. They will fly by day in warm sunshine but are inactive on dull days.

Barred Hook-tip *Drepana cultraria* Fabricius, family Drepanidae. This is a common moth throughout central Europe, its range extending to Asia Minor. In the British Isles it is confined to the southern half of England and parts of Wales. Its favoured habitats are beech woods, preferably on chalky soil. The caterpillar is similar to that of the Oak Hook-tip but the markings are paler. It feeds on the foliage of beech (*Fagus*). When full grown, the caterpillar spins a silken cocoon between two leaves and pupates inside. There are two broods a year and moths are on the wing in spring and again in summer. The males fly freely in sunlight but females are not active by day unless disturbed. This species can be distinguished from the Oak Hook-tip by the presence of two dark bands on each forewing.

Pebble Hook-tip *Drepana falcataria* Linnaeus, family Drepanidae. This moth is common in most parts of Europe except for high mountain regions and its range extends into western and central Asia. In the British Isles it is widespread and there is a distinct race in Scotland, ssp. *scotica* Bytinski-Salz, which has a whitish ground colour to the wings. Habitats are woodlands, marshes and heathland where the foodplant grows. The caterpillar is green with a brown back and raised humps on the segments immediately behind the head. It feeds on the foliage of birch (*Betula*), preferring shrubby plants and will also eat the leaves of alder (*Alnus*). When full grown it pupates between two leaves spun together with silk. There are two broods a year and moths may be found in spring and again in summer, those of the second brood being generally smaller with lighter markings.

Chinese Character *Cilix glaucata* Scopoli, family Drepanidae. This is a common species in many parts of central and southern Europe and its range extends eastwards to central Asia. In the British Isles it is common in many parts of England and Wales and occurs locally in Ireland and southern Scotland. The usual habitats are

Peach Blossom *Thyatira batis*

Oak Hook-tip *Drepana binaria*

Pebble Hook-tip *Drepana falcataria*

Scalloped Hook-tip *Falcaria lacertinaria*

hedgerows and woodland margins. The caterpillar is reddish-brown with a dark line along the back and raised humps on the segments behind the head. It has a distinctively pointed tail. Foodplants are hawthorn (*Crataegus*), blackthorn (*Prunus*), apple (*Malus*) and pear (*Pyrus*). The pupa is formed in a silken cocoon spun amongst the foliage or under loose bark. There are two generations a year and moths may be found in spring and again in summer. When at rest with their wings folded over their backs, they strongly resemble bird droppings. The common name derives from the small white markings on the forewing which are said to resemble Chinese script.

Peach Blossom *Thyatira batis* Linnaeus, family Thyatiridae. This widespread and beautiful species is common in many parts of northern and central Europe and also occurs in temperate regions of Asia. It is common in many southern parts of the British Isles but is more local in Scotland and Northern Ireland. This is generally a woodland species but is also found in parks and large gardens. The caterpillar is brown with

whitish markings and has a series of raised humps along the back. It feeds on the foliage of bramble and raspberry (*Rubus*). When full grown it pupates in a silken cocoon spun among leaves. There is usually one brood a year in Britain with moths on the wing in June and July but sometimes a partial second generation appears in autumn.

Buff Arches *Habrosyne pyritoides* Hufnagel, family Thyatiridae. This moth is locally common in northern and central Europe and also occurs in southern France and northern Italy. In the British Isles it is quite common in southern regions but is scarcer further north and is not found in Scotland. It is a woodland species found in forests and parkland where the foodplant occurs in the undergrowth. The caterpillar is reddish-brown with a dark line down the back and a single, black-ringed whitish spot on each side. It feeds mainly on bramble (*Rubus*) and is also said to eat the foliage of hawthorn (*Crataegus*) and hazel (*Corylus*). It pupates in an earthen cocoon below ground or under moss. There is usually one brood a year with moths

flying in June and July but occasionally a partial second generation of moths may be found in the autumn.

Figure of Eighty *Tethea ocularis* Linnaeus, family Thyatiridae. This is a common and widespread insect throughout Europe and its range extends eastwards into central Asia. In the British Isles it is more local in occurrence and is found only in the Channel Islands, England and the border regions of Wales. The preferred habitats of this species are woods and parkland. The caterpillar is yellowish-white with an indistinct grey band down the back and a yellowish-brown head marked with black. It feeds on the foliage of aspen and poplar (*Populus*), hiding by day in a curled up leaf and coming out at night. When full grown it pupates in a silken cocoon spun amongst the leaves at the foot of the tree. There is one brood a year and moths are on the wing in May and June. The common name of this species refers to the whitish marks on the forewing.

♂   ♀

Alsophila aescularia

♂   ♀

Pseudoterpna pruinata

Geometra papilionaria

Hemithea aestivaria   *Hemistola chrysoprasaria*

Jodis lactearia   *Timandra griseata*

Lifesize

Grass Emerald *Pseudoterpna pruinata* caterpillar

Grass Emerald *Pseudoterpna pruinata* Hufnagel, family Geometridae. This is a common moth in central and southern Europe and its range extends into western Asia. In the British Isles it is widespread and seems to occur almost everywhere except for northern Scotland. Its habitats are moors, heaths and common land where the foodplants grow. The caterpillar is green with a dark line down the back and a broad white line tinged with pink along each side. It feeds on the foliage of broom (*Cytisus*), petty whin (*Genista anglica*) and furze (*Ulex*) and when at rest holds itself stiffly at an angle to the stem so that it appears to be part of the foodplant. The attractive green pupa is formed within a frail silken cocoon spun amongst dead leaves and other plant debris on the ground. This species is single-brooded and moths may be found in June and July.

Large Emerald *Geometra papilionaria* Linnaeus, family Geometridae. This handsome species is widely distributed in Europe, occurring as far north as the Arctic Circle, and is also found in temperate Asia. In the British Isles it is widespread in all parts except for the extreme north of Scotland. Its habitats are woodlands, hedgerows, moorland and fens. The caterpillar is brown at first and remains so throughout the winter when it hibernates on a twig. When the buds begin to open in spring it becomes green with brown warts along its back and so continues to blend with its surroundings. It feeds on the foliage of birch (*Betula*), hazel (*Corylus*) and beech (*Fagus*). Pupation takes place within a silken cocoon spun amongst dead leaves on the ground. There is one brood a year and moths are on the wing from June until August, according to locality. The beautiful green colour of the wings fades rapidly once the moth is dead.

Common Emerald *Hemithea aestivaria* Hübner, family Geometridae. As its name suggests, this is a common species in many parts of central and southern Europe, its distribution extending eastwards through temperate Asia. In the British Isles it occurs commonly in the south but becomes scarcer further north and does not seem to be found in Scotland. Its favoured habitats are forest borders, hedgerows and wooded margins of fields. The caterpillar is green marked with reddish-brown and with blackish V-shaped markings along the back. Immediately behind the head is a prominent notched projection. It feeds on mugwort (*Artemisia*) and other low-growing plants when newly hatched but after hibernation it eats the foliage of oak (*Quercus*), hawthorn (*Crataegus*) and other deciduous trees and shrubs. Pupation takes place in a frail silken cocoon spun amongst the leaves of the foodplant. There is one brood a year and moths are on the wing from June until August, according to locality.

March Moth *Alsophila aescularia* Denis & Schiffermüller, family Geometridae. This moth is common in western, central and eastern Europe. In the British Isles it is widespread and often common although it does not seem to occur in northern Scotland. Habitats are hedgerows, woodlands, orchards and gardens. The caterpillar is yellowish-green with whitish longitudinal lines and may be distinguished from other looper caterpillars by the presence of an extra, but very small, pair of prolegs. It feeds on a wide range of deciduous trees and shrubs and is often a pest of fruit trees and ornamentals. When full grown it pupates below ground. There is only one brood a year and moths emerge in the early spring, thus giving rise to the common name. While the females are wingless and spider-like, the males are fully winged and fly actively at night. When at rest they roll their wings over each other and cling tightly to the branch or tree trunk so that they merge into the background.

March Moth *Alsophila aescularia* at rest

Small Emerald *Hemistola chrysoprasaria* Esper, family Geometridae. The range of this delicately coloured moth extends throughout most of Europe eastwards to central Asia. In the British Isles it is mainly confined to southern and eastern counties of England although it does occur rarely in Ireland. Habitats are hedgerows, mostly in chalky areas, where the foodplant abounds. The caterpillar is yellowish-green with a reddish-brown head and there are lines of white dots down the back and along the sides. The first and last body segments have raised pointed projections on the back. The foodplant of this species is traveller's joy (*Clematis*). It hibernates through the winter and completes its growth in the following spring. When full grown it spins leaves together with silk and turns into a green pupa within the shelter thus formed. Moths are on the wing from May until August according to the locality and fly in the evening.

Little Emerald *Jodis lactearia* Linnaeus, family Geometridae. This species is common in central and southern Europe and its range continues eastwards into temperate Asia. In the British Isles it is quite widespread and common although it does not occur in northern parts of Scotland. Habitats are hedgerows and woodland. The caterpillar is long and thin and is green in colour with reddish spots down the back. There are two raised points on the back of the segment immediately behind the head and also on the last segment. The caterpillar feeds on the foliage of oak (*Quercus*), hawthorn (*Crataegus*), birch (*Betula*) and other deciduous trees and shrubs. When full grown it spins a loose silken cocoon amongst the leaves and pupates inside. There is one brood a year and moths may be found from May until July, according to locality and climatic conditions. The delicate green colour of the wings soon fades after the moth dies.

Blood Vein *Timandra griseata* Petersen, family Geometridae. This distinctive little moth is widespread and common in Europe from southern Scandinavia to the Mediterranean and it also occurs in North Africa. In the British Isles it is most common in southern England but is also found in northern England, Wales, parts of Scotland and very locally in Ireland. Habitats are damp places such as roadside ditches, field margins and hedgerows. The caterpillar is greyish-brown with white markings down the back. When at rest it can expand the segments behind the head so that it takes on a curious shape rather like a miniature cobra. Foodplants are dock, sorrel (*Rumex*), orache (*Atriplex*) and other low growing plants. Pupation takes place in a silken cocoon spun amongst the leaves. There are one or two generations a year and moths may be found between May and September, according to locality. In Britain they are most frequently seen in June.

Small Emerald *Hemistola chrysoprasaria*

Common Emerald *Hemithea aestivaria*

Blood Vein *Timandra griseata*

119

var.

Xanthorhoe fluctuata

var.

Camptogramma bilineata

Cidaria fulvata

♂   ♀

Thera obeliscata

♂   ♀

Operophtera brumata

Lifesize

Garden Carpet *Xanthorhoe fluctuata* Linnaeus, family Geometridae. This is one of the commonest moths in Europe and is found as far north as Lapland. It also occurs in North Africa and ranges eastwards to Siberia. In the British Isles it is widespread and often abundant. This is a common garden species but also occurs in hedgerows and other places where the foodplants grow. The caterpillar varies in colour from grey to green with paler diamond-shaped markings along the back. It feeds on cabbage (*Brassica*), wallflower (*Cheiranthus*), hedge mustard (*Sisymbrium*) and related plants, as well as on gooseberry and currant bushes (*Ribes*). The full

grown caterpillar burrows below ground before pupating in a silken cocoon. There are two or more generations a year and moths may be seen from April until September. The wing pattern is very variable with greater or lesser development of the forewing bands and a ground colour ranging from grey to pure white.

Yellow Shell *Camptogramma bilineata* Linnaeus, family Geometridae. This very common moth occurs throughout Europe, its range extending to North Africa and central Asia. In the British Isles it is widespread and abundant and is represented by four named subspecies. It is

found in hedgerows, gardens and any place where suitable foodplants are available. The caterpillar varies in colour from brown to green, with a dark line down the back and one along each side below which the body colour is much paler. When at rest it curls itself into a characteristic question-mark shape. It feeds on the foliage of chickweed (*Stellaria*), dock (*Rumex*), grasses and other low-growing plants. When full grown it burrows below ground and pupates in a cocoon of earth and silk. Moths are on the wing from June until August, according to locality. The ground colour and extent of black banding of the wings is very variable and many forms have been named.

Barred Yellow *Cidaria fulvata* Forster, family Geometridae. This species is widespread and often common in Europe, its range extending eastwards to central Asia. In the British Isles it is common in England and Wales but has a scattered distribution in Scotland and Ireland. It is usually found in hedgerows and open scrub where the foodplants grow. The caterpillar is green with yellowish divisions between the segments, three greyish lines down the back and a yellowish-white line along each side. It feeds on the foliage of dog rose (*Rosa canina*) and burnet rose (*R. pimpinellifolia*) and in captivity will eat the leaves of various garden rose varieties. When full grown it spins a flimsy silken cocoon amongst the foliage and pupates inside. There is only one brood a year and moths may be found from June until August, according to locality. They hide under the leaves by day but may be seen in flight quite early in the evening.

Grey Pine Carpet *Thera obeliscata* Hübner, family Geometridae. This species is found in many parts of northern, central and eastern Europe. In the British Isles it is widespread and occurs in most localities where the foodplants grow. This is an insect of coniferous forests. The caterpillar is bright green with three white lines down its back and a yellow line along each side. It may be distinguished from other closely related species by the fact that it has pink thoracic legs. Scot's pine (*Pinus sylvestris*) is the favourite food, but caterpillars will also feed on the needles of silver fir (*Abies alba*) and various species of spruce (*Picea*). Caterpillars overwinter and complete their development in the following spring. There is only one brood a year and moths are on the wing in May and June.

Winter Moth *Operophtera brumata* Linnaeus, family Geometridae. This is a very common moth in central and northern Europe but is scarcer in southern Europe. Its range extends eastwards to Siberia. In the British Isles it occurs almost everywhere and is usually common. Habitats are woodlands, hedgerows, orchards and gardens. The caterpillar is green with pale divisions between the segments, a dark line along the back with a white line on each side and a yellowish stripe along the line of the spiracles. This species will feed on the foliage of almost any deciduous tree or shrub and is a notorious pest of apple (*Malus*) and other fruit trees. The full grown caterpillar drops to the ground and pupates in the soil at the foot of the tree. Moths emerge in late autumn and winter and males may be on the wing at any time between October and February. The spider-like, wingless females are flightless and climb up the tree trunk to mate.

Garden Carpet *Xanthorhoe fluctuata* at rest

Barred Yellow *Cidaria fulvata* at rest

Grey Pine Carpet *Thera obeliscata* at rest

Winter Moth *Operophtera brumata* at rest

Yellow Shell *Camptogramma bilineata* at rest

Eupithecia venosata

Eupithecia centaureata

Eupithecia vulgata

Odezia atrata

♂

♀

var.

var.

Abraxas grossulariata

var.

Abraxas sylvata

Lifesize

Netted Pug *Eupithecia venosata*

Common Pug *Eupithecia vulgata* Haworth,
family Geometridae. This widespread species is
common in Europe, occurring in northern
Scandinavia and ranging eastwards to central
Asia. In the British Isles it is common almost
everywhere and is represented by three
subspecies. Habitats are hedgerows, waste land,
gardens and any place where suitable foodplants
grow. The caterpillar is pale reddish-brown with
a series of darker lozenge-shaped marks along the
back and a pale yellowish line along each side. It
feeds on the leaves of hawthorn (*Crataegus*),
sallow (*Salix*), bramble (*Rubus*) and many other
plants and when full grown pupates on the
ground in an earthen cocoon. There are two
broods a year with moths on the wing in May and
June and again in August. They vary greatly in
colour from pale greyish-brown to almost black
and are often difficult to distinguish from closely
related species.

Lime-speck Pug *Eupithecia centaureata* Denis &
Schiffermüller, family Geometridae. This
common moth is found in many parts of Europe
and also occurs in North Africa, Asia Minor and
central Asia. In the British Isles it is widespread
and may be found almost everywhere except for
northern Scotland. Habitats are waste ground
and gardens where the foodplants grow. The
caterpillar is green or yellowish in colour and
sometimes has a series of reddish markings down
the back. It feeds on the flowers of ragwort
(*Senecio*), knapweed (*Centaurea*), yarrow
(*Achillea*), golden-rod (*Solidago*) and various
other plants. When full grown it leaves the
foodplant and pupates in an earthen cocoon on
the ground. There may be one or two broods
each year with moths on the wing from May to
August and again from September to October.
When at rest with its wings spread out it can
often be mistaken for a bird-dropping.

Chimney Sweeper *Odezia atrata* Linnaeus,
family Geometridae. This distinctive little moth
is widespread in central and northern Europe,
occurring as far north as Lapland. In the British
Isles it is widely distributed, but very local and
does not occur in northern Scotland. Its favoured
habitats are damp places such as woodland
borders, wet fields and hedgerow ditches. The
caterpillar is green with three dark lines along the
back, the central line becoming reddish at the
tail. A pale line runs along each side below the
line of reddish spiracles. It feeds on the flowers of
the earthnut (*Conopodium majus*), rough chervil
(*Chaerophyllum temulentum*) and other related
umbellifers. Pupation takes place below ground.

Netted Pug *Eupithecia venosata* Fabricius,
family Geometridae. This attractive little moth,
which at one time was known as the Pretty
Widow Moth, is widespread throughout Europe
and also occurs in North Africa and parts of
temperate Asia. In the British Isles it may be
found in many areas where the foodplants grow.
The caterpillar is greyish-brown above and pale
green or yellow below and has three dark lines
down the back. The head is blackish-brown. The
foodplants of this species are various types of
campion (*Silene* and *Lychnis*). Feeding takes
place within the seed capsules but, when full
grown, the caterpillar leaves the foodplant and
pupates below ground. There is only one brood a
year and moths may be found in May and June.
This species shows considerable geographic
variation, particularly in the ground colour of the
forewings which may be almost white, smoky
grey or yellowish-brown.

Chimney Sweeper *Odezia atrata*

Common Pug *Eupithecia vulgata*

Magpie *Abraxas grossulariata* caterpillar

Magpie *Abraxas grossulariata* eggs

There is one generation a year and moths can be found in June and July. They are active by day and may be seen in some numbers flying about flowers in bright sunshine.

Magpie *Abraxas grossulariata* Linnaeus, family Geometridae. This common and beautiful species is found throughout Europe as far north as southern Scandinavia and its range extends eastwards across Siberia. In the British Isles it is widespread and sometimes abundant. Its favoured habitats are hedgerows, waste ground, gardens and allotments. The caterpillar is very distinctive and similar to the moth in coloration. It is yellowish-white with an intricate pattern of black over the body and a reddish line along each side. Sometimes a form occurs in which the caterpillar is almost completely black. Foodplants are blackthorn (*Prunus*), hawthorn (*Crataegus*), *Euonymus* and various other plants but this species is chiefly known for its attacks on gooseberry and currant bushes (*Ribes*) and is sometimes a serious pest. Pupation takes place in an open cocoon spun amongst the leaves. Moths are on the wing in

summer and will fly by day. This is an extremely variable species and there are a great many named varieties.

Clouded Magpie *Abraxas sylvata* Scopoli, family Geometridae. The range of this attractive relative of the common Magpie moth extends through central Europe eastwards to central Asia. In the British Isles it is most commonly found in western England and Wales although it also occurs in other parts of England and southern Scotland and a few localities in Ireland. The habitats of this species are woodlands where the foodplants grow. The caterpillar is yellowish-white marked with black lines and with a yellow stripe along each side. Its head is shining black. Foodplants are wych elm (*Ulmus glabra*), common elm (*Ulmus procera*) and beech (*Fagus*). There is one brood a year and moths are on the wing from May to July according to locality. Moths may be seen by day at rest on the undergrowth and are attracted to the flowers of dog's mercury (*Mercurialis perennis*). This is a very variable species but it does not have as many named varieties as the common Magpie.

Clouded Magpie *Abraxas sylvata*

Magpie *Abraxas grossulariata*

Plagodis dolabraria

Opisthograptis luteolata

Apeira syringaria

♂   ♀

Selenia dentaria

♂   ♀

Selenia tetralunaria

♂   ♀

♂   ♀ var.

Odontopera bidentata

Lifesize

Lilac Beauty *Apeira syringaria* caterpillar

Brimstone *Opisthograptis luteolata* caterpillar

Scorched Wing *Plagodis dolabraria* Linnaeus, family Geometridae. This distinctive little moth is widespread in Europe and its range extends eastwards across temperate Asia. Widespread in England and also occurs in Wales, Ireland and locally in Scotland. It is found in woodland rides and clearings. The caterpillar is brown with darker markings along the back and has a large wart towards the tail which resembles the joint of a twig. It feeds on the foliage of birch (*Betula*), oak (*Quercus*), sallow (*Salix*) and beech (*Fagus*) and, when full grown, pupates under moss on the tree trunk. Moths are on the wing from April until August, according to locality, but in Britain they are most frequently found in May and June. They fly at night but by day they rest on tree trunks.

Brimstone Moth *Opisthograptis luteolata* Linnaeus, family Geometridae. An aptly named species common throughout Europe. In the British Isles it is widespread and frequently common. Habitats are hedgerows, light woodland and open country where the foodplants occur. The caterpillar has both brown and green forms but both have a distinctive double-pointed hump on the back at the middle of the body. It feeds on the foliage of hawthorn (*Crataegus*), blackthorn (*Prunus*) and various other deciduous shrubs and trees. It is very well camouflaged and resembles a small twig. Pupation take place in a silken cocoon on or near the ground. There are two broods a year but these overlap so that moths may be found in any month between April and October. They fly by day and are often mistaken for small butterflies.

Lilac Beauty *Apeira syringaria* Linnaeus, family Geometridae. This beautiful species, sometimes also known as the Lilac Thorn, is widespread, ranging from Scandinavia to southern Europe and eastwards to Siberia. In Britain, most frequently found in southern England and Wales but also occurs in northern England and parts of Ireland. Habitats: woodland clearings, hedgerows and gardens. The caterpillar is yellowish or reddish-brown in colour with darker markings but is most easily recognised by the

124

Early Thorn *Selenia dentaria*

Purple Thorn *Selenia tetralunaria*

Brimstone *Opisthograptis luteolata*

Scorched Wing *Plagodis dolabraria* at rest

Lilac Beauty *Apeira syringaria*

Scalloped Hazel *Odontopera bidentata*

remarkable pointed, tentacle-like projections on the back in the middle of the body. Although these appear to be so conspicuous, they break up the shape of the caterpillar and make it difficult to find on the foodplant. It feeds on the foliage of honeysuckle (*Lonicera*), lilac (*Syringa*) and privet (*Ligustrum*) and when full grown pupates in a cocoon on the underside of a leaf. There are one or two broods a year with moths on the wing in early summer and sometimes again in autumn.

Early Thorn *Selenia dentaria* Fabricius, family Geometridae. This moth is common throughout Europe and ranges eastwards across temperate Asia. In the British Isles it is widespread and especially common in the south. Its habitats are woodlands and hedgerows. The caterpillar is reddish-brown or sometimes darker purplish and has two pairs of raised points on the back towards the tail. When at rest it strongly resembles a small twig of a thorn bush. It feeds on the foliage of hawthorn (*Crataegus*), blackthorn (*Prunus*), birch (*Betula*) and many other deciduous trees and bushes. When full grown it descends to the ground to pupate. There are usually two broods a year in the south,

including England, while in northern localities there is only one. Moths are on the wing from April to May and again in July and August. When at rest with their wings folded together over their backs they often look like dead leaves.

Purple Thorn *Selenia tetralunaria* Hufnagel, family Geometridae. This species is widespread in Europe and its range extends eastwards to Siberia. In the British Isles it occurs in many parts of England, particularly in the south, and also in Wales and Scotland, but is seldom common. It is found in woodlands where the foodplants grow. The caterpillar is reddish-brown with darker markings and has a number of wart-like protuberances on the body which resembles a piece of twig. It feeds on the foliage of birch (*Betula*), alder (*Alnus*), oak (*Quercus*), sallow (*Salix*) and many other deciduous trees. When full grown it spins a cocoon amongst the leaves and pupates inside. There are usually two generations a year with moths on the wing in April and May and again in July and August. Moths of the spring generation are often larger and brighter in coloration. Occasionally moths of a third brood appear in late autumn.

Scalloped Hazel *Odontopera bidentata* Clerck, family Geometridae. This moth occurs throughout much of Europe, where it is common, and its range extends into temperate Asia. In the British Isles it occurs almost everywhere except for the Orkneys and Shetlands. Its habitats are woodlands and hedgerows. The caterpillar varies in colour from green to brown and there is a mottled form which resembles lichen. It feeds on the foliage of oak (*Quercus*), birch (*Betula*), sallow (*Salix*) and almost every other deciduous tree. When full grown it pupates under moss on the trunk of the tree. There is only one brood a year and moths are usually on the wing from May to June although they may occasionally occur in April.

Ourapteryx sambucaria

Colotois pennaria
♂   ♀

Apocheima pilosaria
♂   ♀

Lycia hirtaria
♂   ♀

Lifesize

Pale Brindled Beauty *Apocheima pilosaria* at rest

on the foliage of oak (*Quercus*), birch (*Betula*), sallow (*Salix*), hawthorn (*Crataegus*) and many other deciduous trees and shrubs. When full grown it burrows below ground to pupate within a cocoon of silk and soil particles. This species is single-brooded and moths are to be found from September to November, according to locality. It is called the feathered thorn because of the large feathered antennae of the male.

Pale Brindled Beauty *Apocheima pilosaria* Denis & Schiffermüller, family Geometridae. This is a common and widespread moth in central and eastern Europe. In the British Isles it is found almost everywhere and is often common although it appears to be rather scarce in Ireland. Its habitats are hedgerows and woodlands where the foodplants grow. The caterpillar is greyish-brown marked with reddish-brown and has a series of reddish points along the back. Like many other geometrid caterpillars, this species is a very effective twig-mimic, the reddish markings matching the colour of the leaf buds. It feeds on the foliage of most deciduous trees and shrubs and when full grown burrows below ground to pupate at the base of the foodplant. Moths are on the wing from November to April according to locality and the occasional specimen appears in June. In Britain they are most usually encountered from January to March. They fly at night but the male appears to be much more active than the female.

Brindled Beauty *Lycia hirtaria* Clerck, family Geometridae. This common and widespread moth occurs in most parts of Europe and its range extends to Asia Minor. In the British Isles it is widely distributed but is most common in southern England. Its habitats are woodlands, orchards, parks and gardens. The caterpillar is reddish-brown with an intricate pattern of red lines and yellow spots or pale grey with the markings entirely yellow. It feeds on the foliage of almost any deciduous tree but is particularly common on lime (*Tilia*), willow (*Salix*) and fruit trees such as apple (*Malus*) and pear (*Pyrus*). Pupation takes place below ground in an earthen cocoon. There is one brood a year and moths may be found in March and April. While the males fly at night, the females are wingless and on emerging from the pupa on the ground have to climb up a tree trunk to find a mate.

Swallow-tailed Moth *Ourapteryx sambucaria* Linnaeus, family Geometridae. This large and distinctive geometrid moth is common throughout much of Europe excepting the extreme north and its range extends eastwards into temperate Asia. In the British Isles it is common almost everywhere except in Scotland where it is confined to the south. Its habitats are woodland margins, parks and gardens. The caterpillar is long and thin and is brown with fine dark lines along the length of the body. Foodplants are ivy (*Hedera*), privet (*Ligustrum*), hawthorn (*Crataegus*) and many other deciduous shrubs and trees. The caterpillar overwinters among twigs of the foodplant and is extremely difficult to detect. When full grown in early

summer it pupates in a silken cocoon suspended from the underside of a twig. There is one brood a year and moths are on the wing in July and August although an occasional specimen has been seen in the autumn.

Feathered Thorn *Colotois pennaria* Hübner, family Geometridae. This moth is common and widespread in Europe and also occurs in Asia Minor. In the British Isles it occurs almost everywhere except for the extreme north of Scotland but is most common in southern localities. Its habitats are woodlands and hedgerows. The caterpillar is greyish-brown with reddish-brown markings and a pair of reddish points on the back near the tail. It feeds

Pale Brindled Beauty *Apocheima pilosaria* caterpillar

Feathered Thorn *Colotois pennaria*

Brindled Beauty *Lycia hirtaria*

f. carbonaria   Biston betularia   f. carbonaria

Erannis defoliaria

Peribatodes rhomboidaria

Lifesize

Peppered Moth *Biston betularia* at rest

Willow Beauty *Peribatodes rhomboidaria* Denis
& Schiffermüller, family Geometridae. This
delicately patterned moth is fairly common in
central and southern Europe although it is rather
local in occurrence. In the British Isles it is quite
widespread but does not occur in the extreme
north of Scotland. Its habitats are woodlands,
parks and gardens. The caterpillar is reddish-
brown with paler mottling and with a pair of
small warts on the back about one third of the
way down the body. It feeds on the foliage of a
wide range of trees and shrubs including ivy
(*Hedera*), privet (*Ligustrum*), birch (*Betula*), yew
(*Taxus*), and fir (*Abies*). Pupation takes place
within a silken cocoon attached to a twig.
Although there is only one brood a year in
northern localities, with moths on the wing in
July and August, there may be a partial second
brood in some regions producing moths in
autumn.

Mottled Umber *Erannis defoliaria* Clerck,
family Geometridae. This is a common species
and occurs in many parts of Europe. In the
British Isles it is widespread and frequently
abundant, particularly in the south. Its habitats
are woodlands, hedgerows, parks and gardens.
The caterpillar is variable, ranging in colour
from pale yellowish-brown to dark reddish-
brown with many intermediates, but may usually
be recognised by a series of bright yellow patches
along each side. It feeds on the foliage of almost
any deciduous tree or shrub but is particularly
common on oak (*Quercus*), birch (*Betula*),
hawthorn (*Crataegus*) and sometimes on fruit
trees where it may be a minor pest. The full
grown caterpillar leaves the foodplant to pupate
on the ground. This species is single-brooded
and moths appear from October to December.
The males fly at night but the females are
virtually wingless and may be found climbing up
the tree trunks at dusk.

Peppered Moth *Biston betularia* Linnaeus,
family Geometridae. This well-known moth is
found in many parts of Europe extending into
northern Fennoscandia and eastwards into
temperate Asia. In the British Isles it is
widespread and often common. Its habitats are
woodlands and parks. The caterpillar is either
moss green or greyish-brown with a strongly
notched head and a number of warts along the
body which resemble the joints of a twig. It feeds
on the foliage of virtually every deciduous tree

and shrub and is sometimes found on fruit trees
in gardens. When full grown it leaves the
foodplant to pupate below ground. There is one
brood a year and moths are on the wing from May
until August according to the locality. The black
form *carbonaria* Jordan is often common in
industrial regions where it blends well with sooty
tree trunks on which it rests, and was the subject
of Dr Kettlewell's celebrated experiments on
industrial melanism.

Mottled Umber *Erannis defoliaria* caterpillar

Willow Beauty *Peribatodes rhomboidaria*

Peppered Moth *Biston betularia* caterpillar

129

Alcis repandata

♂   ♀

Ematurga atomaria

♂   ♀

♂ var.   ♀ var.

Bupalus piniaria

♂   ♀

Theria primaria

Lifesize

Bordered White *Bupalus piniaria* caterpillar

Common Heath *Ematurga atomaria* Linnaeus, family Geometridae. This species is very common throughout Europe, its range extending eastwards to Siberia. In the British Isles it occurs on heathlands everywhere, except for the Shetlands, and is often abundant. The caterpillar is very variable, ranging in colour from greenish-brown to grey, but is often recognisable by a series of small white lines along the back. It feeds on the foliage of heather (*Calluna*), heath (*Erica*), broom (*Cytisus*), clover (*Trifolium*) and various trefoils. When full grown it burrows below ground to pupate. Moths are on the wing from May to September, according to locality, although in Britain they are most frequently encountered in May and June. It is a day-flying species and is often seen fluttering about heather and bracken in bright sunlight. The wing pattern is quite variable and a number of distinct forms have been named including a blackish variety (ab. *unicolorata* Staudinger).

Bordered White *Bupalus piniaria* Linnaeus, family Geometridae. This species is widespread in coniferous forests throughout Europe, its range extending eastwards to Siberia. In the British Isles it is common in suitable localities in England, Wales and Scotland but rather local in Ireland. The caterpillar is green wth longitudinal pale yellow stripes and is very well camouflaged on its foodplant. It eats the needles of pine (*Pinus*), spruce (*Picea*), fir (*Abies*) and many other conifers. The defoliation caused by this species is sometimes severe and foresters know the caterpillar as the Pine Looper. Pupation takes place amongst fallen needles on the ground. There is one generation a year and moths are on the wing between May and July, according to locality. This is a variable species and in Britain males from the south have a yellowish ground colour while those from the north are usually white. Conversely northern females are generally darker than those from the south.

Early Moth *Theria primaria* Haworth, family Geometridae. The distribution of this moth in Europe is rather uncertain because until recent years it has been confused with a closely related species *Theria rupicapraria* Denis & Schiffermüller, under which name most British specimens have been wrongly identified. In the British Isles the Early Moth is widespread and common except in northern Scotland. Its habitats are hedgerows and woodland margins. The caterpillar is light green or dark green, sometimes almost black, with white lines along the back and sides. It feeds on the foliage of hawthorn (*Crataegus*), blackthorn (*Prunus*) and bilberry (*Vaccinium*) and when full grown leaves the foodplant to pupate on the ground. There is one brood a year in January and February. While the male is fully winged and flies at night, the wings of the female are so reduced that it is flightless and may be found sitting on twigs after dark.

Mottled Beauty *Alcis repandata* Linnaeus, family Geometridae. Although similar to the Willow Beauty, this species is more common and widespread in Europe, its range extending into temperate Asia. In the British Isles it is widely distributed and common with a distinct race on the Scottish mainland (ssp. *muraria* Curtis) and another in the Hebrides (ssp. *sodorensium* Weir). Habitats range from woodland margins and gardens to moorland. The caterpillar is brown with a series of diamond-shaped markings down the back. The underside is very pale, lined with darker brown. It feeds on a very wide range of trees and shrubs including hawthorn (*Crataegus*), birch (*Betula*), bilberry (*Vaccinium*) and heather (*Calluna*). When full grown it leaves the foodplant to pupate on the ground. Moths are normally on the wing in June and July although a second generation has been observed in September. This species may be distinguished from the Willow Beauty by the zigzag pattern of the dark lines crossing the forewings.

Common Heath *Ematurga atomaria*

Mottled Beauty *Alcis repandata*

Early Moth *Theria primaria* at rest

Bordered White *Bupalus piniaria*

Agrius convolvuli

Acherontia atropos

Sphinx ligustri

Hyloicus pinastri

Mimas tiliae

⁴/₅ lifesize

Convolvulus Hawk-moth *Agrius convolvuli* Linnaeus, family Sphingidae. This large hawk-moth is found throughout Africa, Asia and the Pacific. It is a strong flier and moths from Africa migrate into Europe every year, sometimes reaching as far north as Scandinavia. It is a regular migrant to the British Isles although the numbers fluctuate widely. The caterpillars are extremely variable, ranging from green to brown with darker markings and oblique stripes along the sides. The horn is usually reddish with a black tip. As its common name suggests, this species feeds on *Convolvulus* and related plants. When full grown, the caterpillar burrows below ground and hollows out a chamber within which it pupates. Moths do not usually reach Britain before July or August but further south they may be found much earlier. They are attracted to flowers, particularly those of tobacco (*Nicotiana*) from which they take nectar.

Death's-head Hawk-moth *Acherontia atropos* Linnaeus, family Sphingidae. This large and distinctive moth is a native of Africa but migrates northwards into most parts of Europe each year. It is a regular migrant to the British Isles and sometimes arrives in quite large numbers. The caterpillar is very variable in colour and pattern but the usual form which occurs in Europe is yellowish-green with diagonal stripes of blue or purple along the sides. It feeds on the foliage of potato (*Solanum*) and related plants and in some southern regions is regarded as a pest. Pupation takes place in an underground chamber hollowed out by the caterpillar. The moth gets its name from the skull-like markings on its thorax and is the subject of many superstitions. It is also notorious for raiding beehives to feed on the honey and was at one time known as the 'Bee Tyger'. Moths usually reach Britain in autumn but further south they may be found earlier in the year.

Privet Hawk-moth *Sphinx ligustri* Linnaeus, family Sphingidae. This moth is common in many parts of western Europe and occurs as far north as Fennoscandia. It is not as common as it used to be in the British Isles and is mainly confined to the south. There are no recent records from Scotland or Ireland. It is found in open places, particularly in chalky areas and in parks and gardens where its foodplants are grown. The striking caterpillar is bright yellowish-green with a series of purple oblique stripes along the sides and a sharply pointed black and yellow horn. It feeds on the foliage of privet (*Ligustrum*), lilac (*Syringa*), ash (*Fraxinus*) and snowberry (*Symphoricarpos*) and when full grown burrows below ground, sometimes as deep as fourteen centimetres, before pupating. Moths are usually on the wing in summer and are attracted to flowers at night. Although this species is resident in Britain, its population is reinforced by immigrants from continental Europe.

Pine Hawk-moth *Hyloicus pinastri* Linnaeus, family Sphingidae. This widespread hawk-moth occurs throughout Europe, its distribution extending into Fennoscandia and northern Russia. In the British Isles it is restricted to the Channel Islands and southern and eastern counties of England, although its range has

Death's Head Hawk-moth *Acherontia atropos* caterpillar

Pine Hawk-moth *Hyloicus pinastri* caterpillar

Lime Hawk-moth *Mimas tiliae*

Privet Hawk-moth *Sphinx ligustri*

spread in recent years due to the increased planting of pines. It is found in pine forests and occurs up to an altitude of 500 metres in Switzerland. In some places it is regarded as a forest pest. The caterpillar is green with white stripes along the body at first but when full grown it is marked with orange-brown and black. It feeds on the needles of pine (*Pinus*) and spruce (*Picea*) and when full grown pupates below ground. The moth flies at dusk and is particularly attracted to the flowers of honeysuckle (*Lonicera*). Moths are on the wing throughout the summer.

Lime Hawk-moth *Mimas tiliae* Linnaeus, family Sphingidae. This widespread and variable species ranges throughout Europe eastwards to Japan. In the British Isles it is common in southern England but is scarce in Wales and does not occur in Scotland or Ireland. It may be found in woodlands up to 500 metres and in parks and urban areas where lime trees (*Tilia*) are planted in the streets. The caterpillar is yellowish-green with oblique yellow stripes along the sides. The horn is bluish and behind it is a roughened patch spotted with red and yellow. It feeds on the foliage of lime and also elm (*Ulmus*), alder (*Alnus*), birch (*Betula*) and oak (*Quercus*). The full grown caterpillar becomes dull pinkish-brown in colour and leaves the tree to pupate below ground. Moths are on the wing in late spring and early summer. They do not visit flowers but are attracted to light and are frequently found flying around shop windows at night.

Convolvulus Hawk-moth *Agrius convolvuli*

Smerinthus ocellata

Laothoe populi

Marumba quercus

Hemaris tityus

Hemaris fuciformis

Macroglossum stellatarum

Lifesize

Eyed Hawk-moth *Smerinthus ocellata* Linnaeus, family Sphingidae. This hawk-moth is widespread in Europe except for the extreme north. In the British Isles it is locally common in England, Wales and Ireland but absent from Scotland. Habitats are open woodland, gardens, orchards and river banks where sallows and willows (*Salix*) grow. The green caterpillar has a distinctive blue horn when full grown which distinguishes it from that of the poplar hawk-moth. Sometimes a form occurs with bright red spots along the sides. It feeds on the foliage of sallow, willow, apple (*Malus*) and poplar (*Populus*). The pupa is formed in an underground chamber in the autumn and the moth emerges in the following spring. Moths are on the wing in late spring and early summer, flying at night. The distinctive eye-spots on the hindwing are normally hidden when the moth is at rest but are suddenly revealed if the moth is attacked and are believed to startle would-be predators.

Poplar Hawk-moth *Laothoe populi* Linnaeus, family Sphingidae. Although less common in the south, this widespread moth is found in almost all parts of Europe even extending to localities within the Arctic Circle. It occurs throughout the British Isles and is the only hawk-moth to occur widely in Scotland. Suitable habitats are woodland margins, parkland and other generally damp situations where the foodplants occur. The caterpillar is either yellowish-green or bluish-green, sometimes with pale red spots along the sides, and the horn is green. It feeds on poplar, aspen (*Populus*), sallow and willow (*Salix*) and when full grown burrows a few centimetres below ground before pupating. In some areas this moth is double-brooded but in the north there is only one generation a year. Moths fly at night in late spring and summer and are attracted to light. They rest in a curious and characteristic position with the hindwings pushed forward in front of the forewings.

Oak Hawk-moth *Marumba quercus* Denis & Schiffermüller, family Sphingidae. The range of this large hawk-moth in Europe is restricted to southern regions, particularly along the Mediterranean coast and its distribution extends into Asia Minor. It does not occur in the British Isles. Its habitats are wooded, hilly areas where the foodplant grows. The caterpillar is yellowish-green with oblique yellow stripes along the sides; the horn is blue. It feeds on the undersides of leaves of oak (*Quercus*), particularly cork oak (*Q. suber*), preferring young shrubby growth to mature trees. When full grown it turns reddish-brown and leaves the foodplant to pupate in an earthen cocoon below ground. There is only one generation a year and moths are on the wing in June and July. Unlike the closely related Poplar Hawk-moth, this species rests with its wings folded in the conventional manner.

Narrow-bordered Bee Hawk-moth *Hemaris tityus* Linnaeus, family Sphingidae. This remarkable bee mimic is widespread throughout Europe occurring as far north as Lapland and ranging southwards to Asia Minor. In the British Isles it is widespread but local and not common. Habitats are woodland margins, rough pastures, marshy heaths and other damp localities. The caterpillar is whitish-green or blue-green with a yellowish line along each side of the back and a conspicuous series of purplish red patches; the roughened horn is reddish-brown. It feeds on the lower leaves of scabious (*Scabiosa*), concealed on the underside and is only apparent by the holes that it has caused. The full grown caterpillar changes colour to a reddish-brown before leaving the foodplant to pupate in a silken cocoon on the

Narrow-bordered Bee Hawk-moth *Hemaris tityus*

Poplar Hawk-moth *Laothoe populi* at rest

Broad-bordered Bee Hawk-moth

Eyed Hawk-moth *Smerinthus ocellata* displaying 'eyes'

Poplar Hawk-moth *Laothoe populi* caterpillar

ground. The freshly emerged moth has a layer of grey scales on the wings but these are shed during its first flight leaving only the brown borders and veins. It flies by day in spring and summer and may be seen hovering over flowers and probing for nectar.

Broad-bordered Bee Hawk-moth *Hemaris fuciformis* Linnaeus, family Sphingidae. This widespread bee mimic is common in many parts of Europe. In the British Isles it occurs locally in Wales and southern and central England. This is a woodland species found in rides and clearings and also in nearby meadows. The caterpillar is bright green with a bluish-green head, a brown horn and a series of reddish-brown patches surrounding the spiracles. It feeds on the foliage

of honeysuckle (*Lonicera periclymenum*), bedstraw (*Galium*) and snowberry (*Symphoricarpos*) usually concealed on the underside of a leaf. When full grown it becomes purplish-brown all over and leaves the foodplant to pupate in a flimsy cocoon of silk and debris on the ground. The moth sheds most of its scales during the first flight leaving only brown borders surrounding the transparent wings. It flies by day from May to July and visits flowers, particularly those of rhododendrons and lilac (*Syringa*).

Humming-bird Hawk-moth *Macroglossum stellatarum* Linnaeus, family Sphingidae. This common migrant hawk-moth is resident in southern Europe but flies northwards each year,

reaching as far as Fennoscandia. It is a regular migrant to many parts of the British Isles and is even recorded from the Shetlands. As it is such an active traveller, it may be found in almost any terrain but is most frequently encountred in parks and gardens. The caterpillar is green or brown with a broad, darker band along the back and a bluish horn. It feeds on bedstraw (*Galium*) and wild madder (*Rubia peregrina*). When full grown it turns a reddish-purple colour and spins a loosely woven silken cocoon on the ground within which it pupates. Moths are on the wing throughout the year in southern Europe but in the British Isles they are usually seen in spring and summer. They fly by day and visit flowers, particularly those of jasmine (*Jasminum*).

135

Daphinis nerii

Hyles euphorbiae

Hyles galii

Hyles lineata

Deilephila elpenor

Deilephila porcellus

Hippotion celerio

⁴/₅ lifesize

Oleander Hawk-moth *Daphnis nerii* Linnaeus, family Sphingidae. Although a native of Africa and southern Asia, this magnificent moth migrates into Europe and will breed during the summer in some southern localities. It is an extremely rare visitor to the British Isles but has been recorded as far north as Aberdeen. Most specimens recorded in northern Europe have been found in towns or gardens where they have been attracted to light. The caterpillar measures up to 15cm in length and is olive green with two large blue eye-spots on the third segment behind the head. The horn is yellow with a black tip. Foodplants are oleander (*Nerium oleander*), periwinkle (*Vinca*) and grape-vine (*Vitis vinifera*). Pupation takes place within a large brown silken cocoon spun on the ground. While this moth may be found in southern Europe from spring to autumn, it usually reaches the British Isles in late summer.

Spurge Hawk-moth *Hyles euphorbiae* Linnaeus, family Sphingidae. This widely distributed species is common in many parts of central and southern Europe and it has even been introduced into Canada to control weed species of *Euphorbia*. Although found in the Channel Islands, its occurrence in other parts of the British Isles is rare and records are almost all from southern England. It is often found in coastal localities although it may also be found inland. The caterpillar is brilliantly patterned in red, black and yellow or green and is very variable. It feeds on various species of *Euphorbia* but seems to have a preference for sea spurge (*E. paralias*) or cypress spurge (*E. cyparissias*). When fully fed it constructs a cocoon of silk and sand just below the surface of the ground within which it pupates. In southern Europe the moth is on the wing in spring with a second brood in late summer but specimens reaching the British Isles usually arrive in summer.

Bedstraw Hawk-moth *Hyles galii* Rottemburg, family Sphingidae. This species is found all over Europe including southern Fennoscandia although it does not survive the winter in northern regions. It is an irregular migrant to the British Isles but has been recorded from most parts including the Shetlands. It seems to prefer sandy areas and caterpillars are sometimes found in coastal areas of Britain. The caterpillar is olive green or brown with two lines of black-ringed yellow spots along the back and a curved red horn. It feeds on bedstraw (*Galium*), willow-herb (*Epilobium*) and *Fuchsia*. The pupa is found on the surface of the ground or just below it in a silken cocoon. Moths fly at dusk and sometimes visit flowers in gardens. There are two broods a year in southern Europe and moths are on the wing in spring and late summer although in Britain they usually arrive in summer.

Striped Hawk-moth *Hyles lineata* Fabricius, family Sphingidae. This widespread moth occurs around the world except for polar and tropical regions. It is only a true resident in southern parts of Europe but migrates northwards each year, sometimes in huge numbers. Whilst it is a fairly regular migrant to the British Isles it seldom arrives in large numbers. The race occurring in Europe is known as ssp. *livornica* Esper. The caterpillar is dark greenish-black dotted with yellow and with a pinkish-yellow line down the back. The horn is red with a black tip. It feeds on bedstraw (*Galium*), dock (*Rumex*), vine (*Vitis*), *Fuchsia* and other plants and when full grown pupates in a flimsy cocoon of silk on the ground. The moth has two broods a year in parts of southern Europe although further south it has three. Found in Britain in spring and summer, often visiting flowers such as honeysuckle (*Lonicera*) at dusk, and are attracted to light.

Small Elephant Hawk-moth *Deilephila porcellus*

Oleander Hawk-moth *Daphnis nerii*

Spurge Hawk-moth *Hyles euphorbiae*

Spurge Hawk-moth caterpillar

Elephant Hawk-moth *Deilephila elpenor*

Elephant Hawk-moth *Deilephila elpenor* caterpillar

Elephant Hawk-moth *Deilephila elpenor*
Linnaeus, family Sphingidae. This common
hawk-moth is found throughout Europe
including Fennoscandia. It is widespread and
common in England and Wales and also occurs in
Ireland and southern Scotland. The usual
habitats of this species are rough waste land,
woodland clearings and river valleys where the
foodplant is abundant. The caterpillar is green or
greyish-brown with a network of fine black lines
and with prominent eye-spots on the fourth and
fifth segments. The front segments of the
caterpillar taper towards the head, sometimes
giving the appearance of an elephant's trunk. It
feeds mainly on willow-herb (*Epilobium*) but will
also eat the foliage of bedstraw (*Galium*), *Fuchsia*
and other plants. Pupation takes place on the
ground in a cocoon of silk, earth and leaf
fragments. Moths are on the wing in summer and
will visit flowers such as valerian (*Valeriana*) and
honeysuckle (*Lonicera*).

Small Elephant Hawk-moth *Deilephila porcellus*
Linnaeus, family Sphingidae. This moth is
common in most parts of Europe and occurs in
southern Fennoscandia. In the British Isles it is
widespread in England and Wales but local in
Scotland and Ireland. It is frequently found in
chalk or limestone districts and the usual habitats
are open meadows, heathland and coastal
sandhills. The caterpillar is usually greyish-
brown although a green form also occurs. It is
similar in appearance to the Elephant
Hawk-moth but is smaller and has two
diminutive, wart-like processes on the tail
instead of the usual horn. The usual foodplant is
bedstraw (*Galium*) but the foliage of willow-herb
(*Epilobium*) and purple loosestrife (*Lythrum
salicaria*) is also eaten. The pupa is formed in a
loose cocoon of silk and leaf litter on the ground.
Moths are on the wing in late spring and summer
and often visit flowers, particularly those of
honeysuckle (*Lonicera*) and *Rhododendron*.

Silver-striped Hawk-moth *Hippotion celerio*
Linnaeus, family Sphingidae. Although this
moth is a resident of Africa and southern Asia it
migrates northwards into Europe each year and
is quite common along the Mediterranean coast.
It is a regular but scarce migrant to the British
Isles and has been reported from the Channel
Islands, England and southern Scotland. In
southern Europe it may be found in vineyards but
moths occurring in Britain are usually found in
gardens or attracted to the lights of houses. The
caterpillar is green or brown with a black horn.
On the fourth segment there are two conspicuous
yellow-ringed eye-spots on the back. The
foodplants are grape-vine (*Vitis vinifera*), virginia
creeper (*Parthenocissus*), bedstraw (*Galium*) and
Fuchsia. The full grown caterpillar usually
burrows underground before pupating. In the
tropics this species has up to four broods a year,
but in southern Europe only two. Migrants to
Britain usually arrive in autumn.

137

Phalera bucephala

Cerura vinula

Furcula bifida

Notodonta dromedarius

Stauropus fagi

Eligmodonta ziczac

Peridea anceps

Pheosia gnoma

Lifesize

Buff-tip *Phalera bucephala* Linnaeus, family Notodontidae. This distinctive moth is common throughout Europe from Fennoscandia to the Iberian Peninsula and eastwards to Siberia. In the British Isles it is common in England and Wales but more local in Scotland and Ireland. Its habitats are woodlands, parks and gardens. The caterpillar is orange-yellow with longitudinal black bands and is covered with short, downy hairs. It feeds on the foliage of many deciduous trees, particularly oak (*Quercus*), sallow (*Salix*) and hazel (*Corylus*). When young, the caterpillars are gregarious and will completely strip a branch before moving *en masse* to a fresh one. Pupation takes place in an earthen cell below ground. There is one brood a year and moths are on the wing from May until July. When at rest the moth bears a striking resemblance to a twig.

Puss Moth *Cerura vinula* Linnaeus, family Notodontidae. The range of this beautiful moth extends throughout Europe eastwards across Siberia to Japan. In the British Isles it is widespread, occurring as far north as Orkney, but most common in southern England. Its habitats are hedgerows, light woodland and other places where the foodplants grow. The distinctive caterpillar is bright green with a dark purple saddle-shaped marking on the back and a two-pronged tail from which red whip-like flagellae are protruded if it is alarmed. The caterpillar can squirt formic acid from glands behind the head. The foodplants are sallow, willow (*Salix*) and poplar (*Populus*). When full grown the caterpillar constructs a tough papery cocoon from silk and chewed-up wood and attaches it to a tree trunk or fence post before pupation. There is one brood a year and moths may be found from April until July, according to locality.

Poplar Kitten *Furcula bifida* Brahm, family Notodontidae. This moth is widely distributed in Europe occurring as far north as Finland and ranging southwards to Italy and Greece. In the British Isles it is quite common in England and found locally in the Channel Islands and Wales but does not occur in Scotland or Ireland. It may be found in many habitats where the foodplant is common, including gardens and tree-lined streets. The caterpillar is yellowish-green with a saddle-like purple marking on the back which is outlined with yellow. The tail is divided into two long pointed prongs and overall the caterpillar is like a small version of the Puss Moth. It feeds on the foliage of poplar and aspen (*Populus*) and when full grown pupates in a cocoon of silk and chewed wood fixed to a tree trunk. Two winters may pass in the pupal stage before moths emerge. Moths are on the wing from May until July.

Lobster Moth *Stauropus fagi* Linnaeus, family Notodontidae. This widespread species is found in most parts of Europe, occurring as far north as southern Scandinavia, and ranging eastwards across temperate Asia to Japan. Occurs locally in southern England, parts of Wales and the extreme south-west of Ireland. It is a woodland insect most usually found in beech (*Fagus*) woods but seldom common. The strange lobster-like appearance of the reddish-brown caterpillar is due to the very large thoracic legs and paired tail-processes and a series of pointed humps along the back. This is enhanced when the caterpillar adopts its characteristic defence posture: head reared up and backwards and tail raised and thrown forwards. It will eat the foliage of birch (*Betula*), oak (*Quercus*), hazel (*Corylus*) and sometimes of fruit trees, as well as that of beech. Pupation takes place in a silken cocoon spun amongst dead leaves. On the wing from May until July according to locality and season.

Iron Prominent *Notodonta dromedarius* Linnaeus, family Notodontidae. This moth is widely distributed in central and northern Europe and occurs throughout Fennoscandia. In the British Isles it is also widespread and absent only from Orkney and Shetland. Its habitats are light woodland and other places where the foodplants grow. The caterpillar varies in colour from green to brown but is usually yellow along the back which bears four prominent brownish humps. There is a further hump at the tail. This species usually feeds on the foliage of birch (*Betula*) or alder (*Alnus*) but is sometimes also found on hazel (*Corylus*). Pupation takes place in a cocoon of soil and silk constructed on the ground at the base of a tree. In Britain this species is usually single-brooded with moths on the wing from May until July but occasionally there is a second brood, producing moths in late summer and autumn.

Pebble Prominent *Eligmodonta ziczac* Linnaeus, family Notodontidae. This is a widespread species occurring throughout Europe from Fennoscandia to the Iberian Peninsula and ranging eastwards to central Asia. In the British Isles it is widely distributed and often common. Its habitats are woodland margins, hedgerows and other places where the foodplants flourish, particularly in fenland and similar damp locations. The caterpillar is pale brownish-grey, sometimes flushed with pink, and with a yellow stripe down the back. There are two large humps on the back behind the head and a further one near the tail. The caterpillar feeds on the foliage of willow, sallow (*Salix*) and occasionally poplar (*Populus*). Pupation takes place below ground at the foot of the tree in an earthen cocoon. There is one brood a year in the north and two in the south with moths on the wing in May and June and again in August. Occasionally a third brood of moths appears in October.

Great Prominent *Peridea anceps* Goeze, family Notodontidae. This moth is widespread in Europe ranging from southern Scandinavia to Spain and Italy and eastwards to western Asia. In the British Isles it is widespread in southern England and Wales and also occurs locally in northern England and parts of Scotland. Its preferred habitat is light woodland where the foodplant grows. The caterpillar is green with pale yellow lines down the back and a series of pink-edged, yellow diagonal stripes along each side. It feeds on the foliage of oak (*Quercus*) and when full grown descends to the ground and pupates in an earthen cocoon amongst the roots. This is a single-brooded species and moths are to be found from April until June. Sometimes the pupal stage lasts for two winters before the moth emerges. Moths fly at night but are more frequently seen when at rest on tree trunks or fences during the day.

Lesser Swallow Prominent *Pheosia gnoma* Fabricius, family Notodontidae. This species occurs throughout Europe from Scandinavia to the Iberian Peninsula and ranges eastwards to Siberia. In the British Isles it is widespread and often quite common. Its preferred habitat is birch (*Betula*) woodland. The caterpillar is purplish-brown with a broad yellow stripe down each side and has a shining appearance as though varnished. It feeds on the foliage of various species of birch and when full grown it descends to the ground and pupates in a cocoon of silk and earth amongst the roots of the tree. There are usually two broods a year except in the extreme north and moths are on the wing in May and June and again in August. It may be distinguished from the closely related Swallow Prominent by its smaller size and the distinctive wedge-shaped white markings on the forewing.

Buff-tip *Phalera bucephala* at rest

Pebble Prominent *Eligmodonta ziczac* caterpillar

Great Prominent *Peridea anceps* caterpillar

Lobster Moth *Stauropus fagi* caterpillar

Iron Prominent *Notodonta dromedarius* at rest

Pebble Prominent *Eligmodonta ziczac* at rest

Pheosia tremula

Ptilodon capucina

Pterostoma palpina

Clostera pigra

Diloba caeruleocephala

♂
Thaumetopoea pityocampa
♀

♂
Thaumetopoea processionea
♀

Lifesize

Swallow Prominent *Pheosia tremula* Clerck, family Notodontidae. This moth has a similar distribution to the closely related Lesser Swallow Prominent, its range extending to the Arctic Circle. In the British Isles it is widespread and common. Its habitats are deciduous and mixed woodlands where the foodplants grow. The caterpillar is usually green with a yellow line along each side but sometimes a greyish-brown form may be found. Both forms have a slight hump on the back at the tail end. The foodplants are poplar, aspen (*Populus*) and willow (*Salix*). Full grown caterpillars of the first generation pupate in a cocoon spun amongst leaves but those occurring in the autumn burrow below ground at the foot of the tree and pupate in a cocoon of silk and soil particles. Moths are on the wing in May and June and a second generation appears in August in southern localities. When at rest on bark they are extremely well camouflaged.

Coxcomb Prominent *Ptilodon capucina* Linnaeus, family Notodontidae. This widespread species occurs commonly throughout Europe from Scandinavia to the Iberian Peninsula and ranges eastwards across temperate Asia. In the British Isles it is widespread and often common. Its habitats are deciduous and mixed woodlands and hedgerows. The caterpillar is usually green with a yellow stripe along each side and a pair of bright red, raised points on the back near the tail. Yellowish-brown and purplish forms of this species also occur but they all have the distinctive red processes. Foodplants are birch (*Betula*), poplar (*Populus*), hazel (*Corylus*) and various other deciduous trees and shrubs. The full grown caterpillar leaves the foodplant and burrows into the ground before pupating in a cocoon of silk and soil particles. There are two generations a year and moths are usually on the wing in May and June and again in late summer and autumn. In some regions the broods may overlap and moths can be found throughout the summer. When at rest with their wings folded tent-like across their back, they strongly resemble dead leaves.

Pale Prominent *Pterostoma palpina* Clerck, family Notodontidae. This common and widespread moth occurs throughout lowland Europe as far north as the Arctic Circle and its range extends eastwards across Siberia to Japan. In the British Isles it occurs widely but is most common in southern England. The preferred habitat is deciduous woodland, usually in damp situations where the foodplants thrive. The caterpillar is bluish-green above and dark green below with thin white lines down the back and a yellow band along each side. It feeds on the foliage of poplar, aspen (*Populus*) and willow (*Salix*) and when full grown pupates in the soil at the foot of the tree in a silken cocoon. There is one brood a year in the north and two in the south with moths on the wing from May until June and again in August in some localities. Like many related species this moth resembles a dead leaf when at rest.

Small Chocolate-tip *Clostera pigra* Hufnagel, family Notodontidae. This species occurs in many parts of northern and central Europe, its range extending into temperate Asia. In the British Isles it is widespread but most common in south-eastern England. Its habitats are marshland, fens and other damp situations where the foodplant is found. The caterpillar is pale orange with a broad band of charcoal grey along each side and is covered with short fine hairs. The head is dark grey and there are two prominent black spots on the back. It feeds on the foliage of various species of willow and sallow (*Salix*), particularly dwarf sallow (*S. repens*), and

Figure of Eight *Diloba caeruleocephala* at rest

Coxcomb Prominent *Ptilodon capucina* at rest

Swallow Prominent *Pheosia tremula* at rest

sometimes on young aspens (*Populus*). When fully developed, it constructs a cocoon by spinning leaves together and pupates inside. There are two or more broods a year in southern localities but only one in the north. Moths may be found from May until October, according to locality.

Figure of Eight *Diloba caeruleocephala* Linnaeus, family Notodontidae. This is a common moth throughout Europe and its range extends into Asia Minor. In the British Isles it is common in many parts of England but elsewhere is very local and scarce. Its habitats are hedgerows, woodland margins, orchards and gardens. The distinctive caterpillar is bluish-grey spotted with black and with three yellow bands, one down the back and one along each side. It feeds on the foliage of blackthorn (*Prunus*), hawthorn (*Crataegus*), apple (*Malus*) and various other fruit trees. When full grown it pupates in a cocoon of earth and silk at the base of the tree. There is one brood a year and moths may be found in late autumn. The common name of this species derives from the figure-of-eight-shaped whitish markings on the forewing of the moth. In many respects this moth is unlike others in its family and in the past it has been placed in the family Noctuidae.

Pine Processionary *Thaumetopoea pityocampa* Denis & Schiffermüller, family Thaumetopoeidae. This interesting species occurs in many parts of central and southern Europe and is particularly common in Mediterranean regions including parts of North Africa. It does not occur in northern France, Germany, the Netherlands or the British Isles. Its habitat is pine (*Pinus*) forests where it can

Coxcomb Prominent *Ptilodon capucina* caterpillar

cause extensive damage and be a serious nuisance. The caterpillar is bluish-black with tufts of brown hair. These hairs are easily detached if the caterpillars are handled and may cause severe skin irritation. Caterpillars live in a communal web or 'nest' by day, coming out at night to feed on the surrounding foliage. They move about together in an unbroken column, thus giving rise to their common name. When full grown they descend to the ground where they pupate in silken cocoons. There is one brood a year and moths are on the wing in May and June.

Oak Processionary *Thaumetopoea processionea* Linnaeus, family Thaumetopoeidae. This moth is widespread in Europe, occurring from

Pine Processionary caterpillars on nest

Fennoscandia southwards to the Iberian Peninsula but it does not occur in the British Isles. Its habitat is oak (*Quercus*) woodland. The caterpillar is bluish-black along the back and greyish-brown along the sides which are marked with white. It is covered with hairs which have similar irritant properties to those of the Pine Processionary. Caterpillars rest by day in a large communal silken 'nest', coming out at night to feed on the foliage of oak, their only foodplant. When leaving the nest they move together in a wedge-shaped procession, from which habit they have been given their common name. When full grown they spin their cocoons in a mass in the nest which they have used as a shelter. There is only one brood a year and moths are on the wing in August and September.

141

♂

♀

Orgyia antiqua

♂

♀

Dasychira pudibunda

♂

♀

Euproctis chrysorrhoea

♂

♀

Euproctis similis

Lifesize

Brown-tail *Euproctis chrysorrhoea* caterpillar

Yellow-tail *Euproctis similis* at rest

Vapourer *Orgyia antiqua* Linnaeus, family Lymantriidae. This familiar little moth has an extremely wide distribution, occurring throughout Europe and eastwards across temperate Asia and also in North America. In the British Isles it is widespread and common. Its habitats are woodlands, parks and gardens. The caterpillar is grey with raised red spots, four brush-like tufts of yellow or pale brown hairs on the back and three groups of long, black, plumed hairs placed one either side of the head and one at the tail. It feeds on the foliage of a wide range of deciduous trees and shrubs and sometimes occurs in very large numbers. The hairs of the caterpillars can cause a rash on sensitive skins. When full grown, pupation takes place in a silken cocoon spun on a tree trunk or a nearby support

such as a fence. There are from one to three broods a year and moths may be found from July to October. While male moths are very active and fly by day, the females are wingless and hardly move at all, even laying their eggs on the empty cocoon.

Pale Tussock *Dasychira pudibunda* Linnaeus, family Lymantriidae. This species occurs in many parts of northern and central Europe and ranges eastwards across temperate Asia to Japan. In the British Isles it is widespread in England and Wales, but local in Ireland and absent from Scotland. Its habitats are woodlands and hop gardens where the caterpillars are sometimes known as 'hop dogs'. The hairy caterpillar is usually yellow or pale green although brown

forms also occur. There are four yellow, brush-like tufts on the back behind the head and a red tuft near the tail. It feeds on the foliage of many deciduous trees and also on hops (*Humulus lupulus*). In parts of Scandinavia it sometimes causes serious defoliation of forest trees. Pupation takes place in a silken cocoon usually on or near the ground. There is one brood a year and moths are on the wing in May and June.

Brown-tail *Euproctis chrysorrhoea* Linnaeus, family Lymantriidae. This notorious moth is widespread in central and southern Europe and has been introduced to North America where it is sometimes a pest in orchards. In the British Isles it is confined to the Channel Islands and southern and eastern England. Habitats are hedgerows, orchards, parks and gardens. The hairy caterpillar is brown marked with red and has tufts of white scale-like hairs along each side and two small fleshy red spots on the back towards the tail. The hairs of this caterpillar can cause a severe and painful rash on the skin and may cause serious damage if they penetrate the eye. The foodplants are blackthorn (*Prunus*), hawthorn (*Crataegus*) and various fruit trees. Caterpillars live in a communal nest until full grown when

Vapourer *Orgyia antiqua* caterpillar

Yellow-tail *Euproctis similis* caterpillar

Pale Tussock *Dasychira pudibunda* caterpillar

Pale Tussock *Dasychira pudibunda* at rest

they wander away to find a place to pupate, usually amongst foliage. There is one brood a year and moths may be found in July and August. The female has a large brown tuft on her tail which carries irritant hairs from the caterpillar stage. These are deposited over the eggs to protect them.

Yellow-tail *Euproctis similis* Fuessly, family Lymantriidae. This is a widespread species occurring throughout Europe and ranging eastwards across Siberia to Japan. In the British Isles it is common and widely distributed throughout most of England, Wales and the Channel Islands but is very local in Ireland and southern Scotland. Its habitats are hedgerows, woodlands and scrub, often in coastal districts. The caterpillar is black with a bright red stripe down the back divided by a thin central line of black. There are tufts of white scale-like hairs along each side below which is a further band of red. The foodplants are hawthorn (*Crataegus*), blackthorn (*Prunus*) and various other deciduous trees and shrubs. Unlike the related Brown-tail, the caterpillars do not live in a communal nest and although the body hairs may cause some irritation this is never severe. Pupation takes place in a cocoon spun amongst the foliage. Moths are on the wing in July and August.

Vapourer *Orgyia antiqua*

♂

Leucoma salicis

♀

♂

Lymantria monacha

♀

♂

Lymantria dispar

♀

Lifesize

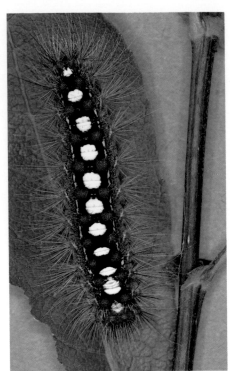

White Satin *Leucoma salicis* caterpillar

Gypsy Moth *Lymantria dispar* caterpillar

White Satin *Leucoma salicis* Linnaeus, family Lymantriidae. This attractive and aptly named moth is widespread in Europe, its range extending across Siberia to Japan. It has been accidentally introduced to North America where it is sometimes a pest. In the British Isles it is locally common in southern and central England and also occurs in some coastal areas of northern England. It is very local in Ireland and there are a few records from Scotland. Habitats are deciduous woodland, parks, gardens and other places where the foodplants grow. The hairy caterpillar is black on the back with a series of large white patches interspersed on either side with red spots. The sides are grey with reddish-brown spots. It feeds on the foliage of

poplar (*Populus*), and sallow (*Salix*) and when full grown pupates in a cocoon spun in crevices of the bark. There is one brood a year with moths on the wing in July and August. They fly by night and may be found resting by day on tree trunks.

Black Arches *Lymantria monacha* Linnaeus, family Lymantriidae. This distinctive species is widespread in Europe from southern Fennoscandia to northern Italy and Greece and ranges eastwards across Siberia to Japan. In the British Isles it is confined to the Channel Islands, southern England and a few localities in Wales. It is found in coniferous and deciduous woodland and in continental Europe it is sometimes a serious forest pest. The hairy caterpillar is greyish-brown with black lines joining a series of

black spots along the back. It feeds on the foliage of oak (*Quercus*), birch (*Betula*), spruce (*Picea*) and pine (*Pinus*) and when full grown pupates in a cocoon under bark. There is one brood a year and moths may be found from July until September. Males fly actively at night but the females are sedentary and can often be found on the tree trunks by day.

Gypsy Moth *Lymantria dispar* Linnaeus, family Lymantriidae. This well-known moth is very common in many parts of Europe, ranging eastwards across temperate Asia to China. It was accidentally introduced to North America in the nineteenth century and is now established there. In the British Isles it is extinct, although at one time it was common in the fens of Huntingdonshire. Its usual habitats are woodlands and orchards, although in Britain it used to occur in damp areas where bog myrtle (*Myrica gale*) and creeping willow (*Salix repens*) grew. The caterpillar is grey with a pale brown line down the back and a series of raised red spots bearing tufts of hairs. Near the head is a series of raised blue spots. In continental Europe the caterpillars feed on the foliage of a wide range of deciduous trees, including fruit trees, and are often serious pests. There is one brood a year with moths on the wing from July until September. Males fly by day but females are inactive and seldom stray far from the cocoon.

Specimens on 'set' plates are uppersides unless otherwise indicated. Where the sexes are similar in appearance, only one is figured. Abbreviations and symbols used in the captions: ♂ male ♀ female △ underside aest. summer form f. form ssp. subspecies var. variety vern. spring form.

Black Arches *Lymantria monacha* at rest

Gypsy Moth *Lymantria dispar*

White Satin *Leucoma salicis* at rest

Miltochrista miniata

Nudaria mundana

var.

Eilema griseola

Eilema lurideola

Utetheisa pulchella

♂ ♀

Parasemia plantaginis

Lifesize

Dingy Footman *Eilema griseola* Hübner, family Arctiidae. This moth is common throughout much of central Europe, its range extending eastwards across temperate Siberia to Japan. In the British Isles it is confined to the Channel Islands, southern England and western Wales but may be quite common in suitable localities. Its habitats are fens, marshes and damp woodlands. The hairy caterpillar is velvety black with a purplish stripe down the back and a broken orange line high up on each side. It feeds on lichens growing on the twigs of trees and shrubs but in captivity will eat mosses and withered leaves of sallow (*Salix*) and various herbaceous plants. Pupation takes place in a cocoon of silk mixed with lichen or moss. There is one brood a year and moths are on the wing in July. A yellow form of this moth (f. *stramineola* Doubleday), peculiar to Britain, was once regarded as a distinct species, called the Straw-coloured Footman.

Common Footman *Eilema lurideola* Zincken, family Arctiidae. This is a common moth found throughout Europe except for the extreme north, its range extending into Asia Minor. In the British Isles it is widespread but is most common in southern England and Wales. Its habitats are hedgerows and woodlands. The hairy caterpillar is grey with black lines down the back and an orange line along each side. It feeds on lichens growing on trees and bushes but will eat the foliage of various plants in captivity and probably also does so in the wild. When full grown it pupates in a cocoon spun in a crevice of the bark. There is one brood a year and moths are on the wing from June until August. Like the Dingy Footman this moth rests in a characteristic position with its wings folded flat over its back. It is attracted to the flowers of traveller's joy (*Clematis*) and thistles (*Carduus*) at dusk.

Crimson Speckled *Utetheisa pulchella* Linnaeus, family Arctiidae. Although this beautiful moth is not a native of central and northern Europe, it is extremely widespread throughout the Mediterranean region, Africa, Asia and Australia. Migrants arrive in central Europe each year and may produce a second generation if conditions are sufficiently warm and sunny. In the British Isles it occurs sporadically as a migrant but is regarded as a rarity. The caterpillar is grey with white lines down the back and sides and a transverse orange bar on each segment. The body is covered with black warts bearing black and grey hairs. Foodplants are forget-me-not (*Myosotis*), borage (*Borago*), heliotrope (*Heliotropium*) and various other herbaceous plants. Pupation takes place in a silken cocoon spun either amongst foliage or on the ground. Continuously brooded in subtropics but those found in Britain usually arrive in the autumn; fly by day in sunshine.

Wood Tiger *Parasemia plantaginis* Linnaeus, family Arctiidae. The distribution of this species extends throughout northern and central Europe and eastwards across Siberia to Japan. In the British Isles it is quite widespread although it seems to be less common in southern England than it was in the past. In Scotland it is represented by a distinct race, ssp. *insularum* Seitz. Habitats are woodland clearings, heaths, moors and downland. The caterpillar is black, densely covered with black and reddish-brown hairs. It feeds on the foliage of various low-growing plants including plantain (*Plantago*), groundsel (*Senecio*) and forget-me-not (*Myosotis*), hibernating through winter. Pupation takes place in a cocoon spun amongst leaves of the foodplant. One brood a year; moths found from June until August. They fly by day, darting about near the ground, and at night.

Rosy Footman *Miltochrista miniata* Forster, family Arctiidae. Common in many parts of central and northern Europe. It is found in the Channel Islands, southern England, Wales and parts of Ireland. Habitats are woodlands, hedgerows and damp, well-wooded heathland. The hairy caterpillar is dark greyish-brown and feeds on various lichens, particularly *Peltigera canina* on the twigs of trees and shrubs. In captivity it will eat withered leaves of oak (*Quercus*) and sallow (*Salix*). It pupates in a silken cocoon interwoven with hairs from the body. There is one brood a year with moths on the wing from June until August, according to locality. Moths fly at night.

Muslin Footman *Nudaria mundana* Linnaeus, family Arctiidae. The distribution of this delicate little moth extends through northern and central Europe and eastwards to Asia Minor. In the British Isles it is widespread and common in suitable localities. Its habitats are rough stony places, particularly on stone walls and lichen-covered rocks. The caterpillar is grey with two lines of raised yellow spots down the back and is covered with grey hairs. It feeds on lichens and algae and when full grown pupates in an open network cocoon spun on the rock. There is one brood a year and moths may be found in June and July. The males fly freely at night but the females are less active and are seldom noticed.

Wood Tiger *Parasemia plantaginis*

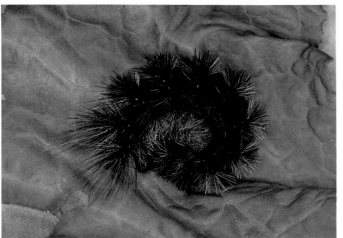
Wood Tiger *Parasemia plantaginis* caterpillar

Rosy Footman *Miltochrista miniata*

Muslin Footman *Nudaria mundana*

Dingy Footman *Eilema griseola*

♂

♀

var.

var.

Arctia caja

♂

♀

Arctia villica

Garden Tiger *Arctia caja*

Garden Tiger *Arctia caja* Linnaeus, family
Arctiidae. This handsome and variable species is
widespread in Europe, occurring as far north as
Lapland and its range extends eastwards across
Siberia to Japan. In the British Isles it occurs
almost everywhere and is often common. Its
habitats are woodlands, waste ground, parks and
other places where suitable foodplants grow. The
caterpillar is black, densely covered with long
hairs which are black on the back and rich
reddish-brown along the sides. It is a common
sight in gardens where it will eat many
herbaceous weeds and cultivated plants and is
known popularly as the 'woolly bear'. The full
grown caterpillar pupates within a yellowish-
white silken cocoon spun at the base of the
foodplant. There is one brood a year with moths
on the wing in July and August. Despite its
bright colours, this moth flies mainly at night and
is seldom encountered by day.

Cream-spot Tiger *Arctia villica* Linnaeus,
family Arctiidae. This moth is found in many
parts of central and southern Europe. In the
British Isles it is represented by ssp. *brittanica*
Oberthür which also occurs in northern France.
It is found locally in southern England and
Wales, mainly in coastal areas, and also occurs in
the Channel Islands. Its habitats are woodlands,
hedgerows and grassy places. The caterpillar is
black with dense reddish-brown hairs and has a
bright reddish-brown head. It feeds on various
low-growing herbaceous plants such as
dandelion (*Taraxacum*), chickweed (*Stellaria*)
and dock (*Rumex*), hibernating through the
winter and completing its growth in the
following spring. Pupation takes place in a silken
cocoon spun amongst foliage or on the ground.
There is one brood a year with moths on the wing
from May until July. They usually fly at night
but are sometimes also active during the day.

Lifesize

Garden Tiger *Arctia caja* at rest

Cream-spot Tiger *Arctia villica*

Garden Tiger *Arctia caja* caterpillar

Diacrisia sannio

♂   ♀

Spilosoma lubricipeda

♀   ♂ var.

Spilosoma lutea

var.

Diaphora mendica

♂   ♀

Phragmatobia fuliginosa

var.

Lifesize

White Ermine *Spilosoma lubricipeda*

White Ermine *Spilosoma lubricipeda* Linnaeus, family Arctiidae. This common moth is widespread throughout Europe, ranging southwards to North Africa and eastwards to Siberia. In the British Isles it occurs almost everywhere except for the Shetlands and is often quite abundant. Its habitats are many and varied and this moth may be found wherever suitable foodplants are growing. The hairy caterpillar is dark greyish-brown with a distinctive orange or red stripe down the back. It will feed on the foliage of almost any low-growing herbaceous plant and is often found on weeds and cultivated flowers in gardens. When full grown it pupates within a silken cocoon spun in a folded leaf or in a sheltered place on the ground. There is usually one brood a year with moths on the wing from May until July but sometimes a small second brood appears in the autumn. This is a very variable species and the black wing markings are sometimes entirely absent or enlarged and joined together to form lines and streaks.

Buff Ermine *Spilosoma lutea* Hufnagel, family Arctiidae. Like its near relative the White Ermine, this species is widespread in Europe and temperate Asia. In the British Isles it is widely distributed and often common but is more local in northern Scotland and in Ireland where it occurs more frequently in coastal regions. Its habitats are many but it shows a preference for damp places with rich vegetation and is often found in gardens. The caterpillar is brown with tufts of reddish-brown hairs, a red stripe down the back and a yellowish-white or pale grey stripe along each side. It feeds on dock (*Rumex*), plantain (*Plantago*) and many other low-growing herbaceous plants but will also eat the foliage of birch (*Betula*) and virginia creeper (*Parthenocissus quinquefolia*). Pupation takes place in a grey cocoon spun amongst leaves or on the ground and moths emerge and are on the wing from May until July. Both the ground colour and the extent of the black markings are very variable and many forms have been named.

Clouded Buff *Diacrisia sannio* Linnaeus, family Arctiidae. This distinctive species is widespread in Europe, its range extending into Asia Minor. In the British Isles it is quite widespread and can be fairly common in suitable localities. Its favoured habitats are heathland and moors but it also occurs in meadows and downland. The caterpillar is reddish-brown with a yellowish-white stripe down the back and is covered with pale brown hairs. It feeds on the foliage of dandelion (*Taraxacum*), dock (*Rumex*), bog myrtle (*Myrica gale*) and a wide range of other low-growing plants, hibernating while still small and completing its development in the following spring. When full grown it pupates in a flimsy cocoon spun amongst vegetation or on the ground. There is one brood a year and moths may be found in June and July. The males fly freely by day but females are more usually active after dusk.

Ruby Tiger *Phragmatobia fuliginosa* caterpillar

Clouded Buff *Diacrisia sannio* at rest

Ruby Tiger *Phragmatobia fuliginosa*

Buff Ermines *Spilosoma lutea*

Muslin Moth *Diaphora mendica* ♂

Muslin Moth *Diaphora mendica* Clerck, family Arctiidae. This moth may be found in many parts of northern and central Europe, its range extending eastwards to Asia Minor. In the British Isles it is widespread and often quite common although in Scotland and Ireland it is more local in occurrence. Its most favoured habitat is light woodland but other places where suitable foodplants grow may be chosen. The caterpillar is greyish-brown with a pale brown head and tufts of yellowish-brown hairs. It feeds on dandelion (*Taraxacum*), plantain (*Plantago*) and many other low-growing plants and will also eat the foliage of birch (*Betula*) and rose (*Rosa*). When full grown it spins a cocoon of silk mixed with hairs and particles of earth within which it pupates. There is one generation a year with moths on the wing in May and June. The males are active at night and are often attracted to light but females are seldom encountered in this way and are more often seen flying by day.

Ruby Tiger *Phragmatobia fuliginosa* Linnaeus, family Arctiidae. This is an extremely widespread species occurring throughout Europe, temperate Asia and North America. In the British Isles it is widely distributed and locally common although it does not occur in the Shetlands. Its habitats range from woodlands to open meadows and moorlands and include almost any place where suitable foodplants grow. The caterpillar is brown, densely covered with hairs which may be yellowish-, reddish- or blackish-brown in colour. It feeds on low-growing herbaceous plants such as dock (*Rumex*) and plantain (*Plantago*) and, when full grown, pupates in a brown silken cocoon spun on the ground or amongst vegetation. There are two generations a year in southern regions but only one in the north and moths may be on the wing from May until September according to locality. In Britain moths are most frequently seen in May and June. They fly at night but may also be encountered occasionally flying in sunshine.

151

var.

Euplagia quadripunctaria

Callimorpha dominula

var.

Tyria jacobaeae

Syntomis phegea

Lifesize

Yellow-belted Burnet *Syntomis phegea*

Scarlet Tiger *Callimorpha dominula* Linnaeus, family Arctiidae. This highly variable moth occurs throughout Europe, extending as far north as southern Fennoscandia and eastwards into temperate Asia. In the British Isles it is very local and confined to southern England and south-western Wales. Its habitats are damp situations such as river banks, fens and moist meadows and woodland clearings. The hairy caterpillar is black with broad yellow broken stripes along the back and sides. It feeds on a wide range of herbaceous plants, such as dock (*Rumex*) and nettle (*Urtica*), but is particularly fond of comfrey (*Symphytum*). It hibernates as a young caterpillar, completing its growth in the following spring and pupating in a cocoon spun amongst leaf litter on the ground. There is one brood a year and moths are on the wing from June until August according to locality. They fly rapidly in bright sunshine.

Cinnabar *Tyria jacobaeae* Linnaeus, family Arctiidae. This distinctive species is widespread in Europe, its range extending eastwards into Asia. In the British Isles it is widely distributed in the south but more local and usually confined to coastal regions in Scotland and Ireland. Its habitats are meadows, waste ground, heathland and sand dunes where the foodplant is abundant. The conspicuous caterpillar is bright orange-yellow with a black band round each segment. The most favoured foodplant is ragwort (*Senecio jacobaea*) but the foliage of groundsel (*S. vulgaris*) and related plants is also eaten. The caterpillars often feed in some numbers together and are seldom attacked by birds as they are distasteful. Pupation takes place in a cocoon on or below the ground. There is one brood a year and moths are on the wing from May until July. They normally fly at night but are easily disturbed by day when they will flutter away to shelter.

Yellow-belted Burnet *Syntomis phegea* Linnaeus, family Ctenuchidae. This moth, known also as the Nine-spotted, is common throughout southern Europe, except in Spain, and also widespread north of the Alps, although rather local in western Europe, occurring in the Netherlands, Belgium and parts of Germany. It does not occur in the British Isles, although a single record of this species from Dover in 1872 has caused it to be listed as British in many books. Its habitats are woodland clearings and other dry, sunny places up to an altitude of 1300 metres. The caterpillar is black with dense black hairs and a reddish-brown head. It feeds on dandelion (*Taraxacum*), scabious (*Scabiosa*) and other low-growing herbaceous plants and when full grown pupates in a flimsy cocoon of silk mixed with hairs, spun amongst the foliage. There is one brood a year with moths on the wing from June until August. They fly by day and are attracted to the flowers of thyme (*Thymus*) and lavender (*Lavandula officinalis*).

Jersey Tiger *Euplagia quadripunctaria* Poda, family Arctiidae. This attractive moth occurs in many parts of central and southern Europe, its range extending into Asia Minor and Iran. Each year vast numbers of these moths migrate to the Adriatic island of Rhodes where they congregate in the famous 'Valley of the Butterflies'. In the British Isles this species is confined to the Channel Islands and to the south coast of Devon where it has been established since about 1880. Its habitats are usually dry sunny places and

moths may often be found in parks and gardens. The hairy caterpillar is dark brown with a broad deep yellow stripe down the back and a series of yellowish-white spots along each side. It feeds on dandelion (*Taraxacum*), plantain (*Plantago*), dead-nettle (*Lamium*) and other herbaceous plants. The pupa is formed within a frail web-like cocoon spun amongst moss and leaf litter. There is one generation a year and moths may be found flying by day from June until September, according to locality.

Scarlet Tiger *Callimorpha dominula*

Jersey Tiger *Euplagia quadripunctaria*

Cinnabar *Tyria jacobaeae*

♂   *Euxoa nigricans*   ♀

♂   *Agrotis segetum*   ♀

♂   ♀

var.   *Agrotis exclamationis*   var.

♂   *Agrotis puta*   ♀

Axylia putris   *Ochropleura plecta*

Lifesize

Garden Dart *Euxoa nigricans* Linnaeus, family Noctuidae. This common moth is widespread in Europe from Fennoscandia to the Iberian Peninsula and its range extends eastwards into western and central Asia. In the British Isles it is widely distributed although it is most common in the south and east of England and is local in Scotland. Its habitats are lowland agricultural land, marshes, fenland and downland. As its name suggests it is also common in gardens. The caterpillar is smooth and yellowish-brown, tinged with green along the sides. It feeds on clover (*Trifolium*), plantain (*Plantago*) and many other herbaceous plants, eating the foliage and sometimes biting through the stems near the ground so that the plants wither and die.

Pupation takes place below ground in an earthen cocoon. There is one brood a year and moths are on the wing in July and August. They fly at night and are attracted to flowers such as those of ragwort (*Senecio*) and *Buddleia*.

Turnip Moth *Agrotis segetum* Denis & Schiffermüller, family Noctuidae. This widespread and common pest species occurs throughout Europe, temperate Asia and parts of Africa. In the British Isles it occurs almost everywhere although it is less common in northern Scotland. Its habitats are agricultural land, allotments, gardens, waste ground and any other place where suitable foodplants grow. The caterpillar is brownish-grey with a purplish sheen and has a pattern of small, dark grey spots. It feeds on the roots and stems of a wide range of herbaceous plants but is particularly known for its attacks on turnips, swedes (*Brassica*) and carrots (*Daucus*). Because of its habit of biting through the base of the stem so that the plant falls over, the caterpillar is popularly known as a 'cutworm'. Pupation takes place in an earthen cell constructed below ground. There is normally one brood a year in Britain with moths on the wing in May and June but occasionaliy a small second generation appears in autumn.

Heart and Dart *Agrotis exclamationis* Linnaeus, family Noctuidae. This is another widespread and common moth, occurring throughout Europe except for the extreme north and also found in western and central Asia. In the British Isles it is very widely distributed and often abundant except in Scotland where it is scarcer. Its habitats are agricultural land, waste ground, gardens and almost any open ground where suitable foodplants grow. The caterpillar is brown above and greyish below and is otherwise like that of the Turnip Moth although the latter has much smaller spiracles. It feeds on the foliage, roots and stems of a wide range of herbaceous plants and is sometimes a pest of turnips (*Brassica rapa*) and potatoes (*Solanum tuberosum*). When full grown it burrows below ground and makes an earthen cocoon in which it usually overwinters before pupating in the spring. There is usually one brood a year in Britain with moths on the wing from May until June but in more southerly regions there is a second generation flying in July and August or later. Moths fly at night and are often attracted to flowers or to honey dew.

Shuttle-shaped Dart *Agrotis puta* Hübner, family Noctuidae. This variable moth occurs in central and southern Europe from southern Germany, Belgium and France to the Iberian Peninsula and the Mediterranean region and is also found in parts of North Africa and western and central Asia. In the British Isles it is mainly confined to the south and does not occur in Scotland or Ireland. In the Scilly Isles there is a distinct race ssp. *insula* Richardson. Habitats are fields, waste ground, marshes and woodland. The caterpillar is greyish-brown mottled with dark brown on the back. It feeds on various low-growing herbaceous plants, such as dock (*Rumex*), knotgrass (*Polygonum*) and dandelion (*Taraxacum*), and when full grown pupates in an underground cocoon. There are probably two broods a year but this is difficult to ascertain as caterpillars develop at different rates and moths may be found at any time from May until September. They fly at night and are attracted to the flowers of *Buddleia* and lime (*Tilia*) and also to honey dew.

Flame *Axylia putris* Linnaeus, family Noctuidae. This is a common moth occurring in many parts of Europe from Fennoscandia to the Iberian Peninsula and ranging eastwards into western and central Asia. In the British Isles it is widespread and common in lowland areas. Its habitats are hedgerows, woodland margins, gardens and other cultivated land. The caterpillar is greyish-brown mottled with reddish-brown or black and with a series of wedge-shaped markings along the back. It feeds at night on the foliage of various low-growing herbaceous plants, such as dock (*Rumex*), plantain (*Plantago*) and bedstraw (*Galium*), and when full grown pupates in an earthen cocoon below ground. There is one brood a year and moths may be found from May until July, according to locality. They fly at night and are attracted to flowers. When at rest the moth often resembles a piece of broken twig or bark.

Flame Shoulder *Ochropleura plecta* Linnaeus, family Noctuidae. This widely distributed moth not only occurs throughout Europe from Fennoscandia to the Mediterranean but is also found in North Africa, temperate Asia and North America. In the British Isles it is widespread and common. Its habitats are meadows, agricultural land, woodland margins, parks and gardens. The caterpillar is brown with two lines of small white dots along the back and a broad cream-coloured band along each side. It feeds on the foliage of almost any herbaceous plant and sometimes attacks cultivated plants such as lettuces (*Lactuca sativa*). When full grown the caterpillar pupates either on or below the ground. There are two generations a year but these overlap and moths may be found at any time between May and September. The peak emergence times in Britain are May, June and August. Moths fly at night and are attracted to flowers, particularly those of ragwort (*Senecio*).

Flame Shoulder *Ochropleura plecta*

Flame *Axylia putris*

Flame *Axylia putris* caterpillar

Heart and Dart *Agrotis exclamationis*

Shuttle-shaped Dart *Agrotis puta*

155

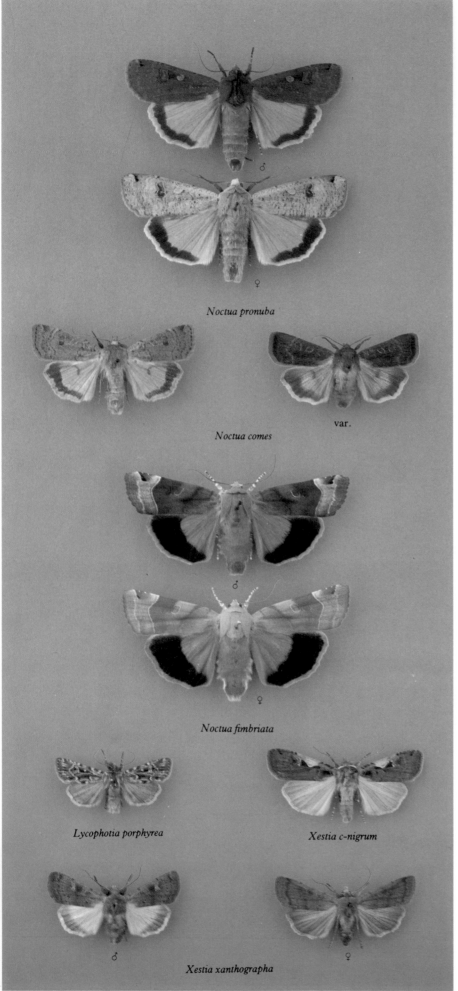

Noctua pronuba

Noctua comes var.

Noctua fimbriata

Lycophotia porphyrea *Xestia c-nigrum*

Xestia xanthographa

Large Yellow Underwing *Noctua pronuba*
Linnaeus, family Noctuidae. This extremely
common and well-known moth occurs
throughout Europe, from Iceland to the
Mediterranean, and is also found in North
Africa, central and western Asia. In the British
Isles it occurs everywhere and is often abundant.
Its habitats are many and varied ranging from
gardens and lowland farms to moorland. The
caterpillar is brown or green with two lines of
black dashes along the back. It feeds on the
foliage, roots and stems of a very wide range of
both wild and cultivated herbaceous plants and
grasses, hiding below ground by day and coming
out at night. It is sometimes a pest of garden
flowers and vegetables. Pupation takes place in
the soil in spring when the overwintered
caterpillars are full grown. There is one brood a
year and moths may be found from June until
October although in Britain they are most
commonly seen in August. They fly at night and
are attracted to flowers and to the bright lights of
houses and shop windows.

Lesser Yellow Underwing *Noctua comes*
Hübner, family Noctuidae. This is a common
moth in many parts of Europe extending from
southern Scandinavia to the Mediterranean and
also occurring in the Canary Islands, North
Africa and Asia Minor. In the British Isles it is
very widely distributed and often abundant. Its
habitats are many and varied and include
hedgerows, heathland and gardens. The
caterpillar is greyish-brown, sometimes tinged
with green, and has two rows of black
wedge-shaped markings on the back extending
from the middle to the tail. When young, the
caterpillars feed on various herbaceous plants,
such as dock (*Rumex*) and clover (*Trifolium*) but,
after hibernating through the winter, they feed
also on the foliage of trees and shrubs such as
birch (*Betula*), sallow (*Salix*) and hawthorn
(*Crataegus*). Pupation takes place in an earthen
cocoon below ground. Moths may be found from
July until September. They fly at night and are
often attracted to flowers of *Buddleia* and other
plants.

Broad-bordered Yellow Underwing *Noctua
fimbriata* Schreber, family Noctuidae. This
species is widespread in Europe from southern
Fennoscandia to the Iberian Peninsula. In the
British Isles it is widely distributed but
apparently does not occur in the extreme north of
Scotland. Its habitats are extensive woodlands
and heavily wooded parkland. The caterpillar is
reddish-brown, finely peppered with dark brown
or black and with large black spots surrounding
the spiracles. It feeds on the foliage of birch
(*Betula*), sallow (*Salix*) and other trees although,
according to some books, it eats low-growing
plants such as dock (*Rumex*) and, when taken
small, can be reared exclusively on this foodplant
in captivity. Pupation takes place in a frail
earthen cocoon below ground. There is one
brood a year and moths are on the wing at first in
July and later at the end of August or in
September, after a period of rest known as
aestivation.

True Lover's Knot *Lycophotia porphyrea* Denis
& Schiffermüller, family Noctuidae. This
species is found in northern Europe within the
Arctic Circle and also ranges south as far as
northern Spain and eastwards into parts of Asia.
In the British Isles it is very widely distributed
and is often common in suitable localities. It is a
heathland species but may be found almost
anywhere where a patch of its foodplant is
established. The caterpillar is reddish-brown
with broken lines of pale whitish-brown marked
with pink. It feeds on heather (*Calluna*) and
heath (*Erica*) and is very difficult to detect when

Lifesize

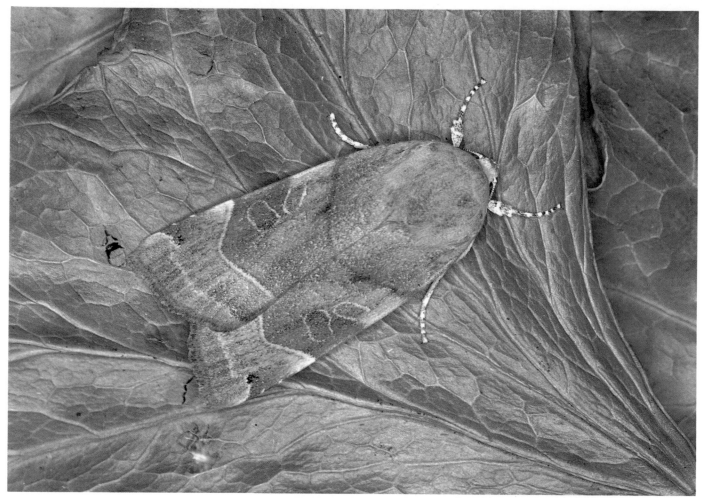

Broad-bordered Yellow Underwing *Noctua fimbriata*

sitting amongst the foliage. It pupates in a frail silken cocoon on or below the surface of the soil. There is one brood a year and moths are on the wing from June until August. They fly mainly at night, visiting the flowers of heather but are occasionally seen during the afternoon.

Setaceous Hebrew Character *Xestia c-nigrum* Linnaeus, family Noctuidae. This common moth has an extremely wide distribution extending throughout temperate Asia and North America and in western Europe occurs from central Fennoscandia to the Iberian Peninsula. In the British Isles it is widespread and particularly common in the south-east. Its habitats range from woods and farmland to marshes and heathlands although this is mainly a lowland species. The caterpillar varies in colour from olive green to pale greyish-brown and has two lines of wedge-shaped, black markings on the back towards the tail and a yellow stripe along each side. It feeds on the foliage of chick-weed (*Stellaria*), groundsel (*Senecio*), dock (*Rumex*), bilberry (*Vaccinium*) and many other low-growing plants. Pupation takes place below ground. The number of broods a year is uncertain but moths are usually found in small numbers in May and June and again in much larger numbers in the autumn. They fly at night and are attracted to flowers and to honey dew.

Square-spot Rustic *Xestia xanthographa* Denis & Schiffermüller, family Noctuidae. This common and variable moth occurs throughout western Europe from southern Fennoscandia to the Iberian Peninsula and eastwards to western Asia. In the British Isles it is widespread and often abundant. Its habitats are woodland margins, open countryside, gardens and almost any other place where suitable foodplants grow. The caterpillar is brown with two rows of

True Lover's Knot *Lycophotia porphyrea*

elongate black markings down the back. It feeds on grasses, a wide range of low-growing herbaceous plants, such as dock (*Rumex*) and plantain (*Plantago*), and also the young shoots of deciduous trees such as sallow (*Salix*) and oak (*Quercus*). It feeds throughout the winter when the weather is not too severe and pupates below ground in the spring. There is one brood a year and moths may be found in August and September. They fly at night and are attracted to flowers such as those of ragwort (*Senecio*), heather (*Calluna*) and *Buddleia*.

Setaceous Hebrew Character *Xestia c-nigrum*

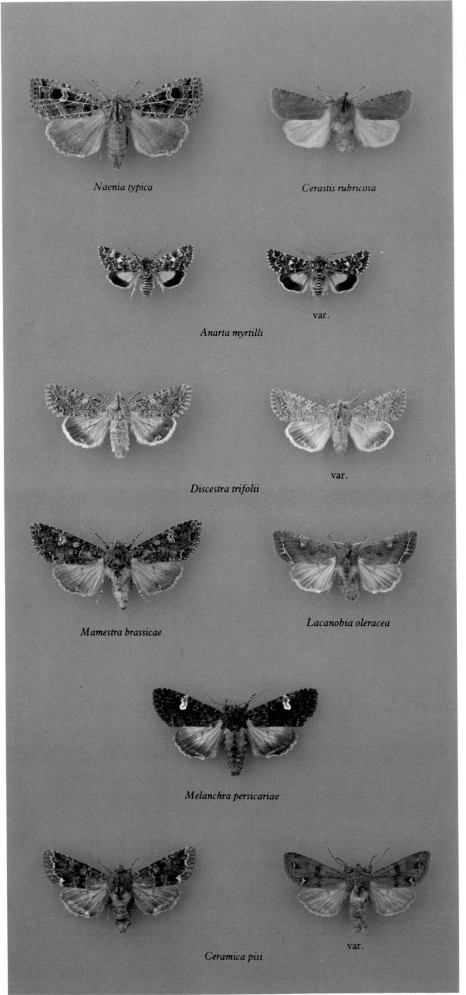

Naenia typica

Cerastis rubricosa

Anarta myrtilli

var.

Discestra trifolii

var.

Mamestra brassicae

Lacanobia oleracea

Melanchra persicariae

Ceramica pisi

var.

Lifesize

Red Chestnut *Cerastis rubricosa* at rest

Gothic *Naenia typica* Linnaeus, family
Noctuidae. This is a widely distributed and
common species in western Europe extending
from southern Fennoscandia to the Iberian
Peninsula and eastwards into temperate Asia. In
the British Isles it is quite common in lowland
areas although not so abundant as it used to be.
Its habitats are woodland margins, agricultural
land, river banks and gardens. The caterpillar is
pale greyish-brown, finely speckled with dark
brown and with two pairs of oblique black
markings on the back near the tail. It feeds on
dock (*Rumex*), dandelion (*Taraxacum*) and many
other low-growing plants, and also on the foliage
of shrubs and trees such as hawthorn (*Crataegus*),
blackthorn (*Prunus*) and sallow (*Salix*). Pupation
takes place below ground in a cocoon of silk and
earth. There is one brood a year and moths are on
the wing from June until August, according to
locality. They fly at night and are attracted to the
blossom of privet (*Ligustrum*).

Red Chestnut *Cerastis rubricosa* Denis &
Schiffermüller, family Noctuidae. This aptly
named moth is found in many parts of Europe
from Fennoscandia southwards but becomes
rather scarce in the Mediterranean region. Its
range also extends into temperate Asia. In the
British Isles it is widespread and usually
common. Its habitats range from woodland
margins to wet moorland. The caterpillar is deep
reddish-brown with two rows of pale yellow
dashes along the back. Above each yellow dash is
a black patch surrounding a white spot. The
foodplants are low-growing herbaceous plants,
such as dock (*Rumex*), chickweed (*Stellaria*) and
groundsel (*Senecio*), and the foliage of sallow
(*Salix*) is also eaten. The full grown caterpillar
burrows below ground to pupate in a frail
earthen cocoon. There is one brood a year with
moths on the wing in March and April. They fly
at night and are strongly attracted to the
blossoms of sallow.

Beautiful Yellow Underwing *Anarta myrtilli*
Linnaeus, family Noctuidae. This attractive
little moth is extremely widespread in Europe,
occurring from the Arctic Circle to the
Mediterranean and is found at altitudes of up to
2000 metres in the Alps. In the British Isles it is
widespread and common in suitable areas but
does not occur in the Shetlands. Its habitats are
heathland, moorland, mountains and even sand
dunes where the foodplants grow. The superbly
camouflaged caterpillar is bright green with spots
and dashes of yellow and white. It feeds mainly
by day on the foliage of heather (*Calluna*) and
heath (*Erica*) and when full grown pupates on the

Bright-line Brown-eye *Lacanobia oleracea*

Broom Moth *Ceramica pisi*

Dot Moth *Melanchra persicariae* caterpillar

Dot Moth *Melanchra persicariae*

Gothic *Naenia typica*

ground in a cocoon of silk and leaf debris, often attached to a root or stone. In northern areas there is one brood a year with moths on the wing in June but, in the south, moths may be found from April until August and there are probably two broods. They fly in bright sunshine, resting on heather in dull weather, and feed on various heathland flowers.

Nutmeg *Discestra trifolii* Hufnagel, family Noctuidae. This is a widespread and common species not only occurring throughout western Europe from southern Fennoscandia to the Iberian Peninsula, but also in many parts of temperate Asia and North America. In the British Isles it is widely distributed but most common in south-eastern England and rare in Ireland. Its habitats are agricultural land and waste ground, generally on light sandy or gravelly soils and, in Britain, often in coastal regions and river valleys. The caterpillar is green or brown with two rows of black markings down the back and a white-edged pink stripe along each side. It feeds mainly on orache (*Atriplex*) and goosefoot (*Chenopodium*) but also on other plants such as knotgrass (*Polygonum*) and onion (*Allium cepa*). Pupation takes place below ground in a fragile cocoon. There is one brood a year in the north with moths on the wing in June and July but in southern regions the first brood appears in May and June and a second in August and September.

Cabbage Moth *Mamestra brassicae* Linnaeus, family Noctuidae. The range of this common moth extends throughout Europe and eastwards to India, Siberia and Japan. In the British Isles it is widespread and frequently abundant. It has a wide range of habitats but is most often encountered on agricultural land and in gardens,

where, as its name suggests, it is often a minor pest of cabbages (*Brassica oleracea*) and related crops. The caterpillar is brown or green with two lines of black dashes along the back and a broad line of pale brown or green along each side, bordered on its upperside with orange. It feeds on a wide range of herbaceous plants as well as those of the cabbage family and when full grown pupates below ground in a fragile cocoon. There is one brood a year but, due to different rates of development, moths may be found in almost any month of the year although they are most common in the summer.

Dot Moth *Melanchra persicariae* Linnaeus, family Noctuidae. This distinctive and appropriately named moth is widespread in Europe and ranges eastwards across temperate Asia. In the British Isles it is very common in the south, becoming less frequent further north, and is absent from most of Scotland. It has a wide range of habitats but is probably most often found in parks and gardens where the caterpillar feeds on cultivated plants. The caterpillar is very variable in colour and may be green, brown or purplish with a series of dark chevron-shaped markings along the back and a prominent hump near the tail. Foodplants include most low-growing plants and the foliage of trees and shrubs. Pupation takes place in a cocoon below ground. There is one brood a year but moths emerge over a long period and may be found from June until August. They fly at night and are attracted to flowers.

Bright-line Brown-eye *Lacanobia oleracea* Linnaeus, family Noctuidae. This is a common species in Europe ranging from central Fennoscandia to the Mediterranean and eastwards to temperate Asia. In the British Isles

it is widespread and frequently abundant, particularly in the south. Habitats range from gardens to open countryside. The caterpillar is very variable in colour and may be green, brown, pink or any shade between. It is covered with small white spots and has a yellow line along each side edged above with black. It feeds on a wide range of herbaceous plants but seems to show a preference for orache (*Atriplex*) and goosefoot (*Chenopodium*). It will also attack both the leaves and fruits of tomato (*Lycopersicon esculentum*) and is known to market gardeners as the Tomato Moth. Pupation takes place in an earthen cocoon below ground. There is one brood a year in the north and two in the south with moths on the wing from May until the autumn, according to locality. They fly at night and are attracted to flowers.

Broom Moth *Ceramica pisi* Linnaeus, family Noctuidae. This moth has a wide distribution occurring from Iceland to central Europe and ranging eastwards into temperate Asia. In the British Isles it is widespread although absent from the Shetlands. Its habitats range from woodlands to marshes and moorlands although it is most common in open situations. The caterpillar varies in colour from green to reddish- or purplish-brown and has broad yellow stripes down the back and sides. It feeds on a very wide range of herbaceous plants, deciduous trees and shrubs, and is often found on bracken (*Pteridium aquilinum*) where this is plentiful. Although feeding usually takes place at night, caterpillars may be found basking on the foliage by day. When full grown they burrow below ground and pupate in an earthen cocoon. There is one brood a year and moths are on the wing between May and July, according to locality. They fly at night and are attracted to flowers and honey dew.

Cerapteryx graminis

Panolis flammea

var.

Orthosia stabilis

var.

var.

Orthosia incerta

var.

var.

var.

Orthosia gothica

Lifesize

Pine Beauty *Panolis flammea* Denis & Schiffermüller, family Noctuidae. Widespread in Europe occurring from central Fennoscandia to the Iberian Peninsula and eastwards into temperate Asia. In Britain widespread and quite common although there are few records from Ireland. An insect of coniferous forests but will also establish itself in parks and gardens where suitable trees are grown. The caterpillar is green with a series of white stripes down the body, those along the sides being bordered below with orange. The head is chestnut brown. Foodplants are various species of *Pinus*, particularly Scots pine (*P. sylvestris*). Pupation takes place in a fragile cocoon in a crevice of the bark or amongst leaf litter on the ground. In continental Europe this species is sometimes a serious pest and in recent years major outbreaks have occurred in conifer plantations in northern Scotland. Moths are on the wing from March until May and are attracted to the blossoms of sallow (*Salix*) at night.

Common Quaker *Orthosia stabilis* Denis & Schiffermüller, family Noctuidae. This common moth is widespread from southern Scandinavia to southern Europe and eastwards into temperate Asia. In Britain it is widely distributed but most abundant in England, Wales and southern Scotland. It seems to prefer woodlands and woodland margins. The caterpillar is green, peppered with small yellowish-white dots and with pale yellow lines down the back and sides. There is a distinctive pale yellow cross-bar near the tail. The caterpillar feeds on the young foliage of many deciduous trees, particularly oak (*Quercus*) and sallow (*Salix*) and when full grown pupates below ground at the foot of the tree. There is one brood a year with moths usually on the wing from March until May although they will sometimes emerge in mid-winter if the weather is mild. They fly at night and are strongly attracted to the blossoms of sallow (*Salix*).

Clouded Drab *Orthosia incerta* Hufnagel, family Noctuidae. Common in many parts of Europe, occurring as far north as Scandinavia and ranging eastwards to central Asia. In Britain widespread and generally common. Habitats: woodlands, orchards, gardens. The caterpillar is pale bluish-green dotted with white and with a broad white line down the back and a narrower one along each side. It feeds on the foliage of oak (*Quercus*), willow (*Salix*) and other deciduous trees and shrubs. Pupation takes place below ground in an earthen cocoon. Single brooded; moths on the wing in March and April although occasionally they emerge in winter. They fly at night and are attracted to the blossoms of sallow (*Salix*) and sometimes to sap from damaged birch (*Betula*) trees.

Hebrew Character *Orthosia gothica* Linnaeus, family Noctuidae. This common moth occurs throughout Europe, even in northern Scandinavia within the Arctic Circle, and eastwards into Siberia. Widespread and generally common in Britain and one of four species to occur on St Kilda. Found almost everywhere and does not seem to have a preferred habitat. The caterpillar is green, finely dotted with white and slender yellow lines down the back and a broad white stripe along each side, bordered above with black. It feeds on the foliage of dock (*Rumex*), dandelion (*Taraxacum*) and a wide range of herbaceous plants, deciduous trees and shrubs. When full grown it pupates below ground in an earthen cocoon. There is one brood a year with moths on the wing in spring although some may emerge during winter. They fly at night and are attracted to the blossom of sallow (*Salix*).

Antler Moth *Cerapteryx graminis* Linnaeus, family Noctuidae. This distinctively marked moth occurs from Iceland and northern Fennoscandia to central Europe and eastwards into central Asia. Its habitats are fields, downland and moorland. The caterpillar is brown and rather glossy with yellowish-white lines down the back and sides. It feeds on various grasses, particularly the coarse types such as purple moor grass (*Molinia caerulea*), and will also eat rushes (*Scirpus* and *Juncus*). Sometimes huge populations build up and devastate whole tracts of upland grassland. Pupation takes place on the ground amongst grass roots. One brood a year with moths on the wing from July until September, according to locality. They fly at night but are also active by day and visit various flowers such as those of thistle (*Cirsium* and *Carduus*).

Antler Moth *Cerapteryx graminis*

Pine Beauty *Panolis flammea* caterpillar

Common Quaker *Orthosia stabilis*

Hebrew Character *Orthosia gothica* at rest

Hebrew Character *Orthosia gothica* caterpillar

Clouded Drab *Orthosia incerta* at rest

161

Mythimna pallens

var.

Cucullia absinthii

Cucullia umbratica

♂

♀

Cucullia verbasci

Brachionycha sphinx

Lifesize

Wormwood *Cucullia absinthii* Linnaeus, family Noctuidae. This moth occurs widely throughout central Europe and its range extends eastwards into temperate Asia. In the British Isles it is mainly confined to England and Wales although there are a few records from Ireland. Its habitats are coastal regions and other places where the foodplant is established. The caterpillar is greyish-brown with patches of olive green along the back and it is wonderfully camouflaged when on the foodplant. It feeds on the flowers and seeds of wormwood (*Artemisia absinthium*) and sometimes of other *Artemisia* species. The full grown caterpillar constructs a very tough cocoon of silk and earth on the ground in which it pupates. There is one brood a year and moths are on the wing in July.

Shark *Cucullia umbratica* Linnaeus, family Noctuidae. This is a common and widespread moth in Europe which also occurs in North Africa, Asia Minor and central Asia. In the British Isles it is widespread but is most common in southern England. Its habitats are waste ground, gardens and other places where the foodplants grow. The caterpillar is pale greyish-brown with black spots and a black head. It feeds on the foliage and flowers of sow thistle (*Sonchus*) and lettuce (*Lactuca*) and when full grown pupates in a loose, hammock-shaped cocoon spun on the foodplant. There is one brood a year and moths may be found from May until July according to locality. They fly at night and are attracted to flowers, particularly those of honeysuckle (*Lonicera*), sweet william (*Dianthus barbatus*) and thistle (*Carduus*). When at rest on fences or rough wooden posts they are well camouflaged.

Mullein *Cucullia verbasci* Linnaeus, family Noctuidae. The distribution of this moth extends from southern Scandinavia to southern Europe, North Africa and Asia Minor. In the British Isles it is mainly confined to England and Wales although there are a few records from Ireland. Its habitats are open ground and gardens where the foodplants grow. The distinctive caterpillar is pale bluish-green, sometimes almost white, patterned with black spots and yellow bands. It feeds on mullein (*Verbascum*), figwort (*Scrophularia*) and sometimes *Buddleia*. It is most conspicuous on its foodplant but is probably distasteful to many birds. The full grown caterpillar burrows below ground and pupates in a large, tough cocoon of silk and earth. There is one brood a year and moths are on the wing in April and May. Although the caterpillar is often encountered, moths are seldom seen, partly because they are nocturnal and very well camouflaged, resembling small dead sticks when at rest.

Sprawler *Brachionycha sphinx* Hufnagel, family Noctuidae. This moth is common in parts of central Europe and its distribution extends eastwards into western Asia. In the British Isles, however, it is mainly confined to England where it occurs locally in most counties but is scarce in the north. It is also found in Ireland but very rarely. Its habitat is deciduous woodland. The caterpillar is yellowish-green with three white lines down the back and a yellow line along each side. It rests in a characteristic position with its head and thorax reared up and when disturbed falls to the ground with its legs spread wide apart, thus giving rise to the name 'Sprawler'. It feeds on the foliage of oak (*Quercus*), beech (*Fagus*) and other deciduous trees and when full grown pupates below ground. There is one brood a year with moths on the wing from October until December. It rests by day on fences or tree trunks and is very well camouflaged.

Common Wainscot *Mythimna pallens* Linnaeus, family Noctuidae. This widely distributed species is found in many parts of Europe and temperate Asia and also occurs in North America. In the British Isles it is widespread and frequently common except in northern Scotland where it is more local in occurrence. Its habitats are marshes, damp meadows and other places where the foodplants thrive. The caterpillar is pale brown with white lines along the body and a darker brown band along each side. It feeds at night on various grasses, such as cock's-foot (*Dactylis*) and meadow-grass (*Poa*), hiding amongst the roots by day. When full grown it pupates in an earthen cocoon below ground. There are two broods a year in the south with moths on the wing in July and again in September but in northern regions there is only one brood which appears in late July. They fly at night and are attracted to flowering grasses.

Mullein *Cucullia verbasci* at rest

Wormwood Shark *Cucullia absinthii*

Common Wainscot *Mythimna pallens*

Sprawler *Brachionycha sphinx* at rest

Red Sword-grass *Xylena vetusta* caterpillar

var.

Xylena vetusta

♂

♀

Xylena exsoleta

var.

Allophyes oxyacanthae

Eupsilia transversa   var.

Lifesize

Red Swordgrass *Xylena vetusta* Hübner, family
Noctuidae. This moth is widespread in Europe
and is found from Lapland to the Iberian
Peninsula and eastwards to Siberia. In the British
Isles it is generally more common in the north
than the south but is nevertheless widely
distributed. Its habitats are damp, open
countryside, bogs, moorland and mountains up
to 1000 metres. The caterpillar is green or brown
with three white or yellow lines down the back
and a broad orange or yellow stripe along the side
edged above with black. It feeds on the foliage of
dock (*Rumex*), knotgrass (*Polygonum*) and other
herbaceous plants but in Scotland is most
frequently found on bog myrtle (*Myrica gale*).
Pupation takes place within a cocoon of silk and
earth on the ground. Moths are on the wing in
September and October and again in the
following March and April after hibernation.
They fly at night and are attracted to the blossom
of ivy (*Hedera*).

Sword-grass *Xylena exsoleta* Linnaeus, family
Noctuidae. This moth is widespread in Europe
except for the extreme north and its range
extends to Asia Minor and eastwards across
Siberia to Japan. In the British Isles it is widely
distributed but most common in Scotland and
northern England. Its habitats range from
agricultural land to fens and moorland. The
striking caterpillar is green with yellow lines
along the back between which are white spots
ringed with black. Along each side is a broad
white band edged above with bright red. It feeds
on restharrow (*Ononis*), thistle (*Carduus*), dock
(*Rumex*) and many other low-growing plants as
well as the foliage of some deciduous trees.
Pupation takes place below ground in an earthen
cocoon. Moths emerge in the autumn and are
often attracted to ivy (*Hedera*) blossom at night.
After hibernation through the winter they
reappear in the spring and are then found feeding
at sallow (*Salix*) blossom.

Green-brindled Crescent *Allophyes oxyacanthae*
Linnaeus, family Noctuidae. This beautiful
moth is widespread in Europe occurring from
Scandinavia to the Mediterranean. In the British
Isles, where it was known by early entomologists
as 'Ealing's Glory', it is widely distributed
although absent from northern Scotland. Its
habitats are hedgerows and woodland. The
caterpillar is purplish-brown patterned with a
fine network of black lines and has two small
pointed projections on the back near the tail. It
feeds on the foliage of hawthorn (*Crataegus*),
blackthorn (*Prunus*) and apple (*Malus*) and when
full grown pupates in a cocoon on the ground.
There is one generation a year and moths are on
the wing in September. They fly at night and are
attracted to the blossom of ivy (*Hedera*) and
sometimes to overripe fruits of blackberry
(*Rubus*).

Sword-grass *Xylena exsoleta* at rest

Satellite *Eupsilia transversa* caterpillar

Green-brindled Crescent caterpillar

Satellite *Eupsilia transversa*

Satellite *Eupsilia transversa* Hufnagel, family Noctuidae. This common moth is widely distributed in Europe and ranges eastwards into Siberia. In the British Isles it is widespread and found almost everywhere. It is mainly an insect of deciduous woodlands but may be found wherever suitable trees are growing. The caterpillar is velvety-black with fine white lines down the back and a few white patches along the sides, mainly near to the head. It feeds on the foliage of various trees, such as oak (*Quercus*), beech (*Fagus*) and elm (*Ulmus*), but will also feed on low-growing herbaceous plants. It is also known to attack and eat other caterpillars, including those of its own species. When full grown it pupates in an earthen cocoon below ground. There is one brood a year and moths may be found from September until as late as November in mild seasons. They fly at night and are attracted to ivy (*Hedera*) blossom and to the rotting fruits of blackberry (*Rubus*) and apple (*Malus*).

Green-brindled Crescent *Allophyes oxyacanthae* at rest

var.

var.

Conistra vaccinii

var.

Acronicta megacephala

Acronicta aceris

Acronicta leporina

Acronicta alni

Acronicta tridens

Acronicta psi

Lifesize

Miller *Acronicta leporina* caterpillar

Poplar Grey *Acronicta megacephala*

greyish-brown with black markings and red spots on the back. Towards the tail is a distinctive white marking. When at rest on leaves it often bends itself into a characteristic 'U' shape. As its common name suggests, it feeds chiefly on various species of poplar (*Populus*) but will also eat the foliage of willow (*Salix*). When full grown it constructs a cocoon of silk and wood fragments in a crevice of the bark and pupates within. There is one brood a year with moths usually on the wing from May until August. They often fly around poplar trees at dusk.

Sycamore *Acronicta aceris* Linnaeus, family Noctuidae. This common moth is widespread throughout Europe and its range extends eastwards into temperate Asia. In the British Isles it is mainly confined to the southern half of England although it also occurs in several localities in Ireland. Its habitats are woodlands, parks and tree-lined streets. The distinctive caterpillar is covered with dense tufts of long yellow hairs with additional tufts of bright red or orange hairs on the back. Down the middle of the back is a line of white diamond-shaped markings ringed with black. As its name suggests, one of the main foodplants is sycamore (*Acer*), but the foliage of other deciduous trees, such as oak (*Quercus*) and horse-chestnut (*Aesculus*), is also eaten. Pupation takes place in a cocoon spun on or under the bark. Moths are on the wing in June and July. They fly at night but may be found resting on tree trunks during the day.

Miller *Acronicta leporina* Linnaeus, family Noctuidae. This species is common in many parts of northern and central Europe, its range extending eastwards into Siberia. In the British Isles it is widespread but rather local in occurrence and most frequently found in south-eastern England. Its habitats are woodlands, heaths and wet moorland. The remarkable caterpillar is pale green or yellow, clothed with long, silky-white or yellow hairs which are swept forward over the head and backwards over the tail. It feeds on the foliage of birch (*Betula*), alder (*Alnus*) and occasionally oak (*Quercus*) or poplar (*Populus*). When full grown it pupates in a crevice of the bark or in a depression hollowed out in dead wood and covered with silk and body hairs. One brood a year; moths on the wing in May and June. They fly at night and rest by day on tree trunks or undergrowth.

Chestnut *Conistra vaccinii* Linnaeus, family Noctuidae. This widespread moth occurs from northern Europe southwards to northern Italy and eastwards across temperate Asia to Japan. In the British Isles it is very widely distributed and usually common. Its habitat is deciduous woodland. The caterpillar is reddish-brown, sometimes tinged with green and has three pale brown lines down the back. It feeds on the foliage of various trees, such as oak (*Quercus*), elm (*Ulmus*) and willow (*Salix*), and will also eat low-growing plants such as dock (*Rumex*). It often conceals itself between two touching leaves. When full grown it pupates in a thick silken cocoon below ground at the roots of the foodplant. One brood a year but moths are seen both in October and March after hibernation. In autumn they feed at ivy (*Hedera*) blossom and rotting fruits, in the spring they are attracted to catkins of sallow (*Salix*).

Poplar Grey *Acronicta megacephala* Denis & Schiffermüller, family Noctuidae. This moth is common and widespread throughout Europe, except in the extreme north, and its range extends into Asia Minor and parts of Siberia. In the British Isles it is widespread but more frequently found in the south. Its habitats are woodlands, parks and gardens. The caterpillar is

Miller *Acronicta leporina* at rest

Sycamore *Acronicta aceris* caterpillar

Alder Moth *Acronicta alni* caterpillar

Alder Moth *Acronicta alni*

Grey Dagger *Acronicta psi* caterpillar

Alder Moth *Acronicta alni* Linnaeus, family Noctuidae. This is a widespread moth in Europe, its range extending eastwards into central Asia. In the British Isles it is widely distributed but rather local in occurrence and is most frequently found in parts of southern England. Its habitat is deciduous woodland. The striking caterpillar is black with a series of bright yellow patches down the back and a line of long, black paddle-shaped hairs along each side. In its earlier instars it is grey with a white patch on the back and when at rest, curled up on a leaf, the caterpillar strongly resembles a bird dropping. The foodplants are oak (*Quercus*), alder (*Alnus*), blackthorn (*Prunus*) and many other deciduous trees and shrubs. Pupation takes place in a shelter excavated in rotten wood. There is one brood a year and moths may be found in May and June. This retiring species is not usually attracted to sugar or to ordinary light and, until the invention of the mercury vapour light trap, was considered to be a rarity.

Dark Dagger *Acronicta tridens* Denis & Schiffermüller, family Noctuidae. This moth is common and widespread in Europe and ranges

eastwards to Siberia. In the British Isles it is widely distributed in England and Wales but rare in Scotland and Ireland. Its habitats are wooded country where the foodplants grow. The caterpillar is black with a broad orange and white stripe down the back and a line of red markings along each side. There is a prominent black hump on the back towards the head. It feeds on the foliage of many deciduous trees and shrubs, including hawthorn (*Crataegus*), blackthorn (*Prunus*) and wild apple (*Malus*). Pupation takes place in a silken cocoon spun in a crevice of the bark. There is one brood a year in Britain with moths on the wing in June but further south there may be a second brood in autumn. Contrary to its common name this moth is generally paler than its close relative, the Grey Dagger from which it is almost indistinguishable except on internal characteristics. It is said that the Dark Dagger is smoother and more oily in appearance.

Grey Dagger *Acronicta psi* Linnaeus, family Noctuidae. This species is widespread and often common in lowland Europe and also occurs in North Africa and temperate Asia. In the British

Isles it is widely distributed and found commonly in England and Wales. Its habitats are woodlands, hedgerows, orchards, parks and gardens. The distinctive caterpillar is dark grey to bluish-black with a broad yellow stripe down the back. Along each side is a line of red spots and below this is a broad band of white. Behind the head there is a slender black projection in the middle of the back which is sometimes tipped with red. Foodplants include various deciduous trees and shrubs such as hawthorn (*Crataegus*), birch (*Betula*), plum (*Prunus*) and apple (*Malus*). The full grown caterpillar pupates in a crevice of the bark. One brood a year; moths on the wing in June. This moth is similar to the Dark Dagger but its caterpillar is very different.

167

Acronicta rumicis

var.

Cryphia domestica

var.

Amphipyra pyramidea

Dypterygia scabriuscula

Mormo maura

Thalpophila matura

Euplexia lucipara

Lifesize

Knot Grass *Acronicta rumicis* Linnaeus, family Noctuidae. This is a common and widespread species throughout most of Europe and also occurs in North Africa and temperate Asia. In the British Isles it is found almost everywhere. Its habitats range from woodlands to moorlands and mountainsides up to 1000 metres. The hairy caterpillar is dark purplish-brown with a row of red spots surrounded by black down the back, on either side of which is a line of large white spots. Lower down on each side is a white line dotted with red. It feeds on the foliage of many low-growing plants, including knotgrass (*Polygonum*) and heather (*Calluna*), and also on trees and shrubs such as hawthorn (*Crataegus*) and bramble (*Rubus*). Pupation takes place in a silken cocoon spun at the base of the foodplant. There is one brood a year and moths are on the wing from June until September, according to locality and climate.

Marbled Beauty *Cryphia domestica* Hufnagel, family Noctuidae. This widely distributed little moth occurs throughout Europe from southern Scandinavia to northern Italy and ranges eastwards into temperate Asia. In the British Isles it is widely distributed and often common although it appears to be absent from northern Scotland. Its habitat is open countryside where lichens grow freely. The caterpillar is a slate-coloured, bluish-grey with a broad orange-yellow band along the back spotted with black. It feeds in the early morning on various lichens and hides for the rest of the day within a shelter spun from silk mixed with fragments of lichen and moss. Pupation takes place within a similar shelter. There is one brood a year with moths on the wing in July and August. They fly at night and are sometimes attracted to the flowers of red valerian (*Centranthus ruber*). When at rest on lichen-encrusted walls or tree trunks they are very well camouflaged.

Copper Underwing *Amphipyra pyramidea* Linnaeus, family Noctuidae. The exact distribution of this moth is not yet known due to confusion with the closely related Svensson's Copper Underwing, *Amphipyra berbera* Rungs, which was only recently recognised as occurring in the British Isles. The Copper Underwing is apparently widespread in Europe and also in the British Isles where it is more common in the south and absent from Scotland. Its habitats are woodlands, parks and wooded countryside. The caterpillar is green dotted with white and with white lines along the back and sides. Near the tail is a pyramidal hump which is usually tipped with yellow. It feeds on the foliage of oak (*Quercus*), birch (*Betula*), sallow (*Salix*) and other deciduous trees and shrubs. Pupation takes place in an earthen cocoon on the ground. Moths are on the wing in July and August. The Copper Underwing may usually be recognised by its bright colours and more distinct markings, whereas Svensson's Copper Underwing is duller and the caterpillar has a red-tipped hump.

Old Lady *Mormo maura* Linnaeus, family Noctuidae. This large and distinctive moth is widely distributed in central and southern Europe. In the British Isles it is widespread and locally common except in the extreme north of Scotland. Its habitats are open woodland, hedgerows and gardens. The caterpillar is brown with a darker diamond-shaped pattern on the back and a white line along each side above which is a series of oblique white streaks. It may be distinguished from similar caterpillars by its orange spiracles. It feeds on low-growing plants, such as dock (*Rumex*) and chickweed (*Stellaria*) in the autumn, but after hibernation it eats the newly developed spring foliage of sallow (*Salix*) and hawthorn (*Crataegus*) and other trees and

Copper Underwing *Amphipyra pyramidea* caterpillar

Straw Underwing *Thalpophila matura* at rest

Marbled Beauty *Cryphia domestica*

Copper Underwing *Amphipyra pyramidea* at rest

Small Angle Shades *Euplexia lucipara* caterpillar

shrubs. Pupation takes place underground. There is one generation a year and moths are on the wing in July and August. They hide themselves away in hollow trees, caves and wooden outbuildings by day and are sometimes even found in houses.

Bird's Wing *Dypterygia scabriuscula* Linnaeus, family Noctuidae. This moth, so called because of the distinctive pattern of its forewings, is common in many parts of Europe and ranges eastwards into temperate Asia. In the British Isles it is most common in southern and eastern England, becoming scarce further north and in Scotland. Its habitats are woodlands and wooded countryside. The caterpillar is reddish-brown dotted with yellow and black. Along the back is a black-edged white line flanked on either side by a black line. Foodplants are dock, sorrel (*Rumex*), knotgrass (*Polygonum*) and related species. The full grown caterpillar pupates within a silken cocoon on the surface of the ground. Usually one

brood a year in Britain with moths seen in May and June but in favourable seasons a second generation may appear in the autumn.

Straw Underwing *Thalpophila matura* Hufnagel, family Noctuidae. This is a widespread and common moth in central and southern Europe, ranging eastwards into temperate Asia. In the British Isles it is widely distributed but does not occur in northern Scotland. Its habitats are open grassland, chalk downland and any dry and stony places where the foodplants grow. The caterpillar is yellowish- or reddish-brown with a line of blackish-brown markings on the back, flanked either side by a brown line. It feeds on meadow grass (*Poa*), mat grass (*Nardus*) and other grasses which flourish in dry situations. Pupation takes place underground. There is one brood a year with moths on the wing in July and August. They hide amongst grass and herbage by day, but fly at night and are sometimes attracted to sap oozing from wounded trees.

Small Angle Shades *Euplexia lucipara* Linnaeus, family Noctuidae. This widely distributed moth occurs in many parts of Europe, temperate Asia and North America. In the British Isles it is widespread but most common in the south. Its habitats are open woodlands, wooded countryside and gardens. The caterpillar is green or reddish-brown with a series of dark V-shaped markings on the back and a white line along each side. It feeds on the foliage of birch (*Betula*), sallow (*Salix*) and various low-growing plants but is particularly noted for feeding on bracken (*Pteris*) and other ferns, sometimes to the extent of becoming a garden pest. Pupation takes place just below the soil surface. One generation a year; moths are usually on the wing in June and July although a few are sometimes found in the autumn. They fly at night, sometimes attracted to the flowers of privet (*Ligustrum*) or to honey dew.

Phlogophora meticulosa

var.

var.

Cosmia trapezina

var.

var.

Apamea monoglypha

var.

♂

♀

Hydraecia micacea

♂

♀

Gortyna flavago

Lifesize

Dun-bar *Cosmia trapezina*

Angle Shades *Phlogophora meticulosa*

Angle Shades *Phlogophora meticulosa* Linnaeus, family Noctuidae. This is a common and widespread moth in Europe ranging from southern Scandinavia to the Mediterranean and also occurring in North Africa and Asia Minor. In the British Isles it is widely distributed and found almost everywhere. Its habitats are hedgerows, agricultural land, waste ground, gardens and other places where suitable foodplants grow. The caterpillar is green or brown with a line of small white dashes down the middle of the back and a series of chevron-shaped dark markings. It feeds on a wide range of low-growing herbaceous plants and shrubs and is sometimes a pest of cultivated plants in greenhouses and gardens. Pupation takes place on the ground in a fragile cocoon. Individuals of this species appear to develop at different rates and to occur in overlapping broods so that both caterpillars and moths may be found at any time of year. Moths fly at night and are attracted to various flowers according to the season. When at rest they often resemble dead, crumpled leaves.

Dun-bar *Cosmia trapezina* Linnaeus, family Noctuidae. This species is widely distributed in Europe, ranging from southern Scandinavia to the Mediterranean, and also occurs in North Africa and Asia Minor. In the British Isles it is

Dark Arches *Apamea monoglypha*

Frosted Orange *Gortyna flavago*

Rosy Rustic *Hydraecia micacea*

widespread but is less common in northern parts of Scotland. Its habitats are woodland rides and clearings and open wooded countryside. The caterpillar is green with black-centred white spots, three narrow, yellow lines down the back and a broad yellow band along each side. It feeds on the foliage of oak (*Quercus*), sallow (*Salix*), birch (*Betula*) and other deciduous trees but will also attack and eat other caterpillars, including those of its own species. The caterpillars of the Winter Moth often form a major part of its diet. Pupation takes place in a silken cocoon on or beneath the ground. There is one brood a year with moths on the wing in July and August. They fly at night and are sometimes attracted to the flowers of ragwort (*Senecio*).

Dark Arches *Apamea monoglypha* Hufnagel, family Noctuidae. This very common moth is widespread throughout Europe and also occurs in Asia Minor and Siberia. In the British Isles it is found almost everywhere and is often abundant. Its habitats are open grassland, agricultural land and anywhere where suitable foodplants are to be found. The plump caterpillar is greyish-white, sometimes tinged with red or brown, with

shining black spots and head. Its foodplants are various grasses such as meadow grass (*Poa*), couch (*Agropyron*) and cock's-foot (*Dactylis*). It hides by day amongst the grass roots and comes out at night to feed at the base of the stems. Pupation takes place below the surface of the ground. There is one brood a year with moths on the wing throughout the summer and sometimes also in autumn. They fly at night and are attracted to flowers such as those of red valerian (*Centranthus ruber*).

Rosy Rustic *Hydraecia micacea* Esper, family Noctuidae. This common moth has a very wide distribution extending throughout Europe eastwards to Siberia, China and Japan and it also occurs in North America. In the British Isles it is widely distributed and particularly common in coastal districts. Its habitats are open countryside, agricultural land, gardens and other places where the foodplants grow. The caterpillar is greyish-pink with black spots and has a dark line down the back. It feeds on dock (*Rumex*) and plantain (*Plantago*) and is sometimes a pest of potato (*Solanum tuberosum*), tomato (*Lycopersicon esculentum*) and other

cultivated plants, feeding in the stems and boring down into the roots. Pupation takes place underground. There is one brood a year and moths are on the wing in the autumn. They fly at night and are sometimes attracted to the flowers of ragwort (*Senecio*).

Frosted Orange *Gortyna flavago* Denis & Schiffermüller, family Noctuidae. This widely distributed species is found in Europe from southern Scandinavia to the Mediterranean and also occurs in North Africa, central Asia and Japan. In the British Isles it is widespread and often common. Its habitats are agricultural land, waste ground and open countryside, particularly damp and marshy ground where the foodplants flourish. The caterpillar is yellowish-pink with large black spots and a brown head. It feeds within the stems of thistle (*Cirsium* and *Carduus*), burdock (*Arctium*) and other plants and sometimes causes damage to potato (*Solanum tuberosum*) and tomato (*Lycopersicon esculentum*) plants. When full grown it pupates in the hollowed-out stem of the foodplant near to the ground. There is one brood a year and moths may be found from August until October.

Helicoverpa armigera

var.

Pseudoips fagana

♂   ♀

Colocasia coryli

var.

Diachrysia chrysitis

Diachrysia chryson

Polychrysia moneta

Autographa gamma

Lifesize

Green Silver-lines *Pseudoips fagana* caterpillar

Burnished Brass *Diachrysia chrysitis*

Scarce Bordered Straw caterpillar

Scarce Bordered Straw *Helicoverpa armigera* Hübner, family Noctuidae. This important pest moth has an extremely wide distribution extending from southern and central parts of Europe to Africa, Asia and Australasia. It is a scarce migrant to Scandinavia and the British Isles although live caterpillars are sometimes imported with fruit and vegetables. The caterpillar is very variable and may be green, brown or purplish with a series of fine pale lines on the back and a pale stripe along each side. It feeds on a wide range of plants and in southern Europe is a pest of tomato (*Lycopersicon esculentum*) and related plants. The caterpillar is know in various parts of the world as the tomatoworm, the bollworm or the corn earworm. Moths are usually found in Europe in the summer and autumn, but imported caterpillars may be found at almost any time of year depending on their country of origin.

Green Silver-lines *Pseudoips fagana* Fabricius, family Noctuidae. This distinctive little moth is common in northern, central and parts of southern Europe and ranges eastwards into Siberia. In the British Isles it is widespread but probably more common in the south. Its habitats are woodlands and hedgerows. The plump caterpillar is spotted and lined with white and has a small red stripe on each of the rear claspers. It feeds on the foliage of oak (*Quercus*), beech (*Fagus*), birch (*Betula*) and hazel (*Corylus*). When full grown it spins a papery, boat-shaped cocoon on the underside of a leaf, in a crevice of the bark or amongst leaf litter, within which it pupates. There is one brood a year and moths are on the wing in June and July. They fly at night and are supposed to be able to produce a high-pitched squeaking noise. During the day they may often be found resting on fronds of bracken.

Nut-tree Tussock *Colocasia coryli* Linnaeus, family Noctuidae. This moth occurs in many parts of northern and central Europe and ranges eastwards into temperate western Asia. In the British Isles it is widespread and sometimes quite common. Its habitats are hedgerows, open woodland and hillsides where bushes of the

Silver Y *Autographa gamma*　　　　　　　　　**Green Silver-lines** *Pseudoips fagana*

foodplant grow. The hairy caterpillar is reddish- or yellowish-brown with a broken black stripe down the back and tufts of hair behind the head which are sometimes bright red. It feeds on the foliage of hazel (*Corylus*), hawthorn (*Crataegus*), birch (*Betula*) and some other deciduous trees and shrubs. When full grown it pupates in a loosely woven silken cocoon constructed in a folded leaf. There are two generations a year and moths are on the wing in May and June and again in August and September. They fly at night but may be found resting on tree tunks and branches by day.

Burnished Brass *Diachrysia chrysitis* Linnaeus, family Noctuidae. This beautiful moth is widespread in Europe and ranges eastwards into temperate Asia. In the British Isles it is widely distributed and common although it does not occur in the Orkneys and Shetlands. Its habitats are hedgerows, meadows, wasteland and gardens. The caterpillar is pale green with a dark green line down the back and oblique dark lines along each side. It feeds on the foliage of stinging nettle (*Urtica dioica*) and other related plants, hibernating through the winter and completing its growth in the following spring. Pupation takes place in a white silken cocoon spun amongst the leaves. There is one brood a year and moths are on the wing from June until autumn. Although most active at night, when they visit many wild and garden flowers, they also fly by day and may be found basking in the sun.

Scarce Burnished Brass *Diachrysia chryson* Hübner, family Noctuidae. Although widespread in Europe from northern Germany to southern France and ranging eastwards into temperate Asia, this moth, as its name suggests, tends to be local and rather scarce. In the British Isles it is mainly restricted to southern and eastern parts of England. Its habitats are damp hedgerows and ditches, particularly in fenland. The caterpillar is green with a darker line down the middle of the back and a dark green line along each side above which is a row of oblique white stripes. It feeds on hemp-agrimony (*Eupatorium cannabinum*) but in captivity is said to eat the leaves of mint (*Mentha*). After hibernating through the winter, the caterpillar completes its growth in spring and pupates on the foodplant. Moths are on the wing in July and August, sometimes by day but more usually at night.

Golden Plusia *Polychrysia moneta* Fabricius, family Noctuidae. This moth is widespread in Europe from Fennoscandia to Spain and ranges eastwards into temperate Asia. In the British Isles it is a relative newcomer, first recorded in 1890, but is now established and widespread in England, Wales and much of Scotland. There are also local records from Ireland. Habitats are hedgerows, parks and gardens. The caterpillar is green dotted with white and with a dark green line down the back and a dark-bordered white line along each side. It feeds on *Delphinium*, monkshood (*Aconitum*) and globe-flower

(*Trollius*) in Britain but in continental Europe has a wider range of foodplants. Pupation takes place within a white or golden yellow silken cocoon spun on the underside of a leaf. There is usually one brood a year in Britain with moths on the wing in June and July although a second generation sometimes appears in August and September. They fly at night and are attracted to the blossoms of many garden flowers.

Silver Y *Autographa gamma* Linnaeus, family Noctuidae. This is a widespread moth, occurring in Europe, North Africa and much of temperate Asia. It is a regular migrant and is found as far north as Lapland. In the British Isles migrants arrive each spring and produce a second generation in the autumn although these do not normally survive the winter. Habitats are agricultural land, waste ground, gardens and open countryside. The caterpillar is pale yellowish-green or dark olive green with wavy white lines down the back and a white stripe along each side. The head is green with a black stripe on each side. The caterpillar feeds on a wide range of low-growing plants and is sometimes a pest of peas (*Pisum sativum*), lettuce (*Lactuca sativa*) and other crops. Pupation takes place in a white silken cocoon spun under the leaves. There are two broods a year in most parts of Europe and may be found from May until November, according to locality. They fly both by day and at night and are attracted to a wide range of flowering plants.

Autographa jota

Autographa pulchrina

Abrostola trigemina

Catocala fraxini

Catocala nupta

Beautiful Golden Y *Autographa pulchrina* Haworth, family Noctuidae. Widespread in northern, central and southern Europe. In Britain it is widespread but appears to be less common in southern England. Its habitats are hedgerows, woodland rides and clearings and gardens. The caterpillar is green with a broad white stripe down the back flanked by fine white lines and a yellowish-white stripe low down on each side. It feeds on a wide range of low-growing herbaceous plants, such as dead-nettle (*Lamium*) and nettle (*Urtica*), and will also eat the foliage of honeysuckle (*Lonicera*) and bilberry (*Vaccinium*). After hibernating through the winter, the caterpillar completes its growth in spring and pupates in a large, flimsy white cocoon spun on the foliage. There is one brood a year and moths may be found in June and July. They fly at dusk and are attracted to various flowers such as those of *Lychnis* and honeysuckle.

Plain Golden Y *Autographa jota* Linnaeus, family Noctuidae. Widely distributed throughout Europe and ranges eastwards into Siberia. In the British Isles it is widespread. Habitats are hedgerows, waste ground and gardens. The caterpillar is yellowish-green dotted with white and with fine, wavy white lines down the back and a thin, pale yellow line along each side. It feeds on stinging nettle (*Urtica dioica*), dead nettles (*Lamium*), groundsel (*Senecio*) and other low-growing plants, as well as the foliage of hawthorn (*Crataegus*) and honeysuckle (*Lonicera*). Hibernation takes place while the caterpillar is quite small and it completes its growth next spring, pupating in a semi-transparent cocoon spun on the foodplant. Moths are on the wing from May until July. They fly at dusk and are attracted to flowers of nettles, honeysuckle and *Lychnis*. Usually distinguished from the closely related Beautiful Golden Y by its less mottled appearance and the thinner Y marking on the forewing.

Dark Spectacle *Abrostola trigemina* Werneburg, family Noctuidae. Widely distributed, occurring throughout Europe and eastwards to eastern Siberia. In Britain it is widespread, although less common in the north. Its habitats are waste ground, agricultural land and gardens. The caterpillar is green speckled with white and has a series of dark wedge-shaped markings down the back. Feeds on hop (*Humulus lupulus*) and stinging nettle (*Urtica dioica*) and when full grown pupates in a silken cocoon spun amongst dead leaves on the ground. Moths are on the wing from June until September. They fly at night and are attracted to the flowers of such plants as red valerian (*Centranthus ruber*), *Lychnis* and campion (*Silene*). Moths may sometimes be seen during the day, resting on fences, although they usually hide amongst vegetation.

Clifden Nonpareil *Catocala fraxini* Linnaeus, family Noctuidae. This large and beautiful moth is widespread in central and northern Europe, occurring in Fennoscandia as far north as the Arctic Circle. It seems that it has extended its range northwards in recent times and at one stage a breeding colony was established in south-eastern England. This now appears to be extinct but occasional specimens have been recorded from many parts of the British Isles, including Orkney, although these have almost certainly migrated from continental Europe. Its habitat is open woodland. The caterpillar is grey mottled with dark brown and is very long and well camouflaged when at rest stretched out on a branch or twig. Its foodplants are ash (*Fraxinus*), poplar and aspen (*Populus*). It pupates in a loose silken cocoon spun amongst dead leaves on the ground. There is one brood a year and moths are on the wing in July and August.

Lifesize

Beautiful Golden Y *Autographa pulchrina*

Plain Golden Y *Autographa jota*

Plain Golden Y *Autographa jota* caterpillar

Red Underwing *Catocala nupta* Linnaeus, family Noctuidae. This large and attractive species is common and widespread throughout most of Europe as far north as southern Scandinavia and ranges eastwards into temperate Asia. In the British Isles it is widely distributed in southern and eastern England but becomes scarcer further north and west and is apparently absent from Ireland, Scotland and northern England. Its habitats are open woodland, hedgerows, parks and gardens. The long caterpillar is grey marked with reddish-brown and has two slight humps on its back, one near the middle of the body, the other near the tail. It feeds by night on the foliage of willow (*Salix*) and poplar (*Populus*) and hides in crevices of the bark by day when it is extremely difficult to find. Pupation takes place in a cocoon spun between dead leaves or under bark. Moths are on the wing in August and September, flying at night, and are sometimes attracted to sap oozing from damaged trees.

Red Underwing *Catocala nupta* at rest

175

Callistege mi

Euclidia glyphica

Scoliopteryx libatrix

Hypena proboscidalis

♂   ♀

Herminia tarsipennalis

Lifesize

Burnet Companion *Euclidia glyphica* Linnaeus, family Noctuidae. This widespread and common little moth is found throughout Europe and also ranges eastwards into Siberia. In the British Isles it is widespread and sometimes abundant in southern localities. Its habitats are hedgerows, wet meadows, woodland margins and downland. The caterpillar is similar to that of the Mother Shipton but has four pairs of claspers instead of three. It feeds on the foliage of various species of clover (*Trifolium*) and when full grown pupates in a cocoon of silk and plant debris spun on the ground. There is one brood a year and moths are on the wing in May and June. They fly in bright sunshine but as soon as the weather becomes cool they remain quiescent, resting on trefoils and other vegetation. They are sometimes attracted to flowers.

Herald *Scoliopteryx libatrix* Linnaeus, family Noctuidae. This widespread moth occurs throughout Europe as far north as Lapland and ranges eastwards across temperate Asia to Japan. It also occurs in North Africa and North America. In the British Isles it is widely distributed and often common. Its habitats are open countryside, parks and gardens. The long slender caterpillar is green with a yellow line along each side. It feeds on the foliage of sallow, willow (*Salix*) and poplar (*Populus*) and when full grown pupates in a white silken cocoon spun amongst the foliage. There is one brood a year and moths are on the wing from August until October and again in spring. Hibernation usually takes place in buildings and moths may be found during the winter in barns, sheds, church towers and similar places. Moths fly at night and are often attracted to ivy blossom and ripe blackberries in the autumn and sometimes to sallow catkins in the spring.

Snout *Hypena proboscidalis* Linnaeus, family Noctuidae. This is a widespread moth in Europe, occurring even in the extreme north of Scandinavia, and ranging eastwards into temperate Asia. In the British Isles it is widely distributed and sometimes very common. Its habitats are hedgerows, ditches, waste ground and other places where the foodplant grows. The slender green caterpillar has a dark line down the back and a number of raised dots scattered over the body, each bearing a short black hair. It feeds on the foliage of stinging nettle (*Urtica dioica*) and pupates in a silken web spun amongst the leaves. There is usually one brood a year with moths on the wing in June and July although sometimes a partial second brood appears in September. Moths fly by night and seldom stray far from the nettle patches where they breed. The common name derives from its large upturned palpi projecting from the head.

Fan-foot *Herminia tarsipennalis* Treitschke, family Noctuidae. This interesting species is widespread and locally common in central Europe and ranges eastwards into Siberia, In the British Isles it is widely distributed in Ireland and south and central England but becomes scarcer and more local further north. Its habitats are hedgerows, open woodland and gardens. The caterpillar is clothed with short downy hairs and is greyish-brown with three dark lines down the back and a series of black streaks along the sides. It feeds on the foliage of wild raspberry (*Rubus idaeus*) and dead or wilted leaves of ivy (*Hedera*), sallow (*Salix*), bramble (*Rubus*) and other trees and shrubs. After hibernation, when the caterpillar is full grown, it pupates amongst dead leaves on the ground. There is one brood a year and moths are on the wing in June and July. This species is named the Fan-foot because of the large tufts of hairs on the forelegs of the male moth.

Mother Shipton *Callistege mi* Clerck, family Noctuidae. This unusual little moth is common throughout most of Europe and ranges eastwards into Siberia. In the British Isles it is found almost everywhere. Its habitats are meadows, downland, marshy places, open woodland and hedge banks. The slender caterpillar is pale yellowish-brown with fine reddish-brown lines down the back and sides and a broad creamy-white stripe low down on each side. It

feeds on clover (*Trifolium*) and melilot (*Melilotus*) and when full grown pupates in a brown cocoon spun within a twisted grass blade. There is one brood a year and moths are on the wing in May and June. They fly by day and are sometimes mistaken for skipper butterflies. The forewing pattern is said to resemble the profile of 'Mother Shipton', a famous Yorkshire witch, but the markings also resemble the letter 'M' and thus gives rise to the scientific name *mi*.

Burnet Companion *Euclidia glyphica*

Mother Shipton *Callistege mi*

Herald *Scoliopteryx libatrix* at rest

Snout *Hypena proboscidalis*

♂

♀

ssp. *thulensis* ♂

ssp. *thulensis* ♀

Hepialus humuli

♂

Hepialus lupulinus

♀

Lifesize

Ghost Moth *Hepialus humuli* Linnaeus, family
Hepialidae. This large and distinctive moth is
widespread in Europe, occurring as far north as
Lapland and ranging eastwards into western
Asia. In the British Isles it is widely distributed
and common. Its habitats are boggy meadows
and agricultural land. The caterpillar is
yellowish-white covered with dark brown raised
spots from which arise short hairs. It feeds on the
roots of grasses and other plants and is often a
pest of horticultural and agricultural crops
particularly in newly ploughed ground.
Presumably because of its burrowing habit, this
species is sometimes known as the 'Otter'. After
overwintering in the ground the caterpillar
completes its growth in the spring and pupates.
Moths are on the wing in summer and males may
sometimes be seen in large numbers hovering
above the vegetation at dusk. The females lay
their eggs while in flight, dropping them
apparently indiscriminately over the foliage.

Common Swift *Hepialus lupulinus* Linnaeus,
family Hepialidae. This common moth is
widespread throughout much of Europe. In the
British Isles it is found almost everywhere. Its
habitats are meadows, agricultural land and
gardens. The caterpillar is similar to that of the
Ghost Moth but is generally smaller and has paler
spots. It feeds on the roots of grasses and various
herbaceous plants and is sometimes a pest of field
crops, particularly in ground only recently
ploughed, and in gardens where it eats both
weeds and cultivated flowers. It overwinters in
the ground, becoming full grown in the spring
when it pupates. Sometimes caterpillars will take
two years to complete their development. There
is normally one brood a year and moths are on the
wing in May and June. They fly at dusk, often in
large numbers, and the females lay their eggs
while hovering over the foliage.

Ghost Moth *Hepialus humuli* ♀

Common Swift *Hepialus lupulinus*

Ghost Moth *Hepialus humuli* ♂

Zeuzera pyrina

♂

♀

Cossus cossus

♂

♀

Lifesize

Goat Moth *Cossus cossus* pupa in opened cocoon

Leopard Moth *Zeuzera pyrina* Linnaeus, family Cossidae. This widely distributed species occurs in central and southern Europe, North Africa, temperate Asia and North America. In the British Isles it is mainly confined to southern England and seems to be quite common in the London area. Its habitats are open woodlands, orchards, gardens and tree-lined streets. The caterpillar is yellowish-white with a wedge-shaped dark brown head. The body is covered with black spots from which arise short hairs. It feeds on a wide range of deciduous trees including fruit trees, burrowing in the wood beneath the bark. This species is sometimes an orchard pest and also disfigures ornamental trees by killing the branches. Caterpillars often take two or three years to reach maturity and then pupate within the burrow near to the surface of the bark. Moths are on the wing in the summer. The females have a long, pointed ovipositor which is often mistaken for a sting.

Goat Moth *Cossus cossus* Linnaeus, family Cossidae. This large and robust moth is widespread in Europe and also occurs in North Africa and temperate Asia. In the British Isles is is widely distributed and was apparently quite common although in recent years it appears to have become quite scarce. Its habitats are woodlands and neglected orchards. The large, fleshy caterpillar is dark red on the back and yellowish-pink below and has a strong goat-like smell from which arises the common name. It burrows in the trunks and branches of various deciduous trees, including fruit trees, and was at one time regarded as an orchard pest. Like other wood-feeding caterpillars, it takes a long time to complete its development and is usually full grown in three or four years. At this stage it often leaves the burrow to pupate in the earth. Moths are on the wing in June and July and are occasionally found resting on tree trunks during the day.

Goat Moth *Cossus cossus*

Leopard Moth *Zeuzera pyrina*

Goat Moth *Cossus cossus* caterpillar

181

Adscita statices

Zygaena trifolii

Zygaena filipendulae

var.

var.   *Zygaena ephialtes*   var.

♂   *Apoda limacodes*   ♀

Sesia apiformis

Lifesize

Forester *Adscita statices*

When full grown, after hibernating through the winter, it pupates in a tough silken cocoon spun on a stem or under a leaf. There is one generation a year and moths are on the wing in May and June. They fly by day and are attracted to flowers, particularly those of ragged-robin (*Lychnis flos-cuculi*).

Six-spot Burnet *Zygaena filipendulae* Linnaeus, family Zygaenidae. This well-known moth occurs throughout Europe and ranges eastwards into western Asia. It is very variable and is represented by many named forms and races. In the British Isles it is widespread and plentiful in most suitable localities. Its habitats are meadows, downland, cliffs and sandhills where the foodplant abounds. The caterpillar is yellowish-green, boldly spotted with black and yellow. It feeds on the foliage of birdsfoot-trefoil (*Lotus corniculatus*), hibernating through the winter and completing its growth in the spring. Pupation takes place in a distinctive, papery, boat-shaped cocoon usually attached to a grass stem well above the ground. Moths are on the wing in June and July, flying actively in hot sunshine. Both moths and caterpillars are brightly coloured to indicate that they are distasteful to would-be predators. All life stages of this species contain significant amounts of cyanide and so are highly poisonous if eaten.

Five-spot Burnet *Zygaena trifolii* Esper, family Zygaenidae. This moth is widespread in Europe and also occurs in North Africa and western Asia. In the British Isles it is restricted to southern England, parts of Wales and the Isle of Man. In south-eastern England moths are found on chalk downland and are referred to as ssp. *palustrella* Verity, while in the west they belong to a marshland race known as ssp. *decreta* Verity. The caterpillar is yellowish- or bluish-green and is boldly marked with black spots. The downland form feeds on the foliage of birdsfoot-trefoil (*Lotus corniculatus*) and pupates on a stem close to the ground, whilst the marshland form feeds on large birdsfoot-trefoil (*Lotus uliginosus*) and pupates high up on grass stems. Moths are on the wing from May until August, depending on locality and habitat, those on downland being earlier and smaller. They fly by day in bright sunshine and, like other burnets, are distasteful to birds.

Variable Burnet *Zygaena ephialtes* Linnaeus, family Zygaenidae. This appropriately named moth occurs in many different forms. It is found in most parts of central and southern Europe and

Forester *Adscita statices* Linnaeus, family Zygaenidae. This attractive little moth is widespread throughout Europe where it is often quite common. In the British Isles it is also widely distributed, except in northern Scotland, but is generally local in occurrence. Its habitats are damp meadows and woodland glades. The caterpillar is yellowish- or greenish-white, shaded with pinkish-brown on the sides and covered with small brown hairy warts. It feeds on sorrel (*Rumex*), mining at first between the upper and lower surfaces of a leaf. Later it eats the lower surface of the leaf, leaving only the upper skin which appears as a translucent 'window'.

Six-spot Burnet *Zygaena filipendulae* newly hatched

Five-spot Burnet *Zygaena trifolii*

Hornet Moth *Sesia apiformis*

Variable Burnet *Zygaena ephialtes*

also occurs in western Turkey. It does not occur in the British Isles. Its habitats are flowery hill slopes, particularly those with open scrub. The caterpillar is yellow or greenish-yellow with a darker line down the back and rows of black spots on either side. It feeds on the foliage of crown vetch (*Coronilla varia*) and related plants and when full grown pupates in a papery cocoon amongst vegetation near the ground. Moths are on the wing in the summer flying by day in bright sunshine. There are two basic types of moth, one with large forewing spots and a red hindwing bordered with black and the other with small forewing spots and a black hindwing. Both of these forms may be found with five or six spots on the forewing or with the red ground colour replaced by yellow.

Festoon *Apoda limacodes* Hufnagel, family Limacodidae. This small moth is widespread in southern and central Europe, occurs as far north as southern Scandinavia and ranges eastwards into temperate Asia. In the British Isles it is confined to southern England and parts of

Ireland. Its habitat is oak (*Quercus*) woodland. The strange caterpillar is flattened and slug-like. It is green spotted with white and has two red dotted yellow lines along the back. It feeds on the foliage of oak and when full grown pupates in a brown cocoon attached to a leaf. The cocoon has a small hinged lid at one end which allows the moth to escape when it is ready to emerge. There is one brood a year and moths are on the wing in June and July. They may be seen flying around tree tops on sunny days.

Hornet Moth *Sesia apiformis* Clerck, family Sesiidae. This remarkable moth is widespread in Europe from Fennoscandia to the Iberian Peninsula and ranges eastwards into temperate Asia. It has also been accidentally introduced into North America. In the British Isles it is widely distributed but of local occurrence, and is most frequently found in eastern England. Its habitats are woodland margins and hedgerows where suitable trees are established. The caterpillar is yellowish-white with a reddish-brown head. It feeds on the roots and lower parts

Festoon caterpillar

of the trunk of poplar (*Populus*) and sallow (*Salix*), usually tunnelling between the bark and the wood but sometimes boring deeper. After two years the full grown caterpillar leaves the burrow to pupate on the bark or in the earth. Moths are on the wing from May until August, according to locality. Despite their striking hornet-like appearance, these moths are quite harmless.

183

Crambus pascuella

Nymphula nymphaeata

Evergestis forficalis

Pterophorus pentadactyla

Eurrhypara hortulata

1½ × lifesize

Grass Moth *Crambus pascuella*

Grass Moth *Crambus pascuella* Linnaeus, family Pyralidae. This common little moth is widespread in Europe, occurring as far north as northern Fennoscandia. In the British Isles it is very widely distributed and is particularly abundant in the south. Its habitats are damp meadows and marshy areas where suitable grasses grow. The caterpillar is greyish-white with a brown head. It feeds at the roots and stem-bases of grasses, particularly meadow grass (*Poa*), and is also said to eat mosses and clover (*Trifolium*). There is one brood a year and moths are on the wing in June and July. They rest by day, head downwards on grass stems with their wings wrapped tightly round their bodies so that they are difficult to see. They are easily disturbed and will rapidly fly off with a zigzag flight to find a safe hiding place. The usual flight period is at dusk.

Brown China-mark *Nymphula nymphaeata* Linnaeus, family Pyralidae. This delicately marked moth is widespread throughout Europe and ranges eastwards into temperate Asia. In the British Isles it is widely distributed and often common. Its habitats are lakes, ponds, reservoirs and slow-moving rivers where the water is almost stagnant. The small caterpillar is remarkable because it lives in the water, constructing a flat, oval, protective case cut out from leaves of the foodplant. It feeds on pond weed (*Potamogeton*), frogbit (*Hydrocharis morsus-ranae*) and other aquatic plants, eating the under surfaces of the leaves and causing large brown blotches. When full grown it pupates in a pale grey cocoon spun on a plant stem a few centimetres above the water level. There is one brood a year and moths are on the wing from June until August. They fly after dusk but may be found at rest on waterside foliage during the day.

Garden Pebble *Evergestis forficalis* Linnaeus, family Pyralidae. This widespread and common moth occurs throughout Europe and ranges eastwards across Siberia to Japan. In the British Isles it is widely distributed, occurring as far north as the Inner Hebrides. Its habitats are agricultural land, hedgerows and gardens. The caterpillar is greyish-green spotted with white and with a yellowish-white line along each side above which is a row of raised black spots. It feeds on the leaves of cabbage, cauliflower (*Brassica*), horseradish (*Armoracia rusticana*) and related plants, sometimes spinning them together with silk to form a shelter. When full grown it burrows below ground and pupates in a tough silken cocoon. Caterpillars of the autumn brood overwinter in their cocoons before pupating in the spring. There are two broods a year and moths are on the wing in May and June and again in August and September. They usually fly at night but are easily disturbed by day and will fly rapidly to a new hiding place.

Small Magpie *Eurrhypara hortulata* Linnaeus, family Pyralidae. This pretty and distinctive little moth is widespread in Europe and ranges eastwards into temperate Asia. In the British Isles it is widely distributed but becomes more local further north. It is known to migrate and has been observed at a lightship more than thirty miles from the coast of Britain. Its habitats are hedgerows, waste land and field margins where the foodplants grow. The caterpillar is yellowish-white with a greyish-green line down the back and a brown head. It feeds mainly on the foliage of stinging nettle (*Urtica dioica*) but will also eat woundwort (*Stachys*), mint (*Mentha*) and other related plants, rolling a leaf or spinning several together with silk. When full grown it changes colour to a bright fleshy pink and spins a transparent silken cocoon in a sheltered place where it overwinters before pupating in the spring. Moths are on the wing in June and July, flying after dusk with a slow hovering flight.

Large White Plume Moth *Pterophorus pentadactyla* Linnaeus, family Pterophoridae. This beautiful and striking moth is widespread throughout Europe. In the British Isles it is found almost everywhere and is usually common. Its habitats are waste ground, gardens and any other place where the foodplant abounds. The caterpillar is green with a yellowish-brown head. The body is covered with little raised bluish warts, each bearing a tuft of greyish hairs. The foodplants are greater bindweed (*Calystegia*) and species of *Convolvulus*. Caterpillars hibernate through the winter before completing their growth in the spring. They pupate under leaves but remain quite active and will wriggle about if disturbed. There is one brood a year and moths may be found in June and July. They are on the wing in the evening and have a characteristic floating flight. When at rest they hold their wings out at right angles to the body and fold their legs backwards so that they look like a letter T.

Large White Plume Moth *Pterophorus pentadactyla*

Small Magpie *Eurrhypara hortulata*

Garden Pebble *Evergestis forficalis*

Brown China-mark *Nymphula nymphaeata*

Nemophora degeerella ♂ ♀

Tineola bisselliella

Yponomeuta padella

Hofmannophila pseudospretella

Endrosis sarcitrella

Cacoecimorpha pronubana ♂ ♀

Tortrix viridana

Cydia nigricana

Cydia pomonella

2 × lifesize

Long-horned Moth *Nemophora degeerella*
Linnaeus, family Incurvariidae. This attractive
and unusual little moth is widespread in Europe,
occurring as far north as Fennoscandia, and
ranges southwards to Asia Minor. In the British
Isles it is generally widespread and locally
common but does not seem to occur in Scotland.
Its habitat is deciduous woodland. The small
caterpillar is white with a yellow head and lives
inside a flattened, pear-shaped case constructed
from leaf fragments spun together with silk. It
feeds on leaf litter and overwinters before
pupating in its case in the spring. There is one
brood a year and moths are on the wing from May
until August, according to locality. They fly at
dusk, often in swarms and may sometimes also
be seen by day. The flight is slow and fluttering
and the long antennae are held out in front.

Common Clothes Moth *Tineola bisselliella*
Hummel, family Tineidae. This well-known and
notorious little moth is found throughout the
world. In the British Isles it is an all too familiar
pest in houses and shops although in recent years
it seems to have declined in numbers probably
due to the increased use of synthetic fibres and
higher standards of hygiene. The small
caterpillar or grub is white with a yellowish-
brown head and, unlike most other clothes
moths, does not live in a protective case. It will
feed on almost any animal fibres such as wool,
felt, furs or feathers. Clean clothes are seldom
attacked so it is a wise precaution to wash all
garments and to seal them in bags before storing
them. Both moths and caterpillars may be found
at any time of year. Clothes moths do not fly
readily but will scuttle away very rapidly if
disturbed.

Small Ermine Moth *Yponomeuta padella*
Linnaeus, family Yponomeutidae. This aptly
named little moth is widespread and common in
Europe, ranging from Fennoscandia to the
Iberian Peninsula and Asia Minor. In the British
Isles it is widely distributed and occurs in most
parts except for the extreme north of Scotland.
Its habitats are hedgerows, woodland margins,
orchards and gardens. The caterpillar is grey
with a darker line down the back flanked on
either side by a row of large black spots.
Caterpillars feed together in a communal web of
silk spun over the foodplant. They feed on
hawthorn (*Crataegus*) and blackthorn (*Prunus
spinosa*) and when full grown pupate in the web.
There is one brood a year and moths are on the
wing in July and August. This is one of a group of
very similar and closely related species, each
attracted to a particular group of foodplants.

Brown House-moth *Hofmannophila
pseudospretella* Stainton, family Oecophoridae.
This cosmopolitan pest moth is found in
temperate regions throughout the world and is
very common and widespread in Europe and the
British Isles. Its habitats are birds' nests, houses
and warehouses. The caterpillar is white with a
brown head and feeds on fabrics, stored foods
and almost any other material of animal or
vegetable origin. This is probably the most
common domestic pest moth in Britain and
frequently causes damage to carpets and other
fabrics, particularly in damp situations.
Infestations in houses often originate from birds'
nests and wasps' nests situated in the loft
although they will also breed in dust and debris
behind skirting boards or between floorboards.
The time taken to complete the life cycle varies
greatly according to conditions so that moths
may be found at any time from May until
September.

White-shouldered House-moth *Endrosis
sarcitrella* Linnaeus, family Oecophoridae. This

Brown House-moth *Hofmannophila pseudospretella*

Small Ermine Moth *Yponomeuta padella*

Long-horned Moth *Nemophora degeerella*

Green Oak Tortrix *Tortrix viridana*

common relative of the Brown House-moth is equally widely distributed and is regarded as a cosmopolitan pest. In the British Isles it is extremely common but seldom causes much damage. Its habitats are birds' nests, beehives, bat roosts, houses and warehouses. The caterpillar is dull white with a brown head and feeds on bird guano, stored foods and other materials of animal or vegetable origin. It lives in a silken web spun over the food and requires rather humid conditions to complete its development. Pupation takes place in a silken cocoon spun amongst the food. This species is virtually continuously brooded under indoor conditions so that moths may be found at any time of year although they are most frequently encountered from March until October.

Carnation Tortrix *Cacoecimorpha pronubana* Hübner, family Tortricidae. This moth is common in southern and parts of central Europe and also occurs in Asia Minor, North Africa, Japan and North America. It was not recorded in the British Isles until 1905 but has now become established in many parts of southern England and in Wales, and is abundant in suitable localities. Its habitats are hedgerows and gardens. The caterpillar is green or brown and lives in a rolled leaf or a spun shoot of the foodplant. It feeds on a very wide range of foodplants although in gardens it is most commonly found on privet (*Ligustrum*) and *Euonymus* hedges. It has received its common name because it is sometimes a serious pest of carnations (*Dianthus*) and other cultivated plants grown under glass. The pupa is formed in a folded leaf. There are two broods a year with moths on the wing from May to July and again in the autumn, flying by day in sunshine.

Green Oak Tortrix *Tortrix viridana* Linnaeus, family Tortricidae. This distinctive little moth is found throughout Europe and occurs also in North Africa and Asia Minor. In the British Isles it is widespread but is particularly abundant in southern England. Its habitat is oak (*Quercus*) woodland. The caterpillar is greyish-green with a

black head and feeds in a rolled or folded oak leaf. Sometimes populations of this species become so large that they completely defoliate the trees and drop to the ground on silken threads to feed on the undergrowth. Caterpillars will also eat the foliage of various other deciduous trees. The pupa is formed in a folded leaf. There is one brood a year with moths on the wing from June until August according to locality. They hide amongst foliage by day, but are easily disturbed and will flutter away.

Pea Moth *Cydia nigricana* Fabricius, family Tortricidae. This moth is found throughout Europe and ranges eastwards across temperate Asia to Japan. In the British Isles it occurs almost everywhere except for the extreme north of Scotland. Its habitats are agricultural land, hedgerows and gardens. The caterpillar is yellowish-white with a brown head and is the common maggot found in pea pods. It feeds on the developing seeds of various plants of the pea family but is particularly known as a pest of cultivated peas (*Pisum sativum*). When full grown the caterpillar leaves the pods and burrows into the ground where it overwinters in

a silken cocoon before pupating in the following spring. There is usually one brood a year although a second brood may occur under favourable conditions. Moths are on the wing from May to August and fly both in the afternoon and at dusk when they may be seen visiting pea blossom.

Codling Moth *Cydia pomonella* Linnaeus, family Tortricidae. This attractively marked little moth is a notorious fruit pest occurring throughout the world wherever apples (*Malus*) are grown. In the British Isles it occurs almost everywhere except for the extreme north of Scotland. Its habitats are orchards and gardens. The caterpillar is yellowish-white at first but when full grown turns a deep pink. This is the common maggot so frequently found when apples are cut open. It will also feed on the fruits of pear (*Pyrus*), quince (*Cydonia*) and walnut (*Juglans*), but this is much less common. The full grown caterpillar overwinters under bark before pupating in the spring. Moths are usually on the wing in July and August although a second brood sometimes appears in the autumn. They rest on tree trunks and foliage by day and fly at dusk.

HAMMERSMITH PUBLIC LIBRARIES

General index

Foodplant index